SPANISH VERBPACK

Also available from Oxford University Press

Pocket Oxford Spanish Dictionary
An intermediate level Spanish dictionary
978–0–19–861072–4

Oxford Colour Spanish Dictionary Plus
Colour headwords throughout
978–0–19–860903–2
978–0–19–860902–5 (US edition)

Spanish Grammar
978–0–19–860343–6

Oxford Spanish Wordpack
978–0–19–860337–5

Oxford Beginner's Spanish Dictionary
A brand new easy-to-use Spanish dictionary
for first-time learning
978–0–19–929856–3

SPANISH VERBPACK

JOHN BUTT

OXFORD
UNIVERSITY PRESS

OXFORD
UNIVERSITY PRESS

Great Clarendon Street, Oxford OX2 6DP

Oxford University Press is a department of the University of Oxford.
It furthers the University's objective of excellence in research, scholarship,
and education by publishing worldwide in

Oxford New York
Auckland Cape Town Dar es Salaam Hong Kong Karachi Kuala Lumpur
Madrid Melbourne Mexico City Nairobi New Delhi Shanghai
Taipei Toronto

With offices in
Argentina Austria Brazil Chile Czech Republic France Greece Guatemala
Hungary Italy Japan Poland Poland Portugal Singapore South Korea Switzerland
Thailand Turkey Ukraine Vietnam

Published in the United States
by Oxford University Press Inc., New York

First published as *Spanish Verbs* 1997
First published as *Spanish Verbpack* 2000

British Library Cataloguing in Publication Data
Data available

Library of Congress Cataloging in Publication Data
Data available

ISBN-13: 978-0-19-860340-5
ISBN-10: 0-19-860340-1

6

Printed in Great Britain by
Clays Ltd, Bungay, Suffolk

CONTENTS

HOW TO USE THIS BOOK

This book is designed as a pocket or handbag reference guide to the Spanish verb system.

It shows 92 common verbs, regular and irregular, fully conjugated in their most important tenses and moods. These verbs, shown on pp.185–276, represent the various patterns that all the other verbs in Spanish conform to. If one knows the rules for conjugating these model verbs, one can conjugate all the other verbs listed in the Verb Directory on pp.1–179.

Books like this one tend to discourage beginners: the number of forms for each verb and the number of verbs listed are initially dismaying. But the picture is in fact a good deal simpler than it seems, and the following notes are designed to make the task of learning Spanish verbs easier.

THE SPANISH VERB SYSTEM

What you need to know

For nearly all the verbs in the language the following forms are in everyday use:[1]

The Infinitive, e.g. **hablar** *to speak* (verb no. 41[2])
The Past Participle, e.g. **hablado** *spoken*
The Gerund, e.g. **hablando** *speaking*

Four Imperative forms, e.g.
habla (familiar singular) **hablad**[3] (familiar plural) *speak!*
hable (polite singular) **hablen** (polite plural in Spain, polite or familiar in Latin America)

Eight Indicative tenses:
The Present, e.g. **hablo** *I speak*
The Preterit,[4] e.g. **hablé** *I spoke*
The Imperfect, e.g. **hablaba** *I was speaking*

---

[1] The anterior preterit (**hube hablabo**, etc.) and the future subjunctive (**hablare**, **hablares**, etc.) are not now used in everyday Spanish and are not discussed in this book.
[2] The numbers in brackets refer to the position of the model in the tables on pp.185–276.
[3] Imperative forms ending in **-d** are not used in Latin America where they are replaced by the imperative forms ending in **-n**.
[4] The American spelling 'preterit' (British 'preterite') is used throughout this book.

The Perfect, e.g. **he hablado** *I have spoken/I spoke*
The Future, e.g. **hablaré** *I will speak*
The Conditional, e.g. **hablaría** *I would speak*
The Pluperfect, e.g. **había hablado** *I had spoken*
The Conditional Perfect, e.g. **habría** or **hubiera hablado** *I would have spoken*

Four Subjunctive tenses (no exact English translation):
The Present Subjunctive, e.g. **hable**
The Imperfect Subjunctive, e.g. **hablara** or **hablase**
The Perfect Subjunctive, e.g. **haya hablado**
The Pluperfect Subjunctive, e.g. **hubiera** or **hubiese hablado**.

All of the above (except the gerund, past participle and imperative) can also appear in the continuous form, e.g. **estar hablando** *to be speaking*, **estoy hablando** *I'm speaking*, **habría estado hablando** *I/he/she would have been speaking*, etc.

As far as regular verbs are concerned, one simply adds the correct endings of the forms listed to the stem left after removing the **-ar**, **-er**, or **-ir** of the infinitive. The simple spelling rules listed on p.xv must be applied if necessary. A few otherwise regular verbs have irregular past participles. These are mentioned in the Verb Directory.

These remarks also apply to most radical changing verbs (see below): only the present indicative, singular familiar imperative, and present subjunctive show irregularities.

In the case of irregular verbs (listed on p.xiv) and also radical changing verbs that are conjugated like **sentir** (no. 78), **pedir** (no. 54), **reír** (no. 68), and **dormir** (no. 34), one needs only to memorize the following forms since all the others can be predicted from them:

The Present Indicative
The Preterit
The Imperfect (but only three verbs are irregular)
The Present Subjunctive
The second-person singular Imperative (only a few verbs are irregular)
The Past Participle (in the case of a few verbs)
The Future (only a few verbs are irregular)

Regular verbs

Regular verbs are divided into three types of conjugations, according to whether their infinitive ends in **-ar**, **-er**, or **-ir**.

The great majority of Spanish verbs are regular **-ar** verbs (about 70% of the verbs listed in the Directory belong to this type), so one should begin by thoroughly learning the conjugation of **hablar** *to speak* (no. 41). The three regular verbs **pagar** (no. 52), **realizar** (no. 65), and **sacar** (no. 74) should be studied next. These conjugate in exactly the same way as **hablar**, but they are affected by the spelling changes listed on p. xv.

The forms of the regular **-er** and **-ir** verbs (exemplified by **comer**, no. 22, and **vivir**, no. 89) can be learned simultaneously, since they are almost identical.

Once these forms are thoroughly memorized, the regular verbs **proteger** (no. 62) and **vencer** (no. 86) should be studied: they are affected by the spelling changes listed on p. xv. However, most verbs ending in **-cer** are in fact slightly irregular and are conjugated like **parecer** (no. 53), and since this type includes a large number of verbs it should be memorized now (only the forms containing **-zc** are irregular).

Verbs like **tañer** (no. 81), **gruñir** (no. 39), and **bullir** (no. 15) should also be noted since they are affected by spelling changes, although this type is not particularly common.

When (and only when) the forms listed above have been thoroughly memorized, students should learn the irregular verbs and radical changing verbs.

Radical changing verbs

These are only partly irregular. Their endings are always regular and correspond to the **-ar**, **-er**, and **-ir** endings of regular verbs, according to the ending of the infinitive. However, there are certain changes that affect one of the vowels in the verb. The only forms affected are the **tú** and **usted/ustedes** imperative, the present indicative and present subjunctive, and, in the case of a few verbs, the preterit and the imperfect subjunctive (but the latter can always be deduced from the former).

The main types of radical changing verb are exemplified by the following model verbs, listed in order of frequency of occurrence in the Directory:

• **Type 1** (121 examples in the Verb Directory)
cerrar (no. 18) *to shut*
comenzar (no. 21, spelling changes) *to start*
negar (no. 49, spelling changes) *to deny*
errar (no. 36, spelling changes) *to wander*

• **Type 2** (71 examples)
contar (no. 24) *to tell, to count*
almorzar (no. 6, spelling changes) *to have lunch*
colgar (no. 20, spelling changes) *to hang up*

• **Type 3** (48 examples)
pedir (no. 54) *to ask for*

reír (no. 68, accents and no second consonant) *to laugh*
regir (no. 66, spelling changes) *to rule*
reñir (no. 69, spelling changes) *to scold*
seguir (no. 77, spelling changes) *to follow*

• **Type 4** (43 examples)
sentir (no. 78) *to feel*
erguir (no. 35, spelling changes) *to prick up (ears)*

• **Type 5** (27 examples)
perder (no. 55) *to lose*

• **Type 6** (22 examples)
mover (no. 48) *to move*
cocer (no. 19, spelling changes) *to cook*

• **Type 7** (4 examples, including **dormirse** and **morirse**)
dormir (no. 34) *to sleep*

• **Type 8** (4 examples)
discernir (no. 32) *to discern*

• **Type 9** (2 examples)
adquirir (no. 3) *to acquire*

• **Type 10** (1 example)
jugar (no. 44, spelling changes) *to play*

Irregular verbs

There are twenty-two common Spanish irregular verbs, although some of them form compound verbs, conjugated like their simple form, e.g. **componer** *to compose* is conjugated like **poner** (no. 58). These are:

andar (no. 7) *to walk*	**poner** (no. 58) *to put*
caber (no. 16) *to fit into*	**producir** (no. 60) *to produce*[5]
caer (no. 17) *to fall*	**querer** (no. 64) *to want*
dar (no. 27) *to give*	**saber** (no. 73) *to know*
decir (no. 28) *to say*	**salir** (no. 75) *to go out*
estar (no. 38) *to be*	**ser** (no. 79) *to be*
haber (no. 40) (aux.)	**tener** (no. 82) *to have*
hacer (no. 42) *to do*	**traer** (no. 83) *to bring*
ir (no. 43) *to go*	**valer** (no. 85) *to be worth*
oír (no. 50) *to hear*	**venir** (no. 87) *to come*
poder (no. 57) *to be able*	**ver** (no. 88) *to see*

As the meanings show, all these verbs are in frequent use, so they must be learned thoroughly.

For a detailed discussion of the uses of the Spanish tenses, see the *Oxford Minireference Spanish Grammar*.

[5] There are several verbs conjugated like **producir**. They are listed with **producir** (no. 60)

Spelling changes

Certain spelling changes affect all verbs, regular and irregular. The most common are:

- Infinitive ends in **-car**: **c** > **qu** before **e** or **i**. See **sacar** (no. 74).
- Infinitive ends in **-gar**: **g** > **gu** before **e** or **i**. See **pagar** (no. 52).
- Infinitive ends in **-zar**: **z** > **c** before **e** or **i**. See **realizar** (no. 65).
- Infinitive ends in **-ger** or **-gir**: **g** > **j** before **o** or **a**. See **proteger** (no. 62) and **rugir** (no. 72).
- Infinitive ends in **-guir**: the **u** disappears before **o** or **a**. See **distinguir** (no. 33).
- Infinitive ends in **-guar**: dieresis needed on **u** before **e**. See **averiguar** (no.13).
- Infinitive ends in **-cer**: a few verbs are conjugated like **vencer** (no. 86) i.e. **c** > **z** before **a** or **o**: these include **ejercer** *to exercise*, **convencer** *to convince*, **mecer** *to rock/sway* and a few others. **Escocer** *to sting* and **torcer** *to twist* are conjugated like **cocer** *to cook* (no. 19). The rest, which are the vast majority, are conjugated like **parecer** (no. 53) and show a slight irregularity: **c** > **zc** before **a**, or **o**.
- Infinitive ends in vowel + **-er** or vowel + **-ir**: a *y* sound is written **y** between vowels. See

poseer (no. 59) and **construir** (no. 23) for examples.

- Infinitive ends in **-cir**. Check verb in list.
- Infinitive ends in **-ñer**, **-ñir**, or **-llir**: diphthong **ió** in preterit > **ó**; **ie** in imperfect subjunctive > **e**. See **tañer** (no. 81), **gruñir** (no. 39), and **bullir** (no. 15).
- Irregular verbs whose preterit stem ends in **-j**: in these verbs, e.g. **decir** (no. 28), **traer** (no. 83) and verbs like **producir** (no. 60) (but not in regular verbs like **tejer** *to weave*/(Lat. Am.) *to knit*) the third-person plural of the preterit ends in **-eron**, not **-ieron**, and the imperfect subjunctive endings begin with **-e**, not **-ie**, e.g. **dijeron**, **dijera**, **dijese**, etc.

Transitive and intransitive verbs

Spanish generally[6] distinguishes clearly between transitive and intransitive verbs, whereas English often does not. Transitive verbs can (and in Spanish usually must) have a direct object: **la vi** *I saw* ***her***, **escribieron una carta** *they wrote* ***a letter***. Intransitive verbs cannot have a direct object: **murió** *he/she died*, **me río** *I laugh*. One cannot die or laugh something or someone.

---

[6] But not always, cf. **aumentar**, which means *to increase* both in the sense of *to make larger* and *to get larger*, or **dormir**, which can mean either *to sleep* or *to put to sleep*.

It is important to keep the distinction clear in Spanish. The Spanish verb **casar** is transitive: it means *to marry* but only in the sense of *to marry someone off to someone else*: **casó a su hija con un abogado rico** *he married his daughter off to a rich lawyer*. **Casarse** is intransitive and must be used for the more normal meaning of the English *to marry*, i.e. *to* **get** *married*. If the forms are confused, incomprehensible Spanish will result: '**caso mañana**' means something like '*tomorrow I'm making someone marry*'; the correct form is **me caso mañana** *I'm getting married tomorrow*. For this reason, the words 'transitive' or 'intransitive' are included in the Directory whenever the English translation does not make the difference clear.

'Reflexive' (i.e. **pronominal**) **verbs**

Pronominal verbs are those whose infinitive is shown in the Verb Directory as ending in **-se**: **arrepentir***se* *to repent*, **ir***se* *to go away*, etc. These verbs are traditionally called 'reflexive' verbs, but this name is inaccurate and misleading.

These verbs are conjugated according to the pattern indicated by the model verb in brackets, but the following pronouns are required (present indicative of **ir***se* *to go away*, no. 43 as an example):

***me* voy**	*I'm going away*
***te* vas**	*you're going away*
***se* va**	*he's/she's going away*
	you (**usted**) *are going away*
***nos* vamos**	*we're going away*
***os* vais**	*you're going away*[7]
***se* van**	*they're going away*
	you (**ustedes**) *are going away*

Such verbs are very common in Spanish and they have a number of different uses, some of which are rather difficult to classify. In most, but not all cases, the pronominal form shows that the verb is intransitive, cf. **acostar** *to put someone to bed* and **acostarse** *to go to bed.* But in some cases (e.g. **arrepentirse** *to repent*) the verb has no non-pronominal counterpart, and in the case of many verbs, especially common verbs of motion, the difference is one of nuance, cf. **salir** *to leave* and **salirse** which means *to walk out* or *to leak*. In a few cases, e.g. **morir** and **morirse** *to die*, no English translation can make the difference in meaning completely clear. For fuller details on this point and on the other uses of pronominal verbs, see the *Oxford Minireference Spanish Grammar*.

---

7 Spain only.

VERB DIRECTORY

The Verb Directory shows in alphabetical order

- All irregular and radical changing verbs in current use
- Common regular verbs

You are given:

- the infinitive and its meaning
- the preposition used if the verb is usually followed by a preposition
- the most common translation(s) of the verb
- an indication of whether the verb is regular. If the word **Reg.** is missing, the verb is irregular in some way.
- in some cases, information as to whether the verb is transitive or intransitive
- the model verb on whose pattern the verb is conjugated
- the number of the model verb in the verb tables on pp. 185–276

Criteria for inclusion

The Directory contains the immense majority of verbs used in plain prose and ordinary conversation. Slang terms are omitted, as are many familiar or popular terms currently used in

Spain and Latin America. Forms used exclusively in Latin America are marked Lat. Am.

For the sake of completion a number of verbs appear that are usually confined to literary usage, and one or two archaic verbs are included (marked 'archaic'). In some cases two or more verbs exist with the same meaning, e.g. **balbucir** and **balbucear** *to stutter*: in such cases the reader is referred to the most commonly used form (in this case **balbucear**). When a form is very rare or literary the equals sign points to the verb of the same meaning that is most commonly used, e.g. **desposarse** = **casarse**.

abalanzar *to balance; to hurl* Reg.	realizar	65
abalanzarse sobre *to rush upon; to lunge at* Reg.	realizar	65
abanderar *to register (a ship); to champion (a cause)* Reg.	hablar	41
abandonar *to abandon* Reg.	hablar	41
abanicar *to fan* Reg.	sacar	74
abaniquear = **abanicar** Reg.	hablar	41
abaratar *to reduce the price of* Reg.	hablar	41
abarcar *to include, cover* Reg.	sacar	74
abarquillar *to wrinkle, curl* (transitive) Reg.	hablar	41
abarquillarse *to become curled, wrinkled* Reg.	hablar	41
abarrotar *to jam full; to overfill* Reg.	hablar	41
abastecer *to supply*	parecer	53
abatir *to knock down; to depress* Reg.	vivir	89
abatirse por *to get depressed about* Reg.	vivir	89
abdicar en *to abdicate in favour of* Reg.	sacar	74
abigarrar *to daub* Reg.	hablar	41
abismar *to spoil completely; to ruin* Reg.	hablar	41
abjurar de *to renounce; to recant* Reg.	hablar	41
ablandar *to make soft* Reg.	hablar	41
ablandarse *to grow soft* Reg.	hablar	41
abnegarse *to go without*	negar	49
abocarse hacia *to head towards* Reg.	sacar	74
abocetar *to sketch* Reg.	hablar	41
abochornar *to make embarrassed* Reg.	hablar	41
abochornarse *to feel embarrassed; to blush* Reg.	hablar	41
abofetear *to slap* Reg.	hablar	41
abogar por *to plead for (*i.e. *to defend)* Reg.	pagar	52
abolir *to abolish*	abolir	1
abollar *to dent; to knock hard* Reg.	hablar	41
abollarse *to become dented* Reg.	hablar	41

abominar de *to abominate* Reg.	hablar	41
abonar *to pay for; to vouch for; to deposit (money); to fertilize* Reg.	hablar	41
abonarse a *to subscribe to; to take out a season ticket for* Reg.	hablar	41
abordar *to approach; to deal with a problem; to accost* Reg.	hablar	41
aborrascarse *to get stormy* Reg.	sacar	74
aborrecer *to loathe*	parecer	53
abortar *to abort; to have a miscarriage* Reg.	hablar	41
abotagarse *to become bloated* Reg.	pagar	52
abotargarse = **abotagarse** Reg.	pagar	52
abotonar *to button* Reg.	hablar	41
abrasar *to burn, scorch* (transitive) Reg.	hablar	41
abrasarse *to burn, scorch* (intransitive) Reg.	hablar	41
abrazar *to hug; to embrace* Reg.	realizar	65
abrevar *to water (cattle)* Reg.	hablar	41
abreviar *to abbreviate* Reg.	hablar	41
abrigar *to shelter; to cherish (an idea, etc.)* Reg.	pagar	52
abrigarse de *to shelter from* Reg.	pagar	52
abrillantar *to polish; to make shiny* Reg.	hablar	41
abrir *to open; to unlock*	abrir	2
abrochar *to fasten (*e.g. *a belt); to button up* Reg.	hablar	41
abrogar *to abrogate; to repeal* Reg.	pagar	52
abrumar *to overwhelm; to oppress* Reg.	hablar	41
absolver *to absolve*	volver	90
absorber *to absorb; to take up (energies, time)* Reg.	comer	22
abstenerse de *to abstain from*	tener	82
abstraer *to abstract*	traer	83
abstraerse *to be lost in thought*	traer	83
abuchear *to boo* Reg.	hablar	41

abultar *to bulge; to inflate (figures)* Reg.	hablar	41
abundar en *to abound in* Reg.	hablar	41
aburguesarse *to become bourgeois/ middle-class* Reg.	hablar	41
aburrir *to bore* Reg.	vivir	89
aburrirse de *to get bored with* Reg.	vivir	89
abusar *to misuse* Reg.	hablar	41
acabar *to end* (transitive and intransitive); **a. de** + infinitive *to have just done something* Reg.	hablar	41
acabarse *to come to an end; to run out (supplies)* Reg.	hablar	41
acaecer *to happen* (third person only)	parecer	53
acalambrarse *to get cramp (muscles)* Reg.	hablar	41
acallar *to silence (criticisms, etc.)* Reg.	hablar	41
acalorar *to make heated; to inflame (passions)* Reg.	hablar	41
acalorarse *to get worked up* Reg.	hablar	41
acampar *to camp* Reg.	hablar	41
acanalar *to groove* Reg.	hablar	41
acaparar *to stockpile, hoard; to take up all of (time, interest, etc.)* Reg.	hablar	41
acaramelar *to caramelize* Reg.	hablar	41
acardenalar *to make black and blue* Reg.	hablar	41
acardenalarse *to become black and blue* Reg.	realizar	65
acariciar *to caress* Reg.	hablar	41
acarrear *to give rise to (a problem, difficulty); to lug, carry along* Reg.	hablar	41
acartonarse *to become wizened* Reg.	hablar	41
acatar *to comply with* Reg.	hablar	41
acatarrarse *to catch a cold* Reg.	hablar	41
acaudalar *to hoard (money)* Reg.	hablar	41

acaudillar *to lead (*i.e. *to be the leader of)* Reg.	hablar	41
acceder a *to accede to; to gain admission to* Reg.	comer	22
accidentarse *to have an accident* Reg.	hablar	41
accionar *to operate (a device)* Reg.	hablar	41
acechar *to lie in wait for; to spy on* Reg.	hablar	41
aceitar *to oil* Reg.	hablar	41
acelerar *to accelerate* Reg.	hablar	41
acendrar *to refine* Reg.	hablar	41
acensuar *to tax* (= **gravar**, **tasar**)	continuar	25
acentuar *to accentuate; to stress*	continuar	25
aceptar *to accept* Reg.	hablar	41
acercar *to bring near or nearer* Reg.	sacar	74
acercarse a *to approach* Reg.	sacar	74
acerrojar *to bolt (*i.e. *lock)* Reg.	hablar	41
acertar *to hit upon, guess right;* **acertar con** *to get right;* **a. a** + infinitive *to manage to*	cerrar	18
acezar *to gasp; to pant* (= **jadear**) Reg.	realizar	65
achacar a *to attribute to* Reg.	sacar	74
achaflanar *to bevel, chamfer* Reg.	hablar	41
achantar *to intimidate* Reg.	hablar	41
achantarse *to back down from (a confrontation)* Reg.	hablar	41
achicar *to make smaller; to take away one's confidence* Reg.	sacar	74
achicarse *to be intimidated; to lack courage* Reg.	sacar	74
achicharrar *to crisp; to scorch* (transitive) Reg.	hablar	41
achicharrarse *to be burnt to a cinder* Reg.	hablar	41
achisparse *to get tipsy* Reg.	hablar	41
achocharse *to become 'gaga', senile* Reg.	hablar	41
acholarse *to be abashed* Reg.	hablar	41

achuchar *to set (dogs, etc.) upon; to unleash (dogs)* Reg.	hablar	41
acibarar *to embitter* (= **amargar**) Reg.	hablar	41
acicalarse *to get dressed up; to smarten oneself up* Reg.	hablar	41
acidificar *to acidify* Reg.	sacar	74
aclamar *to acclaim* Reg.	hablar	41
aclarar *to brighten; to make clear; to clarify* Reg.	hablar	41
aclararse *to see the light; to sort one's ideas out* Reg.	hablar	41
aclimatar *to acclimatize* Reg.	hablar	41
aclimatarse *to become acclimatized* Reg.	hablar	41
acobardar *to intimidate* Reg.	hablar	41
acobardarse ante *to lose one's nerve at* Reg.	hablar	41
acocear *to kick (said of horses)* Reg.	hablar	41
acodar *to bend into an elbow* Reg.	hablar	41
acoger *to welcome; to take in (a guest, etc.)* Reg.	proteger	62
acogerse a *to have recourse to; to seek refuge in* Reg.	proteger	62
acogotar *to kill (an animal by breaking its neck)* Reg.	hablar	41
acolchar *to quilt* Reg.	hablar	41
acolchonar = **acolchar** Reg.	hablar	41
acometer *to attack* Reg.	comer	22
acomodar *to make someone comfortable;* **a. algo a algo** *to adapt something to something* Reg.	hablar	41
acomodarse *to make oneself comfortable; to settle in* Reg.	hablar	41
acompañar *to accompany* Reg.	hablar	41
acompasar *to keep time (rhythm); to keep step* Reg.	hablar	41

acomplejar *to give someone a complex* Reg.	hablar	41
acomplejarse *to get a complex* Reg.	hablar	41
acomunarse *to join forces* Reg.	hablar	41
acondicionar *to condition* Reg.	hablar	41
acongojar *to distress; to grieve* Reg.	hablar	41
aconsejar *to advise* Reg.	hablar	41
aconsejarse de *to seek advice from* Reg.	hablar	41
acontecer *to happen* (3rd-person only)	parecer	53
acopiar *to gather together* (transitive) Reg.	hablar	41
acoplar *to couple; to fit together* (transitive) Reg.	hablar	41
acoplarse a *to adapt oneself to* Reg.	hablar	41
acoquinar *to intimidate* Reg.	hablar	41
acorazar *to armor/(Brit.) armour-plate* Reg.	realizar	65
acorazarse *to protect oneself; to become hardened* Reg.	realizar	65
acordar *to agree on*	contar	24
acordarse de *to remember*	contar	24
acordonar *to cordon off; to lace (shoes)* Reg.	hablar	41
acorralar *to corner (= to force into a corner)* Reg.	hablar	41
acornar *to butt; to gore*	contar	24
acornear = **acornar** Reg.	hablar	41
acortar *to cut short (meeting, etc.)* Reg.	hablar	41
acosar *to harass* Reg.	hablar	41
acostar *to put to bed*	contar	24
acostarse *to lie down; to go to bed*	contar	24
acostumbrar a *to accustom to;* **acostumbra a hacerlo** *he habitually does it* Reg.	hablar	41
acostumbrarse a *to get used to* Reg.	hablar	41
acotar *to mark off; to fence in; to annotate* Reg.	hablar	41

acrecentar *to increase* (transitive)	cerrar	18
acrecentarse *to increase* (intransitive)	cerrar	18
acrecer *to increase* (transitive)	parecer	53
acreditar *to accredit; to authorize; to validate* Reg.	hablar	41
acreditarse *to prove one's value* Reg.	hablar	41
acribillar a *to riddle with (*e.g. *bullets)* Reg.	hablar	41
acriminar *to incriminate* Reg.	hablar	41
acriminarse *to be incriminated* Reg.	hablar	41
acriollarse *to acquire Latin-American ways* Reg.	hablar	41
acrisolar *to refine (a metal)* Reg.	hablar	41
acristalar *to glaze* Reg.	hablar	41
activar *to give an impetus to; to stimulate* Reg.	hablar	41
activarse *to go off (bells, alarms)* Reg.	hablar	41
actualizar *to bring up to date* Reg.	realizar	65
actualizarse *to get up to date* Reg.	realizar	65
actuar *to act (in all senses of the word)*	continuar	25
acuartelar *to quarter (troops); to billet* Reg.	hablar	41
acuatizar = **amarizar** Reg.	realizar	65
acuchillar *to knife* Reg.	hablar	41
acuchillear = **acuchillar** Reg.	hablar	41
acuciar *to plague (*e.g. *with problems)* Reg.	hablar	41
acuclillarse *to squat down* Reg.	hablar	41
acudir a *to come to (an appointment, etc.)* Reg.	vivir	89
acuitar *to afflict* Reg.	hablar	41
acular *to back up (said of horses)* Reg.	hablar	41
acumular *to accumulate* (transitive) Reg.	hablar	41
acumularse *to pile up* (intransitive) Reg.	hablar	41
acunar *to rock in a cradle* Reg.	hablar	41
acuñar *to coin (money, phrases)* Reg.	hablar	41

acurrucarse *to huddle up; to squat* Reg.	sacar	74
acusar *to accuse (of a crime);* **acusar recibo** *to acknowledge receipt* Reg.	hablar	41
acusarse de *to confess to* Reg.	hablar	41
adaptar *to adapt* (transitive) Reg.	hablar	41
adaptarse a *to adapt to* (intransitive) Reg.	hablar	41
adecentar *to make decent; to tidy up* Reg.	hablar	41
adecentarse *to make oneself tidy* Reg.	hablar	41
adecuar a *to adapt to* (transitive) Reg.	hablar	41
adecuarse a *to fit in with* Reg.	hablar	41
adelantar *to move forward; to advance; to overtake* (transitive) Reg.	hablar	41
adelantarse *to go forward; to gain (clocks); to get ahead* Reg.	hablar	41
adelgazar *to lose weight* Reg.	realizar	65
adentrarse en *to penetrate; to go deeper into* Reg.	hablar	41
aderezar *to season (food); to get ready* (transitive) Reg.	realizar	65
adestrar = adiestrar	cerrar	18
adeudar *to owe; to debit (an account)* Reg.	hablar	41
adherir a *to glue to* (transitive)	sentir	78
adherirse a *to adhere to; to stick by (things or principles)*	sentir	78
adiestrar *to train (an animal)* Reg.	hablar	41
adivinar *to guess* Reg.	hablar	41
adjudicar *to adjudicate* Reg.	sacar	74
adjudicarse *to win (trophy, etc.)* Reg.	sacar	74
adjuntar *to enclose (a note, document)* Reg.	hablar	41
administrar *to administrate; to administer (medicine, etc.)* Reg.	hablar	41
administrarse *to handle one's own affairs* Reg.	hablar	41

admirar *to admire; to surprise* Reg.	hablar	41
admirarse de *to be surprised at* Reg.	hablar	41
admitir *to admit (*i.e. *to accept); to confess* Reg.	vivir	89
adobar *to marinade; to pickle* Reg.	hablar	41
adoctrinar *to indoctrinate* Reg.	hablar	41
adolecer de *to suffer from (illness, defects)*	parecer	53
adoptar *to adopt* Reg.	hablar	41
adoquinar *to pave* Reg.	hablar	41
adorar *to adore* Reg.	hablar	41
adormecer *to make sleepy*	parecer	53
adormecerse *to get sleepy; to get numb*	parecer	53
adormilarse *to doze* Reg.	hablar	41
adormitarse = **adormilarse** Reg.	hablar	41
adornar *to decorate* Reg.	hablar	41
adosar algo a *to lean against* (transitive)*; to attach/secure to* Reg.	hablar	41
adquirir *to acquire*	adquirir	3
adscribir a *to assign (someone) to*	escribir	37
adscribirse a *to join (an organization)*	escribir	37
aducir *to adduce; to supply (arguments, evidence)*	producir	60
adueñarse de *to take possession of; to overwhelm* Reg.	hablar	41
adujar *to coil* Reg.	hablar	41
adular *to flatter* Reg.	hablar	41
adulterar *to adulterate* Reg.	hablar	41
advertir *to notice;* **advertir de** *to warn of*	sentir	78
afamar *to make famous* Reg.	hablar	41
afanarse en/por *to strive hard to* Reg.	hablar	41
afear *to make ugly* Reg.	hablar	41
afearse *to lose one's looks* Reg.	hablar	41
afectar *to affect;* + infinitive *to pretend to* Reg.	hablar	41
afeitar *to shave* (transitive) Reg.	hablar	41
afeitarse *to shave* (intransitive) Reg.	hablar	41

afeminarse *to grow effeminate* Reg.	hablar	41
aferrar *to weigh anchor* Reg.	hablar	41
aferrarse a *to cling to* Reg.	hablar	41
afianzar *to make firm/solid; to underwrite* Reg.	realizar	65
afianzarse *to become established* Reg.	realizar	65
aficionar a *to make someone like* Reg.	hablar	41
aficionarse a *to become fond of; to get interested in* Reg.	hablar	41
afilar *to sharpen* Reg.	hablar	41
afiliar a *to sign up* (transitive) Reg.	hablar	41
or	liar	45
afiliarse a *to sign up for* (intransitive) Reg.	hablar	41
or	liar	45
afinar *to tune (motors, instruments); to sing or play in tune* Reg.	hablar	41
afinarse *to get thinner* Reg.	hablar	41
afirmar *to declare; to affirm; to strengthen (a statement)* Reg.	hablar	41
afirmarse *to assert oneself* Reg.	hablar	41
afligir *to afflict*	rugir	72
afligirse *to grieve*	rugir	72
aflojar *to slacken* (transitive) Reg.	hablar	41
aflojarse *to slacken* (intransitive) Reg.	hablar	41
aflorar *to come to the surface (water, minerals, etc.)* Reg.	hablar	41
afluir *to flow (rivers, etc.); to flock (people, crowds)*	construir	23
afrancesarse *to grow Frenchified* Reg.	hablar	41
afrentar *to affront; to insult* Reg.	hablar	41
afrontar *to confront* Reg.	hablar	41
agachar *to bow (the head)* Reg.	hablar	41
agacharse *to crouch; to squat* Reg.	hablar	41
agarrar *to grasp; to grab* Reg.	hablar	41
agarrarse *to stick (*e.g. *food to a saucepan);* **a. a** *to grab hold of* Reg.	hablar	41

agarrochar *to goad* Reg.	hablar	41
agarrotar *to make stiff (muscles); to garrotte* Reg.	hablar	41
agarrotarse *to grow stiff (muscles, etc.)* Reg.	hablar	41
agasajar *to shower attentions on* Reg.	hablar	41
agazaparse *to crouch down* Reg.	hablar	41
agenciar *to manage to; to manage by 'fiddling'* Reg.	hablar	41
agenciarse *to get hold of (by 'fiddling')* Reg.	hablar	41
agigantar *to make huge* Reg.	hablar	41
agigantarse *to grow huge* Reg.	hablar	41
agilizar *to expedite (formalities, etc.)* Reg.	realizar	65
agitar *to agitate; to stir; to flap* (transitive) Reg.	hablar	41
agitarse *to flap, wave* (transitive) Reg.	hablar	41
aglomerar *to agglomerate* Reg.	hablar	41
aglomerarse *to pile up; to form a crowd* Reg.	hablar	41
aglutinar *to agglutinate; to bring together in one group* Reg.	hablar	41
aglutinarse *to form one group* (intransitive) Reg.	hablar	41
agobiar *to overwhelm; to overburden* Reg.	hablar	41
agobiarse *to be overwhelmed, overburdened* Reg.	hablar	41
agolparse *to throng, crowd (*e.g. *ideas in the mind)* Reg.	hablar	41
agonizar *to be in the throes of death* Reg.	realizar	65
agorar *to predict*	agorar	4
agostar *to parch* Reg.	hablar	41
agostarse *to become parched, withered* Reg.	hablar	41

agotar *to exhaust; to use up* Reg.	hablar	41
agotarse *to become exhausted* Reg.	hablar	41
agraciar *to grace* Reg.	hablar	41
agradar *to please* Reg.	hablar	41
agradecer *to thank for*	parecer	53
agrandar *to enlarge* Reg.	hablar	41
agrandarse *to get bigger* Reg.	hablar	41
agravar *to aggravate; to make worse* Reg.	hablar	41
agravarse *to grow worse* Reg.	hablar	41
agraviar *to offend* Reg.	hablar	41
agraviarse *to be offended* Reg.	hablar	41
agredir *to attack; to assault*	abolir	1
agregar a *to add to* Reg.	pagar	52
agregarse a *to join (a group, organization)* Reg.	pagar	52
agriarse *to turn sour* Reg.	hablar	41
or	liar	45
agrietarse *to crack* (intransitive) Reg.	hablar	41
agringarse *to become like a gringo* Reg.	hablar	41
agrumar *to clot* (intransitive)*; to get lumpy* Reg.	hablar	41
agrupar *to divide into groups* Reg.	hablar	41
agruparse *to form groups* (intransitive) Reg.	hablar	41
aguantar *to tolerate; to put up with* Reg.	hablar	41
aguantarse *to restrain oneself; to bear with* Reg.	hablar	41
aguar *to spoil (*e.g. *parties, atmosphere); to water down*	averiguar	13
aguardar *to wait for* Reg.	hablar	41
agudizar *to make more acute; to intensify* Reg.	realizar	65
agudizarse *to grow more intense (*e.g. *feelings, symptoms)* Reg.	realizar	65
aguerrir *to inure, toughen (persons)*	abolir	1
aguijar *to urge on; to goad* Reg.	hablar	41

aguijonear = **aguijar** Reg.	hablar	41
agujerear *to make a hole or holes in* Reg.	hablar	41
aguzar *to sharpen;* **a. el oído** *to prick up one's ears* Reg.	realizar	65
aherrumbrarse *to get rusty* Reg.	hablar	41
ahijar *to adopt (*e.g. *child)*	aislar	5
ahilar *to line up; to go single file*	aislar	5
ahincar *to urge; to press*, but see **aislar** (no. 5) for accents	sacar	74
ahitarse de *to gorge on*	aislar	5
ahogar *to drown* (transitive) Reg.	pagar	52
ahogarse *to drown* (intransitive) Reg.	pagar	52
ahondar *to make deeper;* **ahondar en** *to go deeper into (a subject)* Reg.	hablar	41
ahorcar *to hang (as in executions)* Reg.	sacar	74
ahorcarse *to hang oneself* Reg.	sacar	74
ahormar *to shape, mold/(Brit.) mould* Reg.	hablar	41
ahorrar *to save; to spare* Reg.	hablar	41
ahorrarse *to spare oneself (trouble, bother, etc.)* Reg.	hablar	41
ahoyar *to dig holes in* Reg.	hablar	41
ahuchar *to stash away (money)*	aullar	11
ahuecar *to hollow out* Reg.	sacar	74
ahumar *to smoke (*e.g. *meat, fish)*	aullar	11
ahumarse *to get blackened with soot, smoke*	aullar	11
ahusarse *to taper* (intransitive)	aullar	11
ahuyentar *to frighten away* Reg.	hablar	41
airar *to anger*	aislar	5
airarse *to get angry*	aislar	5
airear *to air; to ventilate* Reg.	hablar	41
airearse *to get some air* Reg.	hablar	41
aislar de *to isolate from*	aislar	5
aislarse de *to cut oneself off from*	aislar	5

ajar *to make something look worn or frayed* Reg.	hablar	41
ajarse *to become worn, rough, or frayed* Reg.	hablar	41
ajardinar *to landscape* Reg.	hablar	41
ajetrearse *to rush around; to be very busy* Reg.	hablar	41
ajuiciar *to bring to one's senses* Reg.	hablar	41
ajustar *to tighten; to adjust* Reg.	hablar	41
ajustarse a *to become adapted to; to obey (norms, rules)* Reg.	hablar	41
ajusticiar *to execute (= to inflict death penalty)* Reg.	hablar	41
alabar *to praise* Reg.	hablar	41
alabarse *to boast* Reg.	hablar	41
alabear *to warp something* Reg.	hablar	41
alabearse *to become warped* Reg.	hablar	41
alambicar *to distill/(Brit.) distil; to make flowery (*e.g. *style)* Reg.	sacar	74
alambrar *to fence with wire* Reg.	hablar	41
alardear de *to boast about* Reg.	hablar	41
alargar *to lengthen; to stretch out (the hand)* Reg.	pagar	52
alargarse *to get longer* Reg.	pagar	52
alarmar *to alarm* Reg.	hablar	41
alarmarse *to get alarmed* Reg.	hablar	41
albergar *to accommodate (*i.e. *to house); to harbor/(Brit.) harbour (feeling, etc.)* Reg.	pagar	52
albergarse *to take shelter* Reg.	pagar	52
alborotar *to make a racket; to make excited, overworked* Reg.	hablar	41
alborotarse *to get excited, overworked* Reg.	hablar	41
alborozar *to fill with joy* Reg.	realizar	65
alborozarse *to be overjoyed* Reg.	realizar	65

alcanzar *to catch up with; to reach; to hit the target;* **a. a** *to manage to* Reg.	realizar	65
alcoholizarse *to become an alcoholic* Reg.	realizar	65
alear *to alloy* Reg.	hablar	41
aleccionar *to lecture (*i.e. *deliver a sermon to)* Reg.	hablar	41
alegar *to put forward (reasons, motives)* Reg.	pagar	52
alegrar *to gladden* Reg.	hablar	41
alegrarse *to be glad* Reg.	hablar	41
alejar de *to move away from* (transitive) Reg.	hablar	41
alejarse de *to move away from* (intransitive) Reg.	hablar	41
alelar *to stupefy* Reg.	hablar	41
alelarse *to become stupefied* Reg.	hablar	41
alentar *to encourage; to cheer on*	cerrar	18
alentarse *to get better; to take heart* Reg.	cerrar	18
alertar de *to alert to (danger, etc.)* Reg.	hablar	41
aletargar *to make lethargic* Reg.	pagar	52
aletargarse *to become lethargic* Reg.	pagar	52
aletear *to beat, flap (wings, fins)* (intransitive) Reg.	hablar	41
alfabetizar *to teach how to read and write* Reg.	realizar	65
alfilerar *to pin* Reg.	hablar	41
alfombrar *to carpet* Reg.	hablar	41
aliar *to ally*	liar	45
aliarse con *to become an ally of*	liar	45
alicatar *to tile* Reg.	hablar	41
alienar *to alienate* Reg.	hablar	41
alienarse *to become alienated* Reg.	hablar	41
aligerar *to lighten; to hasten (pace)* (transitive) Reg.	hablar	41

aligerarse de *to remove (cloak, etc.); to lighten* (intransitive) Reg.	hablar	41
alijar *to smuggle ashore (drugs, contraband, etc.)* Reg.	hablar	41
alimentar *to feed* (transitive) Reg.	hablar	41
alimentarse de/con *to feed on* (intransitive) Reg.	hablar	41
alindar *to mark off* Reg.	hablar	41
alinear *to align* Reg.	hablar	41
alinearse *to get into line* Reg.	hablar	41
alisar *to smooth* Reg.	hablar	41
alistarse *to enlist; to get ready* (transitive) Reg.	hablar	41
aliviar *to alleviate* Reg.	hablar	41
aliviarse *to ease (pain)* (intransitive) Reg.	hablar	41
allanar *to raid (a house); to sweep away (problem)* Reg.	hablar	41
allanarse a *to agree to accept* Reg.	hablar	41
allegar *to gather together* (transitive) Reg.	pagar	52
allegarse a *to approach; to take up (an opinion)* Reg.	pagar	52
almacenar *to store (goods, data on disk)* Reg.	hablar	41
almibarar *to preserve in syrup* Reg.	hablar	41
almidonar *to starch* Reg.	hablar	41
almohadillar *to pad; to cushion* Reg.	hablar	41
almorzar *to eat lunch*	almorzar	6
alojar *to accommodate (*e.g. *in hotel)* (transitive) Reg.	hablar	41
alojarse *to stay, lodge (in a hotel, etc.)* Reg.	hablar	41
alongar *to lengthen* (transitive) Reg.	pagar	52
alquilar *to rent, hire* Reg.	hablar	41
alquilarse *to be for hire* Reg.	hablar	41
alquitranar *to tar* Reg.	hablar	41

alterar *to alter, upset* (transitive) Reg.	hablar	41
alterarse *to get upset* Reg.	hablar	41
altercar *to argue* Reg.	sacar	74
alternar con *to alternate* (transitive)*; to mix with the 'best' set (socially)* Reg.	hablar	41
alucinar *to delude; to astound;* also intransitive = *to hallucinate* Reg.	hablar	41
alucinarse *to hallucinate; to be astounded* Reg.	hablar	41
aludir a *to allude to* Reg.	vivir	89
alumbrar *to illuminate; to be bright* Reg.	hablar	41
alzar *to raise* Reg.	realizar	65
alzarse *to rise* Reg.	realizar	65
amaestrar *to train (an animal)* Reg.	hablar	41
amagar *to hint;* **a. con** + infinitive *to look as though one is going to...* Reg.	pagar	52
amainar *to shorten; to wane* Reg.	hablar	41
amalgamar *to amalgamate* Reg.	hablar	41
amamantar *to nurse (*i.e. *to breastfeed)* Reg.	hablar	41
amancebarse *to set up house together* Reg.	hablar	41
amancillar *to tarnish* Reg.	hablar	41
amanecer *to dawn;* **amanecí cansado** *I woke up tired*	parecer	53
amansar *to tame* Reg.	hablar	41
amar *to love (passionately)* Reg.	hablar	41
amarar = **amarizar** Reg.	hablar	41
amargar *to embitter* Reg.	pagar	52
amargarse *to become bitter (person)* Reg.	pagar	52
amarillear *to turn yellow* Reg.	hablar	41
amarillecer = **amarillear**	parecer	53
amarizar *to land on water (aircraft)* Reg.	realizar	65
amarrar *to moor; to tie up (boat)* Reg.	hablar	41

amartelar *to make jealous* Reg.	hablar	41
amartillar *to cock (a gun); to hammer* Reg.	hablar	41
amasar *to knead; to amass* Reg.	hablar	41
ambicionar *to earnestly desire to; to aspire to* Reg.	hablar	41
ambientar *to give atmosphere to; to set a film, story* Reg.	hablar	41
ambientarse *to adjust to one's surroundings* Reg.	hablar	41
ambular *to walk; to move about* Reg.	hablar	41
amedrentar *to frighten* Reg.	hablar	41
amedrentarse por *to get scared about* Reg.	hablar	41
amelgar *to plow/plough regularly* Reg.	pagar	52
amenazar de *to threaten with;* **a. con** + infinitive *to threaten to* Reg.	realizar	65
amenguar *to wane, diminish*	averiguar	13
amenizar *to make agreeable* Reg.	realizar	65
americanizar *to Americanize* Reg.	realizar	65
ametrallar *to machine-gun* Reg.	hablar	41
amigarse *to make friends* Reg.	pagar	52
amilanar *to intimidate* Reg.	hablar	41
amilanarse *to become intimidated* Reg.	hablar	41
aminorar *to diminish* Reg.	hablar	41
amistarse = **amigarse** Reg.	hablar	41
amnistiar *to grant amnesty*	liar	45
amoblar = **amueblar**	contar	24
amodorrar *to make drowsy* Reg.	hablar	41
amodorrarse *to become drowsy* Reg.	hablar	41
amodorrecer *to make drowsy*	parecer	53
amohecer *to mold/(Brit.) mould*	parecer	53
amohinar *to annoy*	aislar	5
amohinarse *to get annoyed, sulky*	aislar	5
amojonar *to mark off boundaries with posts* Reg.	hablar	41
amolar *to sharpen* (= **afilar**)	contar	24

amoldar *to mold/(Brit.) mould* Reg.	hablar	41
amoldarse a *to adapt to* Reg.	hablar	41
amonedar *to coin; to stamp (an imprint on)* Reg.	hablar	41
amonestar *to admonish* Reg.	hablar	41
amontonar *to pile up* (transitive) Reg.	hablar	41
amontonarse *to become piled up* Reg.	hablar	41
amoratar *to make black and blue* Reg.	hablar	41
amoratarse *to become black and blue* Reg.	hablar	41
amordazar *to muzzle; to gag* Reg.	realizar	65
amorrar *to hang one's head* Reg.	hablar	41
amorrarse *to sulk* Reg.	hablar	41
amortajar *to shroud* Reg.	hablar	41
amortecer *to tone down*	parecer	53
amortiguar *to cushion; to absorb shock*	averiguar	13
amortizar *to be write off (costs, debts)* Reg.	realizar	65
amoscarse *to become annoyed, huffy* Reg.	sacar	74
amotinar *to incite to riot or mutiny* Reg.	hablar	41
amotinarse *to rebel, riot* Reg.	hablar	41
amparar de *to protect from* Reg.	hablar	41
ampararse en *to seek protection in/with* Reg.	hablar	41
ampliar *to expand, extend*	liar	45
amplificar *to amplify (sound, etc.)* Reg.	sacar	74
ampollar *to make blistered* Reg.	hablar	41
ampollarse *to get blistered; to blister* Reg.	hablar	41
amputar *to amputate* Reg.	hablar	41
amueblar *to furnish* Reg.	hablar	41
amunicionar *to supply with ammunition* Reg.	hablar	41
amurallar *to wall* Reg.	hablar	41
amusgar *to throw back the ears (said of animals); to squint to see better* Reg.	pagar	52

anadear *to waddle like a duck* Reg.	hablar	41
analizar *to analyze* Reg.	realizar	65
analizarse *to undergo psychoanalysis, be analyzed* Reg.	realizar	65
anarquizar *to spread anarchy* Reg.	realizar	65
anarquizarse *to become anarchic* Reg.	realizar	65
anatematizar *to anathematize* Reg.	realizar	65
anatomizar *to anatomize* Reg.	realizar	65
anchar *to widen* Reg.	hablar	41
anclar *to anchor* Reg.	hablar	41
ancorar *to anchor* Reg.	hablar	41
andar *to walk; to go; to run (*e.g. *clocks, motors)*	andar	7
aneblarse *to cloud up, grow misty*	cerrar	18
anegar *to flood* Reg.	pagar	52
anegarse *to become flooded* Reg.	pagar	52
anestesiar *to anesthetize* Reg.	hablar	41
anexar *to annex* Reg.	hablar	41
anglicizar *to Anglicize* Reg.	realizar	65
angostar *to narrow* Reg.	hablar	41
angustiar *to distress* Reg.	hablar	41
angustiarse por *to get distressed about* Reg.	hablar	41
anhelar *to desire eagerly; to yearn for* Reg.	hablar	41
anidar *to nest* Reg.	hablar	41
anillar *to fit a ring on (animals, pistons)* Reg.	hablar	41
animar a *to encourage to* Reg.	hablar	41
animarse *to be encouraged; to cheer up; to become more lively* Reg.	hablar	41
aniquilar *to annihilate* Reg.	hablar	41
anochecer *to grow dark (day)*	parecer	53
anonadar *to overwhelm; to leave dumbfounded* Reg.	hablar	41
anotar *to note down; to enrol (*e.g. *for a course)* (transitive) Reg.	hablar	41

anquilosarse *to become stiff (joints, etc.)* Reg.	hablar	41
ansiar *to long for; to yearn to*	liar	45
anteceder *to precede* Reg.	comer	22
antedatar *to antedate; to backdate* Reg.	hablar	41
antedecir *to predict* (usu. **predecir)**	decir	28
antepagar *to pay in advance* Reg.	pagar	52
anteponer a *to put before; to prefer*	poner	58
anticipar *to bring something forward in time; to advance (information, etc.)* Reg.	hablar	41
anticiparse a *to act or happen before; to jump ahead of* Reg.	hablar	41
anticuar (often conjugated like **continuar)** *to antiquate* Reg.	hablar	41
anticuarse (often conjugated like **continuar**) *to become antiquated* Reg.	hablar	41
antiguarse *to attain seniority*	averiguar	13
antipatizar *to arouse a strong dislike* Reg.	realizar	65
antojarse : se me antoja... *I feel like...; it seems to me...* Reg.	hablar	41
anublar *to cloud; to obscure* Reg.	hablar	41
anublarse *to become cloudy* Reg.	hablar	41
anudar *to knot; to tie* Reg.	hablar	41
anular *to annul; to cancel* Reg.	hablar	41
anunciar *to announce; to advertise* Reg.	hablar	41
anunciarse *to promise to be (*e.g. *fruitful, problematic)* Reg.	hablar	41
añadir *to add* Reg.	vivir	89
añejar *to age (e.g. wine)* (transitive)	hablar	41
añilar *to use bluing (on clothes)* Reg.	hablar	41
añorar *to long for* Reg.	hablar	41
aojar *to cast the evil eye* Reg.	hablar	41
apabullar *to crush; to overwhelm* Reg.	hablar	41

apacentar *to pasture*	cerrar	18
apacentarse de *to feed on*	cerrar	18
apaciguar *to pacify*	averiguar	13
apaciguarse *to calm down*	averiguar	13
apachurrar *to crush* Reg.	hablar	41
apadrinar *to act as a godfather; to be best man; to back* Reg.	hablar	41
apagar *to put out; to extinguish; to turn off* Reg.	pagar	52
apagarse *to go out (lights, etc.); to fade away* Reg.	pagar	52
apalabrar *to speak for; to reserve* Reg.	hablar	41
apalabrarse para + infinitive *to agree to do* Reg.	hablar	41
apalancar *to jack; to lever up* Reg.	sacar	74
apalancarse en *to make oneself comfortable in* Reg.	sacar	74
apalear *to beat (with a stick)* Reg.	hablar	41
apandillarse *to band together* Reg.	hablar	41
apantanar *to make swampy* Reg.	hablar	41
apantanarse *to get swampy; to get stuck in the mud* Reg.	hablar	41
apañar *to rig (elections, etc.)* Reg.	hablar	41
apañarse con *to manage with, get by on;* **me las apaño** *I get by* Reg.	hablar	41
aparcar *to park* Reg.	sacar	74
aparear *to make even; to pair; to mate* (transitive) Reg.	hablar	41
aparearse *to mate* (intransitive) Reg.	hablar	41
aparecer *to appear*	parecer	53
aparecerse *to appear (ghosts, visions, etc.)*	parecer	53
aparejar *to prepare (*e.g. *boats); to harness* Reg.	hablar	41
aparentar *to look to be; to feign* Reg.	hablar	41
apartar *to separate* Reg.	hablar	41

apartarse *to move further away/to one side;* **a. de** *to drift off (the subject, etc.)* Reg.	hablar	41
apasionar *to arouse passion (in someone)* Reg.	hablar	41
apasionarse por *to become impassioned, wild about* Reg.	hablar	41
apayasarse *to clown around* Reg.	hablar	41
apear *to help someone alight (*e.g. *from a vehicle)* Reg.	hablar	41
apearse de *to get off; to get out of (vehicle)* Reg.	hablar	41
apechugar con *to put up with; to grin and bear it* Reg.	pagar	52
apedazar *to mend; to patch; to tear to pieces* Reg.	realizar	65
apedrear *to stone, pelt with stones* Reg.	hablar	41
apegarse a *to become attached to; to grow fond of* Reg.	pagar	52
apelar de or **contra** *to appeal against;* **a. a** *to have recourse to* Reg.	hablar	41
apellidar *to give someone a surname* Reg.	hablar	41
apellidarse : **se apellida González** *his surname's González* Reg.	hablar	41
apelmazarse *to squeeze together; to squeeze into one* Reg.	realizar	65
apelotonar *to bunch together; to pile up; to roll (something) into a ball* Reg.	hablar	41
apelotonarse *to roll (oneself) up into a ball; to crowd together* Reg.	hablar	41
apenar *to cause sorrow; to fill (someone) with grief* Reg.	hablar	41
apenarse de/por *to grieve over* Reg.	hablar	41
aperar *to repair* Reg.	hablar	41
apercibir *to warn* Reg.	vivir	89
apercibirse de *to notice* Reg.	hablar	41

apercollar *to grab by the neck* (archaic)	contar	24
apergaminarse *to become withered like parchment* Reg.	hablar	41
apersogar *to tether* Reg.	pagar	52
apersonarse *to appear in person; to show up (somewhere)* Reg.	hablar	41
aperturar *to open (*e.g. *exhibition, conference)* Reg.	hablar	41
apesadumbrar *to fill with grief; to make sad* Reg.	hablar	41
apesadumbrarse *to grieve* Reg.	hablar	41
apestar *to stink* Reg.	hablar	41
apetecer (usually third person only): **no me apetece** *I don't feel like it*	parecer	53
apiadar *to move to pity* Reg.	hablar	41
apiadarse de *to have pity on* Reg.	hablar	41
apicararse *to become a rascal; to turn into a ne'er-do-well* Reg.	hablar	41
apilar *to pile up, heap up* Reg.	hablar	41
apiñar *to squeeze together; to pack (things/people) together* Reg.	hablar	41
apiñarse *to be crowded together; to squeeze together* Reg.	hablar	41
apisonar *to roll with a roller; to flatten* Reg.	hablar	41
aplacar *to placate; to satisfy* Reg.	sacar	74
aplanar *to level, flatten; to astound* Reg.	hablar	41
aplanarse *to cave in; to become discouraged, give up* Reg.	hablar	41
aplastar *to smash, flatten; to leave (someone) speechless* Reg.	hablar	41
aplastarse *to flatten oneself (*e.g. *against a wall)* Reg.	hablar	41
aplaudir *to applaud, clap* Reg.	vivir	89
aplazar *to postpone* Reg.	realizar	65
aplicar a *to apply (match, flame) to; to assign to* Reg.	sacar	74

aplicarse a *to apply oneself to; to devote oneself to* Reg.	sacar	74
aplomar *to plumb; to make straight with a plumb-line* Reg.	hablar	41
aplomarse *to collapse* Reg.	hablar	41
apocar *to lessen; to humiliate; to humble* Reg.	sacar	74
apocarse *to feel humiliated; to feel small* Reg.	sacar	74
apocopar *to apocopate* Reg.	hablar	41
apodar *to nickname* Reg.	hablar	41
apoderar *to give legal powers to; to empower* Reg.	hablar	41
apoderarse de *to take possession of* Reg.	hablar	41
apolillarse *to become moth-eaten* Reg.	hablar	41
apologizar *to praise; to defend* Reg.	realizar	65
apoltronarse *to sprawl in a chair; to become lazy* Reg.	hablar	41
aporrear *to club (*i.e. *to hit with a club)* Reg.	hablar	41
aportar a *to contribute to* Reg.	hablar	41
aportillar *to break down; to breach (wall, etc.)* Reg.	hablar	41
aposentar *to lodge (someone)* Reg.	hablar	41
aposentarse *to take lodging* Reg.	hablar	41
aposesionarse de *to take possession of* Reg.	hablar	41
apostar *to bet*	contar	24
apostarse con *to compete with*	contar	24
apostar *to post a sentry* Reg.	hablar	41
apostarse *to position oneself (*e.g. *near the door, etc.)* Reg.	hablar	41
apostatar de *to apostatize from; to renounce (beliefs)* Reg.	hablar	41
apostillar *to annotate; to add a comment* Reg.	hablar	41

apoyar *to support;* **a. algo contra** *to lean something against* Reg.	hablar	41
apoyarse contra *to lean (oneself) against;* **a. en** *to rely on* Reg.	hablar	41
apreciar *to value; to evaluate; to appreciate* Reg.	hablar	41
aprehender *to apprehend; to confiscate (assets, etc.)* Reg.	comer	22
apremiar *to urge; to harass* Reg.	hablar	41
aprender *to learn* Reg.	comer	22
aprensar *to crush; to press (in a press or crusher); to oppress* Reg.	hablar	41
apresar *to seize; to capture; to grab* Reg.	hablar	41
aprestar *to make ready* Reg.	hablar	41
aprestarse a *to get ready to* Reg.	hablar	41
apresurar *to make someone/something go faster* Reg.	hablar	41
apresurarse *to hurry* (intransitive) Reg.	hablar	41
apretar *to press; to squeeze; to fit tightly*	cerrar	18
apretarse *to get narrower, tighter; to become squashed together*	cerrar	18
apretujar *to jam; to press hard* Reg.	hablar	41
aprisionar *to imprison; to shackle* Reg.	hablar	41
aprobar *to approve; to pass an examination*	contar	24
aprontar *to prepare quickly; to prepare without delay* Reg.	hablar	41
aprontarse *to get ready* Reg.	hablar	41
apropiar a = **adecuar** Reg.	hablar	41
apropiarse de *to appropriate something* Reg.	hablar	41
aprovechar *to make use of; to take advantage of.* **¡Que aproveche!** *bon appetit!* Reg.	hablar	41

aprovecharse de *to take advantage of* Reg.	hablar	41
aprovisionar *to supply with provisions* Reg.	hablar	41
aproximar *to bring near* Reg.	hablar	41
aproximarse a *to approach* Reg.	hablar	41
apuntalar *to prop up, shore up* Reg.	hablar	41
apuntar *to note; to write down; to begin to show; to sprout;* **a. a** *to point at; to point out; to aim at* Reg.	hablar	41
apuntarse *to chalk up (point, victory); to score (victory); to be in agreement; to sign up for* (**para**) *something* Reg.	hablar	41
apuntillar *to kill off (an animal)* Reg.	hablar	41
apuñalar *to stab* Reg.	hablar	41
apuñalear = **apuñalar** Reg.	hablar	41
apuñetear *to punch with the fist* Reg.	hablar	41
apurar *to drain dry; to annoy; to press (someone to do something)* Reg.	hablar	41
apurarse *to fret;* (Lat. Am.) *to hurry* Reg.	hablar	41
aquejar *to afflict; to distress* Reg.	hablar	41
aquietar *to quieten; to calm down; to allay (fears)* Reg.	hablar	41
aquilatar *to assay (metal); to appraise; to appreciate in value* Reg.	hablar	41
aquistar *to gain in value* Reg.	hablar	41
arabizar *to make Arabic; to Arabize* Reg.	realizar	65
arañar *to scratch* Reg.	hablar	41
arar *to plow/(Brit.) plough* Reg.	hablar	41
arbitrar *to referee; to arbitrate* Reg.	hablar	41
arbolar *to raise (flag); to set upright (a pole)* Reg.	hablar	41
arbolarse *to rear up (horse)* Reg.	hablar	41
arborizar *to plant with trees* Reg.	realizar	65

arcaizar *to make archaic*	arcaizar	8
arcar *to arch; to beat (wool);* also = **arquear** Reg.	sacar	74
archivar *to file (= to store away in a file)* Reg.	hablar	41
arder *to burn* (intransitive) Reg.	hablar	41
arenar *to spread with sand; to sprinkle with sand* Reg.	hablar	41
arengar *to harangue* Reg.	pagar	52
argamasar *to mix (cement); to plaster a wall* Reg.	hablar	41
argentar *to silver* Reg.	hablar	41
argüir *to argue (a point)*	argüir	9
argumentar *to argue (a point)* Reg.	hablar	41
aridecerse *to become arid; to become dry*	parecer	53
armar *to arm; to assemble (a mechanism); to kick up (a fuss)* Reg.	hablar	41
armarse de *to arm oneself with; to equip oneself with* Reg.	hablar	41
armonizar *to harmonize* Reg.	realizar	65
arpar = **arañar Reg.**	hablar	41
arponear *to harpoon* Reg.	hablar	41
arquear = *to retch* Reg.	hablar	41
arquearse *to form a vault, arch, curve* Reg.	hablar	41
arracimarse *to cluster; to hang in bunches* Reg.	hablar	41
arraigar *to take root* Reg.	pagar	52
arraigarse *to become deeply settled* Reg.	pagar	52
arramblar con *to sweep away; to make off with; to push to one side* Reg.	hablar	41
arrancar *to pull out, up; to start up (motor)* Reg.	sacar	74
arrasar *to level; to raze to the ground; to sweep away (obstacles)* Reg.	hablar	41

arrasarse en *to become flooded with (tears)* Reg.	hablar	41
arrastrar *to drag* Reg.	hablar	41
arrastrarse *to crawl, creep* Reg.	hablar	41
arrear *to urge on (horses, etc.); to deliver (a blow)* Reg.	hablar	41
arrebañar *to scrape together; to scrape up (remains)* Reg.	hablar	41
arrebatar a *to snatch from* Reg.	hablar	41
arrebatarse por *to become ecstatic over; to get carried away by* Reg.	hablar	41
arrebolar *to redden* Reg.	hablar	41
arrebozar *to wrap up in a cloak* Reg.	realizar	65
arrebozarse *to muffle oneself; to wrap oneself up in a cloak* Reg.	realizar	65
arrebujar *to jumble together* Reg.	hablar	41
arrebujarse en *to snuggle into, wrap oneself in*	hablar	41
arreciar *to grow worse; to get more severe (weather, etc.)* Reg.	hablar	41
arreciarse = **arreciar** Reg.	hablar	41
arrecirse *to grow stiff with cold*	abolir	1
arredrar *to frighten off; to drive back (by intimidation)* Reg.	hablar	41
arredrarse *to be intimidated; to back off* Reg.	hablar	41
arregazar *to tuck up* Reg.	realizar	65
arreglar *to fix; to repair; to put right; to arrange* Reg.	hablar	41
arreglarse con *to come to an agreement with;* **arreglárselas para** *to manage to* Reg.	hablar	41
arregostarse a *to take a liking to* Reg.	hablar	41
arrejuntarse *to live together, cohabit* Reg.	hablar	41
arrellanarse *to sprawl in one's seat* Reg.	hablar	41

arremangar *to turn up (sleeves); to tuck up* Reg.	pagar	52
arremangarse = **arremangar** Reg.	pagar	52
arremeter contra *to rush forth upon; to assault; to charge against* Reg.	comer	22
arremolinarse *to whirl; to mill about in a crowd* Reg.	hablar	41
arrendar *to rent; to lease*	cerrar	18
arrepentirse de *to repent of; to back down from*	sentir	78
arrestar *to arrest* Reg.	hablar	41
arrestarse a *to rush ahead boldly with; to charge headlong into* Reg.	hablar	41
arrezagar *to tuck up* Reg.	pagar	52
arriar *to lower (flag)*	liar	45
arriarse *to become flooded*	liar	45
arribar *to arrive; to make port* Reg.	hablar	41
arriesgar *to risk something* Reg.	pagar	52
arriesgarse *to take a risk* Reg.	pagar	52
arrimar a *to bring close to; to draw (something) close to* Reg.	hablar	41
arrimarse a *to come close to; to snuggle up to* Reg.	hablar	41
arrinconar *to corner; to abandon; to push away; to throw out* Reg.	hablar	41
arrizar *to reef; to lash down* Reg.	realizar	65
arrobar *to enchant; to fill with rapture* Reg.	hablar	41
arrobarse *to be enraptured* Reg.	hablar	41
arrodillarse *to kneel* Reg.	hablar	41
arrogarse *to arrogate* Reg.	pagar	52
arrojar *to throw; to fling* Reg.	hablar	41
arrojarse *to throw oneself; to leap* Reg.	hablar	41
arrollar *to trample upon; to flatten (opponents); to run down; to roll up* Reg.	hablar	41
arropar *to wrap up (with clothing)* Reg.	hablar	41

arroparse *to wrap up warm (with clothing)* Reg.	hablar	41
arrostrar *to face up to; to brave* Reg.	hablar	41
arrostrarse *to pitch into (a fight, the fray)* Reg.	hablar	41
arrugar *to wrinkle* (transitive) Reg.	pagar	52
arrugarse *to wrinkle* (intransitive) Reg.	hablar	41
arruinar *to ruin* Reg.	hablar	41
arruinarse *to go to ruin* Reg.	hablar	41
arrullar *to coo; to lull (to sleep)* Reg.	hablar	41
arrumbar *to take bearings (*i.e. *a ship)* Reg.	hablar	41
arrumbarse *to be seasick* (= **marearse**) Reg.	hablar	41
arrutinarse *to get into a rut/routine* Reg.	hablar	41
artesonar *to stucco; to put decorative panels on* Reg.	hablar	41
articular *to articulate; to join together; to draw up (rules)* Reg.	hablar	41
artificializar *to make artificial* Reg.	realizar	65
asalariar *to fix a salary; to put on the payroll* Reg.	hablar	41
asaltar *to assault* Reg.	hablar	41
asar *to roast; to broil; to grill* Reg.	hablar	41
asarse *to feel extremely hot* Reg.	hablar	41
ascender *to promote (= to raise someone's rank); to ascend*	perder	55
asear *to clean up; to adorn, embellish* Reg.	hablar	41
asearse *to get cleaned up; to smarten oneself up* Reg.	hablar	41
asediar *to besiege; to lay siege to* Reg.	hablar	41
asegurar *to make secure; to assure; to assert; to insure* Reg.	hablar	41
asegurarse *to get insured;* **a. de** *to make certain about* Reg.	hablar	41
asemejar *to make like* Reg.	hablar	41

asemejarse a *to be similar* (= **parecerse a**) Reg.	hablar	41
asenderear *to hound, harry* Reg.	hablar	41
asentar *to seat; to settle (someone, something); to lay down (rules, etc.)*	cerrar	18
asentarse *to settle; to settle down*	cerrar	18
asentir *to assent;* **a. a** *to assent to*	sentir	78
aserrar = **serrar**	cerrar	18
asertar *to assert* Reg.	hablar	41
asesinar *to murder* Reg.	hablar	41
asesorar *to advise* (= **aconsejar**) Reg.	hablar	41
asesorarse de *to seek advice from* Reg.	hablar	41
asestar *to aim (a blow);* **a. a** *to aim at* Reg.	hablar	41
aseverar *to assert* Reg.	hablar	41
asfaltar *to asphalt* Reg.	hablar	41
asfixiar *to asphyxiate* (= **ahogar**) Reg.	hablar	41
asfixiarse *to be asphyxiated* (= **ahogarse**) Reg.	hablar	41
asignar *to assign; to allocate* Reg.	hablar	41
asilar *to give refuge to; to give asylum to* Reg.	hablar	41
asilarse en *to take refuge in* Reg.	hablar	41
asimilar *to assimilate* (transitive) Reg.	hablar	41
asimilarse *to become assimilated;* **a. a** *to resemble (=* **parecerse a***)* Reg.	hablar	41
asir *to grasp*	asir	10
asirse a *to grasp hold of*	asir	10
asistir *to assist* (= **ayudar**)*;* **a. a** *to attend (classes, etc.)* Reg.	vivir	89
asociar con *to associate with; to relate to* Reg.	hablar	41
asociarse *to associate* (intransitive)*; to act jointly* Reg.	hablar	41
asolanar *to parch* Reg.	hablar	41
asolar *to parch, dry up* (transitive) Reg.	hablar	41

asolar (formerly conjugated like **contar**) *to raze, destroy* Reg.	hablar	41
asolear *to sun* Reg.	hablar	41
asolearse *to get sun-tanned; to sun oneself* Reg.	hablar	41
asomar *to show something through an opening; to stick out (head, etc.)* Reg.	hablar	41
asomarse a/por *to lean out of* Reg.	hablar	41
asombrar *to astonish; to amaze* Reg.	hablar	41
asombrarse de *to be astonished at* Reg.	hablar	41
asordar = **ensordecer** Reg.	hablar	41
asosegar = **sosegar**	negar	49
aspirar *to inhale; to aspire;* **a. a** *to aspire to* Reg.	hablar	41
asquear *to disgust; to nauseate* Reg.	hablar	41
asquearse *to feel nauseated* Reg.	hablar	41
astillar *to splinter* Reg.	hablar	41
astringir *to constrict*	rugir	72
asumir *to assume (responsibility, task); to suppose* Reg.	vivir	89
asurar *to burn (food)* (= **quemar**)*; to parch (land)* Reg.	hablar	41
asustar *to scare* Reg.	hablar	41
asustarse de/por *to be scared about/by* Reg.	hablar	41
atacar *to attack; to assault* Reg.	sacar	74
atajar *to intercept; to take a shortcut* Reg.	hablar	41
atajarse *to feel ashamed* (= **avergonzarse**) Reg.	hablar	41
atañer *to concern* (= **concernir**. Third person only)	tañer	81
atar *to tie up* Reg.	hablar	41
atarse en *to get bogged down in* Reg.	hablar	41
atarantar *to stun* Reg.	hablar	41
atarantarse *to be stunned* Reg.	hablar	41

atardecer *to draw towards evening; to grow dark (day)*	parecer	53
atarear *to assign a task to* Reg.	hablar	41
atarearse *to work very hard* Reg.	hablar	41
atarugar *to make someone be quiet; to peg down* Reg.	pagar	52
atarugarse *to get confused; to choke* Reg.	pagar	52
atascar *to clog up* (transitive) Reg.	sacar	74
atascarse *to get stuck; to get clogged up* Reg.	sacar	74
ataviar *to attire; to adorn*	liar	45
ataviarse con *to dress oneself up in*	liar	45
atediar *to bore* (= **aburrir**) Reg.	hablar	41
atediarse *to get bored* (= **aburrirse**) Reg.	hablar	41
atemorizar *to frighten* Reg.	realizar	65
atemorizarse *to get frightened* Reg.	realizar	65
atemperar *to temper* Reg.	hablar	41
atender a *to attend to; to pay attention; to take care; to take into account; to wait on*	perder	55
atenerse a *to abide by*	tener	82
atentar contra *to make an attempt/ assault on* Reg.	hablar	41
atenuar *to lessen; to tone down*	continuar	25
aterirse *to become stiff with cold*	abolir	1
aterrar *to terrify* Reg.	hablar	41
aterrarse *to become frightened* Reg.	hablar	41
aterrar *to cover with earth; to demolish*	cerrar	18
aterrizar *to land* Reg.	realizar	65
aterrorizar *to terrify* Reg.	realizar	65
atesorar *to treasure; to hoard up; to amass* Reg.	hablar	41
atestar *to attest;* **a. de** *to cram, stuff with* (in latter meaning sometimes conj. like **cerrar**) Reg.	hablar	41
atestiguar *to testify; to attest*	averiguar	13

atezarse *to become tanned* Reg.	realizar	65
atiborrar *to stuff, cram full* Reg.	hablar	41
atiborrarse de *to gorge oneself on* Reg.	hablar	41
atiesar *to stiffen* Reg.	hablar	41
atildar *to spruce up* Reg.	hablar	41
atinar a *to guess right;* + infinitive *to manage to* Reg.	hablar	41
atisbar *to catch a glimpse of* Reg.	hablar	41
atizar *to stir up; to poke (a fire); to rouse* Reg.	realizar	65
atolondrar *to confuse, fluster* Reg.	hablar	41
atolondrarse *to get confused* Reg.	hablar	41
atollarse *to get stuck* Reg.	hablar	41
atomizar *to break into fragments; to spray with fine droplets* Reg.	realizar	65
atontar *to stupefy* Reg.	hablar	41
atontarse *to become stupefied* Reg.	hablar	41
atorar *to obstruct* Reg.	hablar	41
atorarse *to be choked* Reg.	hablar	41
atormentar *to torment* Reg.	hablar	41
atornillar *to screw in* Reg.	hablar	41
atosigar *to hassle* Reg.	pagar	52
atracar *to mug; to hold up (*i.e. *rob); to approach land* Reg.	sacar	74
atracarse de *to eat too much of* Reg.	sacar	74
atraer *to attract*	traer	83
atragantarse *to choke, get clogged up* Reg.	hablar	41
atramparse *to be trapped* Reg.	hablar	41
atrancar *to bar; to obstruct* Reg.	sacar	74
atrancarse *to get stuck, blocked* Reg.	sacar	74
atrapar *to trap* Reg.	hablar	41
atrasar *to slow down; to set back; to delay* Reg.	hablar	41
atrasarse *to go slow; to tail behind* Reg.	hablar	41
atravesar *to put or lay across; to cross; to pierce; to go through*	cerrar	18

atreverse a *to dare to* Reg.	comer	22
atribuir *to attribute*	construir	23
atribular *to afflict* Reg.	hablar	41
atrofiar *to atrophy* Reg.	hablar	41
atrofiarse = **atrofiar** Reg.	hablar	41
atronar *to deafen with noise*	contar	24
atropellar *to run over (*e.g. *car)* Reg.	hablar	41
atropellarse *to rush* Reg.	hablar	41
atufarse *to get angry* Reg.	hablar	41
aturdir *to stun* Reg.	vivir	89
aturdirse *to be stunned, flustered* Reg.	vivir	89
aturrullarse *to get flustered* Reg.	hablar	41
atusar *to smooth hair, clothes* Reg.	hablar	41
augurar *to augur; to foretell* Reg.	hablar	41
aullar *to howl*	aullar	11
aumentar *to increase* (transitive and intransitive) Reg.	hablar	41
aunar *to unite, combine*	aullar	11
auscultar *to examine with a stethoscope* Reg.	hablar	41
ausentarse *to absent oneself; to leave* Reg.	hablar	41
auspiciar *to sponsor* Reg.	hablar	41
autenticar *to authenticate* Reg.	sacar	74
For the conjugation of unlisted verbs beginning with **auto-**, see the root verb		
autoabastecerse *to be self-sufficient*	parecer	53
autofinanciarse *to be self-financing* Reg.	hablar	41
autografiar *to autograph*	liar	45
automatizar *to automate* Reg.	realizar	65
automedicarse con *to self-prescribe (medicine)* Reg.	sacar	74
autorizar *to authorize* Reg.	realizar	65
autorregularse *to be self-regulating* Reg.	hablar	41
auxiliar *to help* (= **ayudar**) Reg.	hablar	41
avalar *to guarantee; to underwrite* Reg.	hablar	41

avalorar *to estimate* Reg.	hablar	41
avanzar *to advance* (transitive and intransitive) Reg.	realizar	65
avasallar *to dominate; to subjugate* Reg.	hablar	41
avecindarse *to take up residence (in a city or town)* Reg.	hablar	41
avenir *to reconcile*	venir	87
avenirse en *to agree on*	venir	87
aventajar *to excel* Reg.	hablar	41
aventajarse *to get ahead of* Reg.	hablar	41
aventar *to fan (fire, flames)*	cerrar	18
aventurar *to venture (an opinion)* Reg.	hablar	41
aventurarse a *to venture to* Reg.	hablar	41
avergonzar *to shame* (transitive)	avergonzar	12
avergonzarse de *to be ashamed at*	avergonzar	12
averiar *to damage*	liar	45
averiarse *to break down (motors, etc.)*	liar	45
averiguar *to find out*	averiguar	13
avezar *to accustom* Reg.	realizar	65
avezarse *to become accustomed* Reg.	realizar	65
aviar *to prepare something; to ready*	liar	45
aviarse para *to get ready to*	liar	45
avinagrar *to sour* Reg.	hablar	41
avinagrarse *to turn sour* Reg.	hablar	41
avisar *to notify; to warn* Reg.	hablar	41
avispar *to put someone in the picture* Reg.	hablar	41
avisparse *to 'wise up', get smart* Reg.	hablar	41
avistar *to glimpse* Reg.	hablar	41
avivar *to enliven, arouse; to stir up (fire)* Reg.	hablar	41
avivarse *to become livelier* Reg.	hablar	41
ayudar *to help* Reg.	hablar	41
ayunar *to fast* Reg.	hablar	41
azorar *to embarrass* Reg.	hablar	41

azorarse *to be abashed, embarrassed* Reg.	hablar	41
azotar *to whip* Reg.	hablar	41
azucarar *to sugar* Reg.	hablar	41
azular *to color/(Brit.) colour blue* Reg.	hablar	41
azularse *to turn blue* Reg.	hablar	41
azulejar *to tile* Reg.	hablar	41
azuzar *to goad (animals); to incite* Reg.	realizar	65
babear *to dribble, slobber* Reg.	hablar	41
babearse *to dribble, slobber over oneself* Reg.	hablar	41
babosear = **babear** Reg.	hablar	41
bailar *to dance* Reg.	hablar	41
bajar *to lower; to take down; to come/go down; to get off* Reg.	hablar	41
bajarse de *to get out of (vehicle); to get down from* Reg.	hablar	41
balancear *to rock; to swing* Reg.	hablar	41
balancearse *to sway* Reg.	hablar	41
balar *to bleat* Reg.	hablar	41
balbucear *to stammer; to stutter; to babble* Reg.	hablar	41
balbucir (= balbucear)	balbucir	14
baldar *to cripple* Reg.	hablar	41
baldear *to wash down, sluice* Reg.	hablar	41
balear (Lat. Am.) *to shoot* Reg.	hablar	41
balizar *to mark with buoys or flares* Reg.	realizar	65
balsear *to cross by raft* Reg.	hablar	41
bambolear *to swing* Reg.	hablar	41
bambolearse *to sway* Reg.	hablar	41
banderillear *to stick banderillas into a bull's neck (in a bullfight)* Reg.	hablar	41
bañar *to bathe* Reg.	hablar	41
bañarse *to take a bath; to go for a swim* Reg.	hablar	41

barajar *to shuffle (cards, etc.)* Reg.	hablar	41
baratear *to sell at a bargain* Reg.	hablar	41
barnizar *to varnish* Reg.	realizar	65
barrenar *to drill* Reg.	hablar	41
barrer *to sweep* Reg.	comer	22
barruntar *to guess* Reg.	hablar	41
basar en *to base on* Reg.	hablar	41
basarse en *to base one's judgement on* Reg.	hablar	41
bascular *to swing* Reg.	hablar	41
bastar *to be enough* Reg.	hablar	41
bastarse *to be self-sufficient* Reg.	hablar	41
bastonear *to beat with a stick* Reg.	hablar	41
batallar *to battle* Reg.	hablar	41
batear *to bat* Reg.	hablar	41
batir *to beat (eggs, wings)* Reg.	vivir	89
bautizar *to baptize* Reg.	realizar	65
beatificar *to beatify* Reg.	sacar	74
beber *to drink* Reg.	comer	22
beberse *to drink up; to drink all of* Reg.	comer	22
becar *to grant a scholarship or fellowship* Reg.	sacar	74
befar *to scoff* Reg.	hablar	41
bendecir *to bless*	maldecir	47
beneficiar *to benefit (someone)* Reg.	hablar	41
beneficiarse de *to profit from* Reg.	hablar	41
besar *to kiss* Reg.	hablar	41
besuquear *to cover/smother with kisses* Reg.	hablar	41
bienquerer *to like*	querer	64
bienquistar *to reconcile* Reg.	hablar	41
bienquistarse *to become reconciled* Reg.	hablar	41
bifurcarse *to fork (= to divide into two branches)* Reg.	sacar	74
biografiar *to write the biography of*	liar	45
birlar *to filch* Reg.	hablar	41
bisecar *to bisect* Reg.	sacar	74

biselar *to bevel* Reg.	hablar	41
blandear *to soften* Reg.	hablar	41
blandir *to brandish*	abolir	1
blanquear *to whiten, bleach* Reg.	hablar	41
blanquecer *to whiten*	parecer	53
blasfemar *to blaspheme* Reg.	hablar	41
blasonar *to boast* Reg.	hablar	41
blindar *to armor/(Brit.) armour-plate* Reg.	hablar	41
bloquear *to block* Reg.	hablar	41
bobear *to talk nonsense* Reg.	hablar	41
bogar *to row* Reg.	pagar	52
boicotear *to boycott* Reg.	hablar	41
bombardear *to bomb; to bombard* Reg.	hablar	41
bombear *to pump* Reg.	hablar	41
bonificar *to subsidize; to give a discount* Reg.	sacar	74
bordear *to border; to go round the edge* Reg.	hablar	41
borrar *to erase* Reg.	hablar	41
borrarse *to fade* Reg.	hablar	41
borronear *to smudge* Reg.	hablar	41
bosquejar *to sketch* Reg.	hablar	41
botar *to throw away* (usu. Lat. Am.)*; to bounce; to launch* Reg.	hablar	41
boxear *to box (sport)* Reg.	hablar	41
bracear *to swing one's arms* Reg.	hablar	41
bramar *to bellow* Reg.	hablar	41
bravear *to boast* Reg.	hablar	41
bregar *to struggle* Reg.	pagar	52
brillar *to shine* Reg.	hablar	41
brincar *to hop; to jump* Reg.	sacar	74
brindar *to toast; to offer (as a favour)* Reg.	hablar	41
brindarse a *to volunteer to* Reg.	hablar	41
bromear *to joke* Reg.	hablar	41
broncear *to tan (someone)* Reg.	hablar	41

broncearse *to get a suntan* Reg.	hablar	41
brotar *to sprout* Reg.	hablar	41
bruñir *to polish*	gruñir	39
brutalizar *to brutalize, ill-treat* Reg.	realizar	65
bucear *to dive (= to swim or work under water)* Reg.	hablar	41
bufar *to snort; to blow* Reg.	hablar	41
bufonear *to clown* Reg.	hablar	41
bullir *to seethe*	bullir	15
burbujear *to bubble* Reg.	hablar	41
burilar *to engrave* Reg.	hablar	41
burlar *to mock; to deceive* Reg.	hablar	41
burlarse de *to make fun* Reg.	hablar	41
buscar *to look for* Reg.	sacar	74
cabalgar *to ride horseback; to gallop* Reg.	pagar	52
cabecear *to nod (in sleep); to nod off* Reg.	hablar	41
cabellar *to grow hair; to put on false hair* Reg.	hablar	41
caber *to fit in; to have enough room:* **¿quepo yo?** *is there room for me?*	caber	16
cablear *to wire; to cable* Reg.	hablar	41
cabrear (familiar) *to make annoyed* Reg.	hablar	41
cabrearse (familiar) *to get annoyed* Reg.	hablar	41
cacarear *to cackle; to crow* Reg.	hablar	41
cachear *to frisk* Reg.	hablar	41
cachondearse de (familiar) *to make fun of* Reg.	hablar	41
caducar *to expire (documents, etc.)* Reg.	sacar	74
caer *to fall; to be located*	caer	17
caerse *to fall over; to fall down*	caer	17
cagar (vulgar) *to shit* Reg.	pagar	52

calafatear *to caulk* Reg.	hablar	41
calar *to soak through; to see through a person* Reg.	hablar	41
calarse *to become soaked* Reg.	hablar	41
calcar *to trace; to copy* Reg.	sacar	74
calcificar *to calcify* Reg.	sacar	74
calcificarse *to become calcified* Reg.	sacar	74
calcinar *to burn (= to burn to death)* Reg.	hablar	41
calcular *to calculate* Reg.	hablar	41
caldear *to heat up* Reg.	hablar	41
caldearse *to become heated* Reg.	hablar	41
calefaccionar *to heat* Reg.	hablar	41
calentar *to heat; to warm; to annoy*	cerrar	18
calentarse *to get hot*	cerrar	18
calibrar *to calibrate* Reg.	hablar	41
calificar *to grade/(Brit.) to mark (exam paper);* **c. de** *to describe as* Reg.	sacar	74
callar *to silence, not to mention; to be silent* Reg.	hablar	41
callarse *to become silent* Reg.	hablar	41
callejear *to loaf around the street* Reg.	hablar	41
calzar *to put shoes on; to wear (shoes)* Reg.	realizar	65
calzarse *to put one's shoes on* Reg.	realizar	65
cambalachear *to barter; to swap* Reg.	hablar	41
cambiar *to change; to exchange* Reg.	hablar	41
cambiarse *to change clothes; to swap places; to move house* Reg.	hablar	41
caminar *to walk* Reg.	hablar	41
campanear *to ring the bells* Reg.	hablar	41
campar *to camp; to stand out* Reg.	hablar	41
campear *to wander freely; to fly freely* Reg.	hablar	41
camuflar *to camouflage* Reg.	hablar	41
canalizar *to channel* Reg.	realizar	65

cancelar *to cancel* Reg.	hablar	41
canjear *to exchange; to cash (a cheque)* Reg.	hablar	41
canonizar *to canonize* Reg.	realizar	65
cansar *to tire* Reg.	hablar	41
cansarse *to get tired* Reg.	hablar	41
cantar *to sing* Reg.	hablar	41
canturrear *to hum* Reg.	hablar	41
canonear *to cannonade* Reg.	hablar	41
capacitar *to enable; to prepare (= to train)* Reg.	hablar	41
capacitarse *to become qualified* Reg.	hablar	41
capar *to castrate* Reg.	hablar	41
capear *to duck out of; to weather (crises); to flourish a cape (bullfighting)* Reg.	hablar	41
capitalizar *to capitalize; to compound (interest)* Reg.	realizar	65
capitanear *to lead; to command* Reg.	hablar	41
capitular *to capitulate* Reg.	hablar	41
capotar *to overturn (car)* Reg.	hablar	41
capotear = **capear** Reg.	hablar	41
captar *to grasp (meaning); to receive (radio, TV signals)* Reg.	hablar	41
capturar *to capture* Reg.	hablar	41
caracolear *to caper* Reg.	hablar	41
caracterizar *to characterize* Reg.	realizar	65
caramelizar *to caramelize* Reg.	realizar	65
carbonatar *to carbonate* Reg.	hablar	41
carbonear *to make charcoal* Reg.	hablar	41
carbonizar *to char; to carbonize* Reg.	realizar	65
carbonizarse *to be reduced to ashes* Reg.	realizar	65
carcajearse *to howl with laughter* Reg.	hablar	41
carcomer *to eat away (envy, disease)* Reg.	comer	22
cardar *to card* Reg.	hablar	41

carduzar *to card* Reg.	realizar	65
carear *to bring face to face* Reg.	hablar	41
carecer *to lack*	parecer	53
cargar *to load; to charge (gun, battery, price)* Reg.	pagar	52
cargarse *to become loaded; to ruin; to kill* Reg.	pagar	52
cariar *to cause decay (in teeth)*	liar	45
cariarse *to become decayed (teeth)*	liar	45
caricaturizar *to caricature* Reg.	realizar	65
carnear *to slaughter; to butcher* Reg.	hablar	41
casar a alguien con alguien *to marry someone off to someone* Reg.	hablar	41
casarse *to get married* Reg.	hablar	41
cascabelear *to jingle* Reg.	hablar	41
cascar *to crack* Reg.	sacar	74
castañetear *to chatter (teeth)* Reg.	hablar	41
castigar *to punish* Reg.	pagar	52
castrar *to castrate* Reg.	hablar	41
catar *to taste (wine, etc.)* Reg.	hablar	41
catear *to flunk, to fail (a student)* (transitive) Reg.	hablar	41
causar *to cause* Reg.	hablar	41
cauterizar *to cauterize* Reg.	realizar	65
cautivar *to captivate; to charm* Reg.	hablar	41
cavar *to dig* Reg.	hablar	41
cavilar *to cavil; to quibble* Reg.	hablar	41
cazar *to hunt* Reg.	realizar	65
cebar *to fatten; to bait (a fishhook)* Reg.	hablar	41
cebarse en/con *to vent one's anger on* Reg.	hablar	41
cecear *to pronounce c before e or i, and also the letter z, as th (as in Spain); to lisp* Reg.	hablar	41
ceder *to yield; to give up* Reg.	comer	22
cegar *to blind*	negar	49

cegarse *to go blind*	negar	49
cejar *to back off; to back down* Reg.	hablar	41
celar *to keep an eye or check on; to conceal* Reg.	hablar	41
celarse de *to be jealous of* Reg.	hablar	41
celebrar *to celebrate; to hold (a meeting, etc.)* Reg.	hablar	41
cellisquear *to sleet* Reg.	hablar	41
cementar *to cement* Reg.	hablar	41
cenar *to have supper/dinner* Reg.	hablar	41
cencerrear *to jingle; to rattle* Reg.	hablar	41
centellear *to sparkle* Reg.	hablar	41
centralizar *to centralize* Reg.	realizar	65
centrar en *to center/(Brit.) centre on (*e.g. *gaze, attention)* Reg.	hablar	41
centrifugar *to centrifuge* Reg.	pagar	52
centuplicar *to increase a hundredfold* Reg.	sacar	74
ceñir *to gird; to encircle*	reñir	69
ceñirse a *to stick to (a text, a subject)*	reñir	69
cepillar *to brush; to plane* Reg.	hablar	41
cercar *to encircle; to fence in; to surround* Reg.	sacar	74
cercenar *to trim; to clip* Reg.	hablar	41
cerciorar *to assure* Reg.	hablar	41
cerciorarse de *to ascertain* Reg.	hablar	41
cerner *to sift*	perder	55
cernerse sobre *to hover over; to loom over*	perder	55
cernir = cerner	discernir	32
cernirse = cernerse	discernir	32
cerrar *to close* (transitive)*; to lock*	cerrar	18
cerrarse *to close* (intransitive)	cerrar	18
certificar *to certify; to register (a letter)* Reg.	sacar	74
cesar de *to cease from; to quit* Reg.	hablar	41
chacharear *to chatter* Reg.	hablar	41

chacotearse de *to make fun* Reg.	hablar	41
chafar *to flatten* Reg.	hablar	41
chaflanar *to chamfer* Reg.	hablar	41
chalar *to make someone lose his head* Reg.	hablar	41
chalarse *to go crazy* Reg.	hablar	41
chamuscar *to singe* Reg.	sacar	74
chancar *to crush (stones)* Reg.	sacar	74
chancletear *to go around in slippers* Reg.	hablar	41
chapalear = **chapotear** Reg.	hablar	41
chapar *to plate (with metal sheets)* Reg.	hablar	41
chaparrear *to rain hard; to pour at intervals* Reg.	hablar	41
chapotear *to splash* Reg.	hablar	41
chapucear *to bodge; to do odd jobs* Reg.	hablar	41
chapurrear *to speak a language brokenly* Reg.	hablar	41
charlar *to chat* Reg.	hablar	41
charlatanear *to chatter* Reg.	hablar	41
charlotear *to chatter* Reg.	hablar	41
charolar *to varnish* Reg.	hablar	41
chascar = **chasquear** Reg.	sacar	74
chasquear *to click the tongue* Reg.	hablar	41
chequear *to check* Reg.	hablar	41
chichear *to hiss* Reg.	hablar	41
chicotear *to lash; to whip* Reg.	hablar	41
chiflar *to whistle at (in disapproval)* Reg.	hablar	41
chiflarse por *to go mad over* Reg.	hablar	41
chillar *to scream* Reg.	hablar	41
chinchar *to bother* Reg.	hablar	41
chiripear *to win by a fluke* Reg.	hablar	41
chirlar *to talk fast and loud* Reg.	hablar	41
chirriar *to squeak (*e.g. *door)*	liar	45
chismear *to gossip* Reg.	hablar	41

chismorrear = **chismear** Reg.	hablar	41
chispear *to spark; to sparkle; to spit with rain* Reg.	hablar	41
chisporrotear *to throw off sparks* Reg.	hablar	41
chistar *to mutter, grumble* Reg.	hablar	41
chitar *to mumble* Reg.	hablar	41
chivarse *to 'grass', 'squeal' (to the police)* Reg.	hablar	41
chocar *to collide; to shock; to knock together* Reg.	sacar	74
chocarrear *to tell coarse jokes* Reg.	hablar	41
chochear *to become doddery (with age)* Reg.	hablar	41
chorrear *to drip* Reg.	hablar	41
chotear *to make fun of; to jeer at* Reg.	hablar	41
chufletear *to jest* Reg.	hablar	41
chulear *to act as a pimp* Reg.	hablar	41
chulearse *to boast* Reg.	hablar	41
chupar *to suck* Reg.	hablar	41
chuparse *to get drunk* Reg.	hablar	41
churruscarse *to become crisp (food)* Reg.	sacar	74
chutar *to shoot (soccer)* Reg.	hablar	41
ciar *to back water (nautical)*	liar	45
cicatear *to be stingy* Reg.	hablar	41
cicatrizar *to heal* Reg.	realizar	65
cicatrizarse *to form a scar* Reg.	realizar	65
cifrar *to encipher; to abridge* Reg.	hablar	41
cimbrar *to shake around, swish* (transitive) Reg.	hablar	41
cimbrarse *to shake around, sway about* (intransitive) Reg.	hablar	41
cimbrearse = **cimbrarse** Reg.	hablar	41
cimentar *to found; to lay the foundation*	cerrar	18
or Reg. like	hablar	41
cincelar *to carve; to chisel* Reg.	hablar	41
cinchar *to cinch, girth* Reg.	hablar	41

circular *to circulate* Reg.	hablar	41
circuncidar *to circumcise* Reg.	hablar	41
circundar *to surround* Reg.	hablar	41
circunnavegar *to circumnavigate* Reg.	pagar	52
circunscribir *to circumscribe*	escribir	37
circunvalar *to surround* Reg.	hablar	41
circunvolar *to fly around*	contar	24
citar *to make an appointment with; to cite* Reg.	hablar	41
citarse con *to have an appointment with* Reg.	hablar	41
civilizar *to civilize* Reg.	realizar	65
cizañar *to sow discord* Reg.	hablar	41
clamar *to cry out for* Reg.	hablar	41
clarear *to grow clearer; to clear up* Reg.	hablar	41
clarearse *to show through; to be transparent (said of fabric)* Reg.	hablar	41
clarecer *to dawn*	parecer	53
clarificar *to clarify* Reg.	sacar	74
clasificar *to classify* Reg.	sacar	74
claudicar *to give in* Reg.	sacar	74
clausurar *to close (meeting, session)* Reg.	hablar	41
clavar *to nail* Reg.	hablar	41
clavetear *to stud* Reg.	hablar	41
claxonar *to sound one's horn (car)* Reg.	hablar	41
climatizar *to air-condition* Reg.	realizar	65
clocar = **cloquear**	trocar	84
cloquear *to cluck* Reg.	hablar	41
cloroformar = **cloroformizar** Reg.	hablar	41
cloroformizar *to chloroform* Reg.	realizar	65
coaccionar *to compel; to pressure* Reg.	hablar	41
coacervar *to heap up; to pile* Reg.	hablar	41
coactar *to coerce* Reg.	hablar	41
coadyuvar *to help* Reg.	hablar	41
coagular *to coagulate* Reg.	hablar	41
coartar *to limit* Reg.	hablar	41

cobardear *to be or act cowardly* Reg.	hablar	41
cobijar *to cover, protect* Reg.	hablar	41
cobrar *to be paid (wages, etc.); to take (money)* Reg.	hablar	41
cocear *to kick (horses)* Reg.	hablar	41
cocer *to cook; to boil; to bake*	cocer	19
cocinar *to do the cooking* Reg.	hablar	41
codear *to elbow* Reg.	hablar	41
codearse con *to hobnob with, mix with (socially)* Reg.	hablar	41
codiciar *to covet* Reg.	hablar	41
codificar *to codify* Reg.	sacar	74
coeditar *to publish jointly* Reg.	hablar	41
coercer *to coerce* Reg.	vencer	86
coexistir con *to coexist with* Reg.	vivir	89
coger *to seize; to pick; to catch; to get* Reg.	proteger	62
cohabitar *to live together* Reg.	hablar	41
cohechar *to bribe* Reg.	hablar	41
cohibir *to restrain; to repress*	prohibir	61
coincidir *to coincide* Reg.	vivir	89
cojear *to limp* Reg.	hablar	41
colaborar *to collaborate* Reg.	hablar	41
colar *to strain (liquids)*	contar	24
colarse en *to slip or sneak in*	contar	24
colchar *to quilt* Reg.	hablar	41
colear *to wag the tail* Reg.	hablar	41
coleccionar *to collect* Reg.	hablar	41
colectar *to collect* Reg.	hablar	41
colegir *to infer, deduce*	regir	66
colgar *to hang; to dangle*	colgar	20
coligarse *to join forces* Reg.	pagar	52
colindar con *to border on* Reg.	hablar	41
colmar *to fill to the brim;* **c. de** *to shower with (*e.g. *blessings)* Reg.	hablar	41
colocar *to place; to lay out* Reg.	sacar	74

colocarse *to get placed; to find a job* Reg.	sacar	74
colonizar *to settle; to colonize* Reg.	realizar	65
colorar *to color/(Brit.) to colour* Reg.	hablar	41
colorear = **colorar**; *to blush, grow red* Reg.	hablar	41
colorir = **colorar**, **colorear**	abolir	1
coludir *to be in collusion* Reg.	vivir	89
columbrar *to glimpse* Reg.	hablar	41
columpiar *to swing* (transitive) Reg.	hablar	41
columpiarse *to swing (*i.e. *on a swing)* Reg.	hablar	41
comadrear *to go around gossiping* Reg.	hablar	41
comandar *to command* Reg.	hablar	41
comanditar *to invest in an undertaking as a silent partner* Reg.	hablar	41
comarcar con *to border on* Reg.	sacar	74
combar *to bend* (transitive) Reg.	hablar	41
combarse *to warp, bend* (intransitive) Reg.	hablar	41
combatir *to combat* Reg.	vivir	89
combatirse con *to struggle against* Reg.	vivir	89
combinar *to combine* Reg.	hablar	41
combinarse para *to get together in order to* Reg.	hablar	41
comedirse *to behave politely/civilly*	pedir	54
comentar *to comment on* Reg.	hablar	41
comenzar a *to begin to; to start to*	comenzar	21
comer *to eat* Reg.	comer	22
comerse *to eat up; to eat the whole of* Reg.	comer	22
comercializar *to market; to commercialize* Reg.	realizar	65
comerciar en *to trade in* Reg.	hablar	41
cometer *to commit* Reg.	comer	22
comisionar *to commission* Reg.	hablar	41
compactar *to compact* Reg.	hablar	41

compadecer *to pity; to feel sorry for*	parecer	53
compaginar *to put in order;* **compaginar con** *to bring in to line with* Reg.	hablar	41
compaginarse con *to tally with* Reg.	hablar	41
comparar *to compare* Reg.	hablar	41
comparecer *to appear (in court)*	parecer	53
compartir *to divide; to share out* Reg.	vivir	89
compartimentar *to compartmentalize* Reg.	hablar	41
compasar *to measure with a compass* Reg.	hablar	41
compeler *to compel* Reg.	comer	22
compendiar *to summarize* Reg.	hablar	41
compenetrarse con *to share feelings and outlook with* Reg.	hablar	41
compensar *to compensate;* **no me compensa** *it isn't worth it for me* Reg.	hablar	41
competer a *to be the responsibility of* Reg.	comer	22
competir con *to compete with*	pedir	54
compilar *to compile (dictionaries, programs)* Reg.	hablar	41
complacer *to please*	parecer	53
complacerse en *to be pleased to*	parecer	53
complementar *to complement* Reg.	hablar	41
completar *to complete* Reg.	hablar	41
complicar *to complicate; to involve* Reg.	sacar	74
complicarse *to get complicated, entangled* Reg.	sacar	74
complotar *to plot* Reg.	hablar	41
componer *to fix; to compose*	poner	58
componerse de *to be composed of; to consist of*	poner	58
comportar *to tolerate; to bear* Reg.	hablar	41
comportarse *to behave* Reg.	hablar	41
comprar *to buy* Reg.	hablar	41

comprender *to include; to understand* (= **entender**) Reg.	comer	22
comprimir *to compress; to hold back (tears)* Reg.	vivir	89
comprimirse *to control oneself, hold oneself back* Reg.	vivir	89
comprobar *to verify; to check*	contar	24
comprometer *to compromise; to commit (someone)* Reg.	comer	22
comprometerse a *to undertake, be committed to* Reg.	comer	22
compulsar = **comparar** *(legal language)* Reg.	hablar	41
compungir *to make remorseful*	rugir	72
compungirse *to feel remorse*	rugir	72
computar *to compute* Reg.	hablar	41
computarizar = **computerizar** Reg.	realizar	65
computerizar *to computerize* Reg.	realizar	65
comulgar *to take communion;* **c. con** *to sympathize with* Reg.	pagar	52
comunicar *to inform* Reg.	sacar	74
comunicarse con *to get in touch, communicate with* Reg.	sacar	74
concadenar = **concatenar** Reg.	hablar	41
concatenar *to link together* Reg.	hablar	41
concebir *to conceive*	pedir	54
conceder *to concede; to grant* Reg.	comer	22
concentrar *to concentrate (in one place)* Reg.	hablar	41
concentrarse en *to concentrate on* Reg.	hablar	41
conceptuar *to judge; to deem*	continuar	25
concernir *to concern* (third person only)	discernir	32
concertar *to arrange (*e.g. *appointment); to harmonize*	cerrar	18
concertarse con *to come to terms with*	cerrar	18
conchabar *to join, mix* Reg.	hablar	41

conchabarse para *to gang together in order to* Reg.	hablar	41
concienciar = **concientizar** Reg.	hablar	41
concientizar *to make aware, raise consciousness in* Reg.	realizar	65
conciliar *to conciliate, reconcile* Reg.	hablar	41
concitar *to incite, stir up* Reg.	hablar	41
concluir *to conclude*	construir	23
concluirse *to come to an end*	construir	23
concordar *to agree*	contar	24
concretar *to make specific* Reg.	hablar	41
concretarse *to become definite, specific, tangible;* **c. a** *to confine oneself to* Reg.	hablar	41
conculcar *to violate, infringe* Reg.	sacar	74
concurrir en *to concur in; to come together in* Reg.	vivir	89
concursar *to declare bankrupt* Reg.	hablar	41
condecorar *to decorate (with medals, etc.)* Reg.	hablar	41
condenar *to condemn* Reg.	hablar	41
condenarse *to acknowledge one's guilt* Reg.	hablar	41
condensar *to condense* (transitive) Reg.	hablar	41
condensarse *to condense* (intransitive) Reg.	hablar	41
condescender *to condescend*	perder	55
condicionar *to condition* Reg.	hablar	41
condimentar *to season (with spices, etc.)* Reg.	hablar	41
condolerse de *to sympathize over*	mover	48
condonar *to cancel (a debt)* Reg.	hablar	41
conducir *to conduct; to drive*	producir	60
conducirse *to behave*	producir	60
conectar *to connect;* **c. con** *to communicate well with* Reg.	hablar	41

conexionarse con *to get in touch with* Reg.	hablar	41
confabularse con *to connive; to scheme with* Reg.	hablar	41
confederarse *to confederate* Reg.	hablar	41
conferenciar con *to confer with* Reg.	hablar	41
conferir a *to bestow on (an award)*	sentir	78
confesar *to confess*	cerrar	18
confesarse = **confesar** Reg.	cerrar	18
confiar *to entrust; to confide*	liar	45
confiarse *to trust; to become confident*	liar	45
configurar *to shape; to form; to configure* Reg.	hablar	41
configurarse *to take shape; to take form* Reg.	hablar	41
confinar *to confine; to lock up;* **c. con** *to border on* Reg.	hablar	41
confinarse *to keep oneself locked away* Reg.	hablar	41
confirmar *to confirm* Reg.	hablar	41
confiscar *to confiscate* Reg.	sacar	74
confitar *to preserve in sugar; to candy* Reg.	hablar	41
confluir *to come together; to flow together*	construir	23
conformar *to shape, fashion* Reg.	hablar	41
conformarse con *to conform to; to reconcile oneself to* Reg.	hablar	41
confortar *to comfort* Reg.	hablar	41
confraternizar *to fraternize* Reg.	realizar	65
confrontar *to confront* Reg.	hablar	41
confrontarse con *to confront* Reg.	hablar	41
confundir *to confuse* Reg.	vivir	89
confundirse *to become confused; to make an error* Reg.	vivir	89
congelar *to freeze (food, funds)* Reg.	hablar	41

congeniar con *to get along well with* Reg.	hablar	41
congestionar *to make congested* Reg.	hablar	41
congestionarse *to become congested* Reg.	hablar	41
conglomerar *to conglomerate* (transitive) Reg.	hablar	41
conglomerarse *to become conglomerated* Reg.	hablar	41
congraciar *to win over* Reg.	hablar	41
congraciarse con *to get into the good books of* Reg.	hablar	41
congratular *to congratulate* Reg.	hablar	41
congregar *to congregate* Reg.	pagar	52
conjeturar *to guess* Reg.	hablar	41
conjugar *to conjugate; to bring together (qualities)* Reg.	pagar	52
conjugarse *to fit together; to be conjugated* Reg.	pagar	52
conjurar *to conspire; to conjure* Reg.	hablar	41
conllevar *to imply; to entail; to tolerate; to put up with* Reg.	hablar	41
conmemorar *to commemorate* Reg.	hablar	41
conmensurar *to make commensurate* Reg.	hablar	41
conminar con *to threaten with* Reg.	hablar	41
conmover *to move (emotionally)*	mover	48
conmoverse *to be moved, touched (emotionally)*	mover	48
conmutar *to exchange* Reg.	hablar	41
connaturalizarse con *to become accustomed to* Reg.	realizar	65
connotar *to connote* Reg.	hablar	41
connumerar *to enumerate* Reg.	hablar	41
conocer *to know; to meet*	parecer	53
conocerse a *to know someone only too well*	parecer	53

conquistar *to conquer; to win over* Reg.	hablar	41
consagrar *to consecrate; to devote* Reg.	hablar	41
consagrarse a *to devote oneself to* Reg.	hablar	41
conseguir *to obtain; to get*	seguir	77
consensuar *to reach a consensus on*	continuar	25
consentir *to allow; to consent*	sentir	78
consentirse *to give way (in an argument)*	sentir	78
conservar *to preserve* Reg.	hablar	41
considerar *to consider* Reg.	hablar	41
consignar *to consign; to dispatch* Reg.	hablar	41
consistir en *to consist in/of* Reg.	vivir	89
consolar *to console*	contar	24
consolarse con *to take consolation in*	contar	24
consolidar *to consolidate* Reg.	hablar	41
consonar *to be in harmony*	contar	24
conspirar contra *to conspire against* Reg.	hablar	41
constar *to be on the record; to be a fact that;* **c. de = consistir en** Reg.	hablar	41
constatar *to verify* Reg.	hablar	41
consternar *to dismay, fill with consternation* Reg.	hablar	41
consternarse por *to be dismayed that* Reg.	hablar	41
constiparse *to catch a cold* Reg.	hablar	41
constituir *to constitute; to set up*	construir	23
constreñir *to constrain*	reñir	69
construir *to construct; to build*	construir	23
consultar *to consult* Reg.	hablar	41
consumar *to consummate, complete, carry through* Reg.	hablar	41
consumir *to consume, use up* Reg.	vivir	89
consumirse *to waste away; to be used up* Reg.	vivir	89
contactar *to contact* Reg.	hablar	41

contagiar *to infect (with an illness)* Reg.	hablar	41
contagiarse *to become infected* Reg.	hablar	41
contaminar *to contaminate; to pollute* Reg.	hablar	41
contaminarse *to become contaminated, polluted* Reg.	hablar	41
contar *to count; to tell (story);* **c. con** *to count on*	contar	24
contemplar *to contemplate* Reg.	hablar	41
contemporizar *to comply; to be flexible, compliant* Reg.	realizar	65
contender *to contend*	perder	55
contener *to contain*	tener	82
contenerse *to control oneself*	tener	82
contenerizar *to containerize* Reg.	realizar	65
contentar *to content* Reg.	hablar	41
contentarse con *to be content with* Reg.	hablar	41
contestar *to answer* Reg.	hablar	41
contextualizar *to back with quotations; to provide a context for* Reg.	realizar	65
continuar *to continue;* + gerund *to continue to*	continuar	25
contonearse *to swagger, strut* Reg.	hablar	41
contorcerse *to writhe*	cocer	19
contornear *to trace the contour of; to go around* Reg.	hablar	41
contornearse *to strut* Reg.	hablar	41

For the conjugation of unlisted verbs beginning with **contra-**, see the root verb (e.g. **contramarchar** will be conjugated like **marchar**)

contratacar = contraatacar		
contraatacar *to counterattack* Reg.	sacar	74
contrabalancear *to counterbalance* Reg.	hablar	41
contrabandear *to smuggle* Reg.	hablar	41
contradecir *to contradict*	decir	28

contraer *to contract (*e.g. *debt, marriage); to make tighter*	traer	83
contraerse *to contract (= to become smaller)*	traer	83
contrahacer *to copy; to counterfeit*	hacer	42
contramarcar *to countermark* Reg.	sacar	74
contrapesar *to counterbalance, counterweigh* Reg.	hablar	41
contraponer *to oppose; to compare*	poner	58
contrariar *to oppose; to vex*	liar	45
contrarrestar *to counteract* Reg.	hablar	41
contrastar *to contrast; to resist* Reg.	hablar	41
contratar *to contract, sign up (a person)* Reg.	hablar	41
contravenir *to transgress*	venir	87
contribuir *to contribute*	construir	23
contristar *to sadden* Reg.	hablar	41
controlar *to check (passports, tickets, etc.); to control* Reg.	hablar	41
controvertir *to dispute*	sentir	78
contundir *to contuse, bruise* Reg.	vivir	89
conturbar *to perturb* Reg.	hablar	41
conturbarse *to be perturbed* Reg.	hablar	41
contusionar *to bruise, damage* Reg.	hablar	41
convalecer *to recover from an illness*	parecer	53
convalidar *to confirm; to validate* Reg.	hablar	41
convencer *to convince*	vencer	86
convenir en *to agree on; to be suitable, appropriate*	venir	87
converger *to converge* Reg.	proteger	62
convergir = **converger**	rugir	72
conversar *to converse* Reg.	hablar	41
convertir *to convert*	sentir	78
convertirse en *to change into, turn into*	sentir	78
convidar *to invite* Reg.	hablar	41
convivir con *to live amicably with* Reg.	vivir	89

convocar *to summon; to call (elections, meeting)* Reg.	sacar	74
convoyar *to escort, convoy* Reg.	hablar	41
convulsionar *to convulse* Reg.	hablar	41
cooperar *to co-operate* Reg.	hablar	41
coordinar *to co-ordinate* Reg.	hablar	41
copar *to surround, corner (an enemy)* Reg.	hablar	41
copear *to have a drink* Reg.	hablar	41
copiar *to copy; to copy down* Reg.	hablar	41
copular *to join one thing with another* Reg.	hablar	41
copularse con *to copulate with* Reg.	hablar	41
coquetear con *to flirt with* Reg.	hablar	41
corcovar *to bend over* Reg.	hablar	41
corcovear *to buck (horse); to prance about* Reg.	hablar	41
corear *to chorus* Reg.	hablar	41
coreografiar *to choreograph*	liar	45
cornear *to butt; to gore* Reg.	hablar	41
coronar *to crown; to cap* Reg.	hablar	41
corregir *to correct*	regir	66
corregirse *to mend one's ways*	regir	66
correlacionar *to correlate* Reg.	hablar	41
correr *to run; to flow; to rush* Reg.	comer	22
corresponder a/con *to correspond to/with;* **me corresponde a mí** *it's my affair/turn* Reg.	comer	22
corresponderse *to correspond (= to harmonize)* Reg.	comer	22
corroborar *to corroborate* Reg.	hablar	41
corroer *to corrode*	roer	71
corromper *to corrupt* Reg.	comer	22
corromperse *to become corrupt, rotten* Reg.	comer	22
corrugar *to corrugate* Reg.	pagar	52
cortar *to cut; to cut off; to omit* Reg.	hablar	41

cortarse *to cut oneself; to be embarrassed* Reg.	hablar	41
cortejar *to court* Reg.	hablar	41
cosechar *to harvest* Reg.	hablar	41
coser *to sew* Reg.	comer	22
cosquillear *to tickle* Reg.	hablar	41
costar *to cost*	contar	24
costear *to defray or pay the cost of; to sail along the coast of* Reg.	hablar	41
cotejar *to collate; to compare* Reg.	hablar	41
cotillear *to gossip* Reg.	hablar	41
cotizar *to quote (price); to contribute one's share* Reg.	realizar	65
cotizarse a *to be priced/quoted at* Reg.	realizar	65
cotorrear *to chatter; to gossip* Reg.	hablar	41
crear *to create* Reg.	hablar	41
crecer *to grow (in size)*	parecer	53
crecerse *to grow (morally, emotionally, in status); to get haughty*	parecer	53
creer *to believe; to think*	poseer	59
creerse *to believe mistakenly*	poseer	59
crepitar *to crackle* Reg.	hablar	41
criar *to rear, breed, bring up*	liar	45
criarse *to be brought up*	liar	45
cribar *to sieve* Reg.	hablar	41
criminalizar *to criminalize* Reg.	realizar	65
crispar *to make tense; to contract (muscles)* Reg.	hablar	41
cristalizar *to crystallize* Reg.	realizar	65
cristianizar *to Christianize* Reg.	realizar	65
criticar *to criticize* Reg.	sacar	74
croar *to croak* Reg.	hablar	41
cronometrar *to clock; to time* Reg.	hablar	41
crucificar *to crucify* Reg.	sacar	74
crujir *to creak; to gnash (one's teeth)* Reg.	vivir	89

cruzar *to cross over (= to go to the other side)* Reg.	realizar	65
cruzarse *to cross (= one over another)* Reg.	realizar	65
cuadrar *to square; to balance (books)* Reg.	hablar	41
cuadrarse *to stand to attention; to square up* Reg.	hablar	41
cuadricular *to divide into squares* Reg.	hablar	41
cuadruplicar *to quadruple* Reg.	sacar	74
cuajar *to coagulate, clot* Reg.	hablar	41
cuajarse *to curdle* Reg.	hablar	41
cualificar *to qualify* Reg.	sacar	74
cuantificar *to quantify* Reg.	sacar	74
cuartear *to cut up (carcass)* Reg.	hablar	41
cubicar *to cube (math)* Reg.	sacar	74
cubrir *to cover*	cubrir	26
cubrirse *to put one's hat on*	cubrir	26
cucharear *to spoon* Reg.	hablar	41
cuchichear *to whisper* Reg.	hablar	41
cuchufletear *to make fun; to joke* Reg.	hablar	41
cuestionar *to question (a statement, assertion)* Reg.	hablar	41
cuidar *to take care of; to watch over; to take good care of* Reg.	hablar	41
cuidarse *to take care of oneself;* **c. de** *to refrain from* Reg.	hablar	41
culebrear *to wiggle* Reg.	hablar	41
culminar *to culminate* Reg.	hablar	41
culpar *to blame* Reg.	hablar	41
cultivar *to cultivate* Reg.	hablar	41
cumplimentar *to carry out (a duty)* Reg.	hablar	41
cumplir *to fulfill/(Brit.) fulfil; to keep a promise* Reg.	vivir	89
cumplirse *to come to pass; to come true* Reg.	vivir	89

cundir *to spread; to yield abundantly; to propagate* Reg.	vivir	89
curar *to cure; to treat (a sick person)* Reg.	hablar	41
curarse *to get well* Reg.	hablar	41
curiosear *to browse around* Reg.	hablar	41
cursar *to take a course in* Reg.	hablar	41
curtir *to tan; to harden, toughen a person* Reg.	vivir	89
curtirse *to become tanned; to become hardened to difficulties* Reg.	vivir	89
custodiar *to watch over; to guard* Reg.	hablar	41
danzar = **bailar** Reg.	realizar	65
dañar *to hurt, damage* (transitive) Reg.	hablar	41
dañarse *to spoil; to get damaged* (intransitive) Reg.	hablar	41
dar *to give; to hit*	dar	27
darse a *to devote oneself to*	dar	27
datar *to date (a document, etc.)* Reg.	hablar	41
deambular *to wander about* Reg.	hablar	41
debatir *to debate, discuss* Reg.	vivir	89
debatirse entre *to struggle between (*e.g. *two opposing ideas)* Reg.	vivir	89
deber *to owe;* + infinitive *must* Reg.	comer	22
debilitar *to make weak* Reg.	hablar	41
debilitarse *to grow weak* Reg.	hablar	41
debutar *to make one's debut* Reg.	hablar	41
decaer *to decay (= to lessen, decline)*	caer	17
decantar *to decant* Reg.	hablar	41
decantarse por *to opt for* Reg.	hablar	41
decapar *to remove, strip (paint)* Reg.	hablar	41
decapitar *to behead* Reg.	hablar	41
decepcionar *to disappoint* Reg.	hablar	41
decidir *to decide* Reg.	vivir	89
decidirse a *to make up one's mind to* Reg.	vivir	89

decir *to say*	decir	28
declamar *to declaim* Reg.	hablar	41
declarar *to declare* Reg.	hablar	41
declinar *to decline (= reject)* Reg.	hablar	41
decolorar = **descolorar** Reg.	hablar	41
decomisar *to confiscate* Reg.	hablar	41
decorar *to decorate* Reg.	hablar	41
decrecer *to decrease*	parecer	53
decrepitar *to crackle* Reg.	hablar	41
decretar *to decree* Reg.	hablar	41
decuplar *to multiply by ten* Reg.	hablar	41
dedicar *to dedicate* Reg.	sacar	74
dedicarse a *to dedicate oneself to* Reg.	sacar	74
deducir *to deduce; to deduct*	producir	60
defecar *to defecate* Reg.	sacar	74
defeccionar *to defect* Reg.	hablar	41
defender *to defend*	perder	55
defenderse *to manage;* **me defiendo en español** *I can get by in Spanish*	perder	55
deferir a *to defer to*	sentir	78
definir *to define* Reg.	vivir	89
definirse *to make one's position clear* Reg.	vivir	89
defoliar *to defoliate* Reg.	hablar	41
deforestar *to deforest* Reg.	hablar	41
deformar *to deform* Reg.	hablar	41
deformarse *to become deformed* Reg.	hablar	41
defraudar *to defraud; to disappoint* Reg.	hablar	41
degenerar *to degenerate* Reg.	hablar	41
degenerarse *to go to seed; to become degenerate* Reg.	hablar	41
deglutir *to swallow* Reg.	vivir	89
degollar *to behead; to slit someone's throat*	agorar	4
degradar *to degrade; to demote* Reg.	hablar	41
degradarse *to become degraded* Reg.	hablar	41
degustar *to taste (e.g. wines)* Reg.	hablar	41

deificar *to deify* Reg.	sacar	74
dejar *to leave; to abandon; to lend; to allow* Reg.	hablar	41
dejarse *to let oneself go (to seed)* Reg.	hablar	41
delatar *to denounce (= to inform on someone)* Reg.	hablar	41
delegar *to delegate* Reg.	pagar	52
deleitar *to delight* Reg.	hablar	41
deletrear *to spell (a word)* Reg.	hablar	41
deliberar *to deliberate* Reg.	hablar	41
delimitar *to delimit* Reg.	hablar	41
delinear *to delineate; to draw* Reg.	hablar	41
delinquir *to transgress; to offend (* i.e. *act criminally)* Reg.	delinquir	29
delirar *to be delirious* Reg.	hablar	41
deludir *to delude* Reg.	vivir	89
demandar *to sue; to demand* Reg.	hablar	41
demarcar *to demarcate* Reg.	sacar	74
demeritar *to discredit (a person)* Reg.	hablar	41
democratizar *to democratize* Reg.	realizar	65
demoler *to demolish*	mover	48
demorar en *to delay in* Reg.	hablar	41
demorarse en *to be late, slow in* Reg.	hablar	41
demostrar *to demonstrate (the truth of)*	contar	24
demudar *to change, alter (*e.g. *facial expression)* Reg.	hablar	41
denegar *to refuse, reject (a request)*	negar	49
denegrir *to blacken*	abolir	1
denigrar *to denigrate* Reg.	hablar	41
denominar *to name (things, not people)* Reg.	hablar	41
denostar *to insult*	contar	24
denotar *to denote* Reg.	hablar	41
dentar *to tooth*	cerrar	18
denudar *to denude* Reg.	hablar	41
denunciar *to denounce; to report (a crime to the police)* Reg.	hablar	41

deparar *to hold in store (* i.e. *fate, the future)* Reg.	hablar	41
departir *to converse* Reg.	vivir	89
depauperarse *to become poor* Reg.	hablar	41
depender de *to depend on* Reg.	comer	22
depilar *to depilate, remove hair* Reg.	hablar	41
deplorar *to deplore* Reg.	hablar	41
deponer *to depose; to lay down (arms)*	poner	58
deportar *to deport* Reg.	hablar	41
depositar *to deposit, place, pay in* Reg.	hablar	41
depositarse *to be deposited (sediment)* Reg.	hablar	41
depravar *to deprave* Reg.	hablar	41
deprecar *to implore* Reg.	sacar	74
depreciar *to depreciate* Reg.	hablar	41
deprimir *to depress* Reg.	vivir	89
deprimirse *to become depressed* Reg.	vivir	89
depurar *to purify (water)* Reg.	hablar	41
derivar de *to derive from* Reg.	hablar	41
derogar *to revoke* Reg.	pagar	52
derramar *to spill (tears)* Reg.	hablar	41
derramarse *to flow, overflow* Reg.	hablar	41
derrengarse *to be exhausted*	negar	49
derretir *to melt (something)*	pedir	54
derretirse *to melt (snow, ice)*	pedir	54
derribar *to tear down, demolish* Reg.	hablar	41
derrocar *to overthrow; to fling down* Reg.	sacar	74
derrochar *to squander* Reg.	hablar	41
derrotar *to defeat* Reg.	hablar	41
derruir = **derribar**	construir	23
derrumbar *to overthrow, demolish* Reg.	hablar	41

For the conjugation of unlisted verbs beginning with **des-** see the root verb.

desabollar *to knock the dents out* Reg.	hablar	41
desabotonar *to undo (buttons)* Reg.	hablar	41
desabotonarse *to unbutton oneself* Reg.	hablar	41

desabrigar *to deprive of shelter; to take off (someone's coat, sweater, etc.)* Reg.	pagar	52
desabrigarse *to take off one's coat, sweater* Reg.	pagar	52
desabrirse *to become embittered* Reg.	vivir	89
desabrochar *to unfasten* Reg.	hablar	41
desacatar *to fail to obey (law)* Reg.	hablar	41
desacelerar *to decelerate* Reg.	hablar	41
desacertar *to make a mistake*	cerrar	18
desacostumbrarse a *to lose the habit of* Reg.	hablar	41
desacreditar *to discredit* Reg.	hablar	41
desactivar *to defuse (bomb)* Reg.	hablar	41
desadaptar *to unsettle* Reg.	hablar	41
desadaptarse *to become unsettled* Reg.	hablar	41
desafiar *to defy*	liar	45
desafilar *to make blunt* Reg.	hablar	41
desafinar *to be out of tune* Reg.	hablar	41
desafinarse *to get out of tune* Reg.	hablar	41
desagradar *to displease* Reg.	hablar	41
desagradecer *to be ungrateful*	parecer	53
desagraviar *to make amends for* Reg.	hablar	41
desaguar *to drain*	averiguar	13
desahogar *to relieve from pain or trouble; to give vent to (passions, desires)* Reg.	pagar	52
desahogarse *to let off steam* Reg.	pagar	52
desahuciar *declare a patient past recovery; to evict*	aullar	11
desajustar *to loosen* Reg.	hablar	41
desajustarse *to get loose (bolt, etc.)* Reg.	hablar	41
desalentar *to discourage*	cerrar	18
desalentarse por *to get discouraged*	cerrar	18
desalinizar *desalinate* Reg.	realizar	65
desaliñar *to make shabby, unkempt*	hablar	41

desamarrar *to unhitch* Reg.	hablar	41
desamortizar = **confiscar** Reg.	realizar	65
desamparar *to abandon* Reg.	hablar	41
desatentarse *to become discouraged*	cerrar	18
desalojar *to evict; to oust* Reg.	hablar	41
desamoblar = **desamueblar**	contar	24
desamueblar *to remove the furniture* Reg.	hablar	41
desandar *to retrace (steps)*	andar	7
desangrar *to bleed* Reg.	hablar	41
desanimar *to discourage* Reg.	hablar	41
desanimarse *to grow discouraged* Reg.	hablar	41
desanudar *to unknot, untie* Reg.	hablar	41
desaparecer *to disappear*	parecer	53
desaparejar *to unharness* Reg.	hablar	41
desapoderar *to remove someone's powers, withdraw authority* Reg.	hablar	41
desaprender *to unlearn* Reg.	comer	22
desapretar *to loosen, slacken* (transitive)	cerrar	18
desapretarse *to become loose*	cerrar	18
desaprobar *to disapprove of*	contar	24
desaprovechar *to use to no advantage* Reg.	hablar	41
desarmar *to disarm; to dismantle* Reg.	hablar	41
desarraigar *to root out* Reg.	pagar	52
desarraigarse *to become uprooted* Reg.	pagar	52
desarreglar *to mess up* Reg.	hablar	41
desarrollar *to develop* (transitive) Reg.	hablar	41
desarrollarse *to evolve, develop* (intransitive) Reg.	hablar	41
desarropar *to pull off bedclothes* Reg.	hablar	41
desarroparse *to throw off one's bedclothes* Reg.	hablar	41
desarrugar *to unwrinkle* Reg.	pagar	52
desarticular *to smash up (*e.g. *a criminal organization); to dislocate* Reg.	hablar	41

desarticularse *to become dislocated* Reg.	hablar	41
desasirse de *to get free from (clutches, etc.)*	asir	10
desasistir *to abandon* Reg.	vivir	89
desasnar (familiar) *to educate* Reg.	hablar	41
desasnarse (familiar) *to get educated* Reg.	hablar	41
desasociar *to disassociate* Reg.	hablar	41
desasosegar *to disquiet*	negar	49
desasosegarse *to become disquieted*	negar	49
desatar *to untie; to unknot; to unleash* Reg.	hablar	41
desatarse *to come untied; to break loose* Reg.	hablar	41
desatascar *to unclog* Reg.	sacar	74
desatinar *to talk or act foolishly* Reg.	hablar	41
desatornillar *to unscrew* Reg.	hablar	41
desatrancar *to break down (door)* Reg.	sacar	74
desautorizar *to deprive of authority; to discredit* Reg.	realizar	65
desavenirse *to fall out (friends, etc.)*	venir	87
desaviar *to mislead; to lead astray; to deprive someone of something necessary*	liar	45
desayunar *to breakfast; to eat breakfast* Reg.	hablar	41
desayunarse = **desayunar** (esp. Lat. Am.) Reg.	hablar	41
desazonar *to upset, make anxious*	hablar	41
desazonarse *to get upset, worried*	hablar	41
desbancar *to relegate, push to one side* Reg.	sacar	74
desbandarse *to stampede, scatter in all directions* Reg.	hablar	41
desbarajustar *to disorder* Reg.	hablar	41
desbaratar *to spoil* Reg.	hablar	41

desbaratarse *to fall into pieces* Reg.	hablar	41
desbarrancarse *to go off the road (vehicle)* Reg.	sacar	74
desbarrar *to talk nonsense* Reg.	hablar	41
desbastar *to rough out; to plane down* Reg.	hablar	41
desbastarse *to become polished* Reg.	hablar	41
desbocarse *to bolt (horse)* Reg.	sacar	74
desbordar *to overflow (limits, channel)* Reg.	hablar	41
desbordarse *to overflow* (intransitive) Reg.	hablar	41
desbravar *to tame; to break in* Reg.	hablar	41
descabalgar *to dismount* Reg.	pagar	52
descabezar *to chop off the head of (an organization)* Reg.	realizar	65
descaecer *to decrease*	parecer	53
descafeinar *to decaffeinate* Reg.	hablar	41
descalabrar *to hit on the head* Reg.	hablar	41
descalabrarse *to fracture one's skull; to hurt one's head* Reg.	hablar	41
descalcificar *to soften (water)* Reg.	sacar	74
descalzarse *to take one's shoes off* Reg.	realizar	65
descansar *to rest* Reg.	hablar	41
descararse *to be insolent* Reg.	hablar	41
descargar *to unload; to discharge* Reg.	pagar	52
descargarse *to go flat (battery); to break (storm)* Reg.	pagar	52
descarriarse *to go wild, off the rails*	liar	45
descarrilar *to derail (a train)* Reg.	hablar	41
descarrilarse *to become derailed* Reg.	hablar	41
descartar *to rule out (an option)* Reg.	hablar	41
descender *to drop (temperature); to descend*	perder	55
descentralizar *decentralize* Reg.	realizar	65
descentrar *to put off center/(Brit.) centre* Reg.	hablar	41

descentrarse *to get off center/(Brit.) centre* Reg.	hablar	41
descerrajar *to break the lock off* Reg.	hablar	41
descifrar *to decipher* Reg.	hablar	41
desclavar *to unnail* Reg.	hablar	41
descolgar *to take down (from a peg, wall, etc.); to pick up (a phone)*	colgar	20
descolgarse *to climb down (a rope)*	colgar	20
descollar *to excel*	contar	24
descolonizar *to decolonize* Reg.	realizar	65
descolorar *to discolor/(Brit.) discolour* Reg.	hablar	41
descolorir = **descolorar**	abolir	1
descompaginar *to disorder, turn upside down (plans)* Reg.	hablar	41
descompaginarse *to go to pieces* Reg.	hablar	41
descomponer *to decompose; to break down into arts*	poner	58
descomponerse *to decay, break up into parts; to feel upset*	poner	58
desconcertar *to disconcert*	cerrar	18
desconcertarse *to get out of order*	cerrar	18
desconchar *to chip* Reg.	hablar	41
desconectar *to disconnect* (transitive and intransitive)*; to switch off* Reg.	hablar	41
desconfiar de *to distrust; to have no confidence in*	liar	45
descongelar *to defrost (something)* Reg.	hablar	41
descongelarse *to defrost (* i.e. *to thaw itself out)* Reg.	hablar	41
descongestionar *to decongest* Reg.	hablar	41
desconocer *to fail to recognize, not to know*	parecer	53
desconsolar *to grieve*	contar	24
desconsolarse *to become grieved*	contar	24
descontaminar *to decontaminate* Reg.	hablar	41

descontar *to discount*	contar	24
descontentar *to displease; to dissatisfy* Reg.	hablar	41
descontinuar *to discontinue*	continuar	25
descontrolarse *to go out of control* Reg.	hablar	41
descorazonar *to dishearten* Reg.	hablar	41
descorazonarse *to become disheartened* Reg.	hablar	41
descorchar *to uncork* Reg.	hablar	41
descornar *to dehorn (cattle)*	contar	24
descorrer *to draw (a curtain)* Reg.	comer	22
descortezar *to remove bark, crust* Reg.	realizar	65
descoser *to unstitch* Reg.	comer	22
descoserse *to become unstitched* Reg.	comer	22
descoyuntar *to dislocate* Reg.	hablar	41
descoyuntarse *to become dislocated* Reg.	hablar	41
descremar *to skim (cream)* Reg.	hablar	41
describir *to describe*	escribir	37
descuartizar *to chop into pieces (a carcass)* Reg.	realizar	65
descubrir *to discover; to uncover*	cubrir	26
descubrirse *to take off one's hat*	cubrir	26
descuerar *to flay* Reg.	hablar	41
descuidar *to neglect* Reg.	hablar	41
desdecir *to fail to confirm (qualities)*	decir	28
desdecirse de *to go back on (a promise)*	decir	28
desdentar *to pull or break the teeth of*	cerrar	18
desdeñar *to disdain* Reg.	hablar	41
desdibujar *to blur* Reg.	hablar	41
desdoblar *to unfold (a sheet of paper, etc.)* Reg.	hablar	41
desdoblarse *to split into two* Reg.	hablar	41
desear *to desire* Reg.	hablar	41
desecar *to dry something out* Reg.	sacar	74
desechar *to discard; to reject* Reg.	hablar	41

desedificar *to give a bad example to* Reg.	sacar	74
desembalar *to unpack* Reg.	hablar	41
desembarazar *to disembarrass, remove hindrances* Reg.	realizar	65
desembarazarse de *to get rid of* Reg.	realizar	65
desembarcar *to disembark* Reg.	sacar	74
desembargar *to lift an embargo; to remove impediments from* Reg.	pagar	52
desembocar en *to flow into (rivers); to lead to* Reg.	sacar	74
desembolsar *to pay out (a sum of money)* Reg.	hablar	41
desembozar *to unmask* Reg.	realizar	65
desembragar *to declutch (car)* Reg.	pagar	52
desembuchar *to tell the truth; to come clean (about something)* Reg.	hablar	41
desempacar *to unpack* Reg.	sacar	74
desempañar *to demist* Reg.	hablar	41
desempatar *to break the tie between* Reg.	hablar	41
desempeñar *to carry out (a role); to play (a part)* Reg.	hablar	41
desempolvar *to blow the dust off* Reg.	hablar	41
desencadenar *to unchain, unleash* Reg.	hablar	41
desencadenarse *to break out (storms, etc.)* Reg.	hablar	41
desencajar *to put out of joint* Reg.	hablar	41
desencajarse *to be thrown out of joint* Reg.	hablar	41
desencantar *to disillusion; to disenchant* Reg.	hablar	41
desenchufar *to unplug* Reg.	hablar	41
desenfadarse *to calm down* Reg.	hablar	41
desenfocar *to go out of focus, become unfocussed* Reg.	sacar	74

desenfrenarse *to lose all one's inhibitions* Reg.	hablar	41
desenganchar *to unhitch* Reg.	hablar	41
desengañar *to disillusion* Reg.	hablar	41
desengañarse *to become disillusioned; to become disappointed* Reg.	hablar	41
desenhebrar *to unthread* Reg.	hablar	41
desenlazar *to untie* Reg.	realizar	65
desenlazarse *to turn out (* i.e. *a story, in the end)* Reg.	realizar	65
desenmarañar *to disentangle* Reg.	hablar	41
desenmascarar *to unmask* Reg.	hablar	41
desenredar *to disentangle* Reg.	hablar	41
desenrollar *to unroll something* Reg.	hablar	41
desenrollarse *to become unrolled* Reg.	hablar	41
desenroscar *to unbolt* Reg.	sacar	74
desentenderse *to ignore; to pretend not to know*	perder	55
desenterrar *to unearth*	cerrar	18
desentonar *to be out of tune; to clash (hue, etc.)* Reg.	hablar	41
desentumecer *to relieve of stiffness*	parecer	53
desentumecerse *to become less stiff*	parecer	53
desenvainar *to unsheath* Reg.	hablar	41
desenvolver *to unwrap*	volver	90
desenvolverse *to do well in (a situation)*	volver	90
desequilibrar *to unbalance* Reg.	hablar	41
desequilibrarse *to become unbalanced* Reg.	hablar	41
desertar *to desert* Reg.	hablar	41
desescombrar *to clear away rubble*	hablar	41
desesperar *to drive to despair* Reg.	hablar	41
desesperarse de *to despair of* Reg.	hablar	41
desestimar *to hold in low esteem* Reg.	hablar	41
desfalcar *to embezzle* Reg.	sacar	74
desfallecer *to grow weak*	parecer	53

desfavorecer *to cease to support (cause, person)*	parecer	53
desfigurar *to disfigure* Reg.	hablar	41
desfilar *to parade; to march past* Reg.	hablar	41
desflorar *to deflower* Reg.	hablar	41
desfogarse *to vent one's anger* Reg.	pagar	52
desfondar *to knock the bottom out of* Reg.	hablar	41
desfondarse *to be utterly distraught; to go to pieces* Reg.	hablar	41
desgajar *to break off (a branch)* Reg.	hablar	41
desgajarse *to split off* (intransitive) Reg.	hablar	41
desganarse *to lose one's appetite; to become indifferent* Reg.	hablar	41
desgarrar *to rip* Reg.	hablar	41
desgastar *to wear away* Reg.	hablar	41
desgastarse *to become worn down* Reg.	hablar	41
desglosar *to break down (figures)* Reg.	hablar	41
desgobernar *to misrule; to govern badly*	cerrar	18
desgoznar *to take (a door) off its hinges* Reg.	hablar	41
desgoznarse *to become unhiñged* Reg.	hablar	41
desgraciar *to make ugly, unattractive* Reg.	hablar	41
desgraciarse *to come to a bad end; to fail* Reg.	hablar	41
desgranar *to remove the grain from* Reg.	hablar	41
desgranarse : esta planta se está desgranando *this plant is dropping its seeds* Reg.	hablar	41
desguarnecer *to dismantle, strip down (mechanism)*	parecer	53
desguazar *to break up (for scrap,* e.g. *cars, planes)* Reg.	realizar	65
deshabituar *to disaccustom; to make someone break a habit*	continuar	25

deshabituarse de *to lose the habit of*	continuar	25
deshacer *to undo; to take apart; to untie*	hacer	42
deshacerse *to dissolve; to break up into pieces*	hacer	42
deshebrar *to unpick* Reg.	hablar	41
deshechizar *to remove a spell or incantation from* Reg.	realizar	65
deshelar *to thaw something*	cerrar	18
deshelarse *to melt* (intransitive)	cerrar	18
desherbar *to weed*	cerrar	18
desheredar *to disinherit* Reg.	hablar	41
deshidratar *to dehydrate* Reg.	hablar	41
deshilachar *to fray (material)* Reg.	hablar	41
deshilar *to unravel* Reg.	hablar	41
deshilvanar *to unbaste (sewing)* Reg.	hablar	41
deshinchar *to deflate* Reg.	hablar	41
deshincharse *to go flat (tires, etc.)* Reg.	hablar	41
deshojar *to defoliate, strip leaves off* Reg.	hablar	41
deshojarse *to lose leaves* Reg.	hablar	41
deshonorar *to dishonor/(Brit.) dishonour* Reg.	hablar	41
deshonrar *to affront; to insult; to seduce (a woman)* Reg.	hablar	41
deshuesar *to bone* Reg.	hablar	41
deshumanizar *to dehumanize* Reg.	realizar	65
deshumedecer *to dehumidify*	parecer	53
designar *to designate* Reg.	hablar	41
desilusionar *to disappoint* Reg.	hablar	41
desilusionarse *to be disappointed* Reg.	hablar	41
desincrustar *to descale* Reg.	hablar	41
desinfectar *to disinfect* Reg.	hablar	41
desinfestar *to rid of vermin, disease* Reg.	hablar	41
desinflar *to deflate something* Reg.	hablar	41
desinflarse *to go flat (tires, etc.)* Reg.	hablar	41
desinformar *to disinform* Reg.	hablar	41

desinhibir *to remove inhibitions from* Reg.	vivir	89
desinhibirse *to lose one's inhibitions* Reg.	vivir	89
desintegrar *to disintegrate something* Reg.	hablar	41
desintegrarse *to become disintegrated* Reg.	hablar	41
desinteresarse *to lose interest* Reg.	hablar	41
desintoxicar *to detoxify; to cure of alcoholism* Reg.	sacar	74
desistir de *to desist from* Reg.	vivir	89
deslavar *to wash partially, incompletely* Reg.	hablar	41
deslegitimar *to discredit* Reg.	hablar	41
desleír *to dilute; to dissolve* (transitive)	reír	68
desleírse *to become diluted; to dissolve* (intransitive)	reír	68
deslenguarse *to talk too much*	averiguar	13
desliar *to undo*	liar	45
desligar *to untie* Reg.	pagar	52
desligarse *to become undone* Reg.	pagar	52
deslindar *to mark out boundaries* Reg.	hablar	41
deslizar *to slide* Reg.	realizar	65
deslizarse *to skid; slip; to slide into bad ways* Reg.	realizar	65
deslucir *to tarnish*	lucir	46
deslucirse *to do poorly*	lucir	46
deslumbrar *to dazzle* Reg.	hablar	41
deslustrar *to tarnish, remove the shine from* Reg.	hablar	41
desmanchar *to remove stains* Reg.	hablar	41
desmandarse *to get out of control (person)* Reg.	hablar	41
desmantelar *to dismantle* Reg.	hablar	41
desmaquillarse *to take off one's make-up* Reg.	hablar	41

desmarcarse de *to step out of line from* Reg.	sacar	74
desmayar *to lose heart* Reg.	hablar	41
desmayarse *to faint* Reg.	hablar	41
desmedirse *to be impudent*	pedir	54
desmedrar *to damage, impair* Reg.	hablar	41
desmedrarse *to become impaired; to decline (from a previous standard)* Reg.	hablar	41
desmejorar *to impair; to make worse* Reg.	hablar	41
desmejorarse *to deteriorate* Reg.	hablar	41
desmelenar *to tousle (hair)* Reg.	hablar	41
desmembrar *to dismember*	cerrar	18
desmentir *to contradict; to deny*	sentir	78
desmenuzar *to crumble something* Reg.	realizar	65
desmenuzarse *to crumble* (intransitive) Reg.	realizar	65
desmerecer *to be unworthy of*	parecer	53
desmesurarse *to become impudent, insolent* Reg.	hablar	41
desmilitarizar *to demilitarize* Reg.	realizar	65
desmitificar *to demythify* Reg.	sacar	74
desmochar *to chop off (the top or tip)* Reg.	hablar	41
desmontar *to take apart (mechanism); dismantle* Reg.	hablar	41
desmontarse de *to alight from* Reg.	hablar	41
desmoralizar *to demoralize* Reg.	realizar	65
desmoronar *to wear something down* Reg.	hablar	41
desmoronarse *to crumble away* Reg.	hablar	41
desmotivar *to discourage, demotivate* Reg.	hablar	41
desmovilizar *to demobilize* Reg.	realizar	65
desnatar *to skim (milk)* Reg.	hablar	41
desnaturalizar *to denaturalize* Reg.	realizar	65

desnaturalizarse *to give up one's nationality* Reg.	realizar	65
desnivelar *to make uneven* Reg.	hablar	41
desnivelarse *to become uneven* Reg.	hablar	41
desnucar *to poleaxe; to break the neck of* Reg.	sacar	74
desnudar *to undress someone* Reg.	hablar	41
desnudarse *to undress oneself* Reg.	hablar	41
desnutrirse *to become undernourished* Reg.	vivir	89
desobedecer *to disobey*	parecer	53
desocupar *to vacate* Reg.	hablar	41
desodorizar *to deodorize* Reg.	realizar	65
desoír *to turn a deaf ear to*	oír	50
desolar *to make desolate*	contar	24
desollar *to skin; to flay*	contar	24
desordenar *to throw into disorder* Reg.	hablar	41
desorbitar *to exaggerate wildly* Reg.	hablar	41
desorbitarse *to go to wild extremes* Reg.	hablar	41
desordenar *to disorder, disarray* Reg.	hablar	41
desorganizar *to disorganize* Reg.	realizar	65
desorientar *to misdirect; to confuse* Reg.	hablar	41
desorientarse *to lose one's way; to become confused* Reg.	hablar	41
desosar = **deshuesar**	desosar	30
desovar *to spawn*	hablar	41
desovillar *to unwind (a ball of string, etc.)* Reg.	hablar	41
desovillarse *to become unwound* Reg.	hablar	41
desoxidar *to de-rust* Reg.	hablar	41
despachar *to complete, carry out; to finish a task; to dispatch* Reg.	hablar	41
despacharse *to finish work; to get on with something* Reg.	hablar	41
despachurrar *to squash* Reg.	hablar	41
despampanar *to trim, prune* Reg.	hablar	41

desparpajar = **desmontar** Reg.	hablar	41
desparramar *to scatter; to spread all over the place* Reg.	hablar	41
desparramarse *to be scattered, spread* Reg.	hablar	41
despatarrar *to dumbfound* Reg.	hablar	41
despatarrarse *to do the splits, open one's legs wide* Reg.	comer	22
despechar *to enrage* Reg.	hablar	41
despedazar *to break to pieces* Reg.	realizar	65
despedir *to fire (dismiss); to give off; to see off*	pedir	54
despedirse de *to say good-bye to*	pedir	54
despegar *to take off (aircraft)* Reg.	pagar	52
despegarse *to come off; to come unstuck* Reg.	pagar	52
despeinar *to mess up the hair* Reg.	hablar	41
despejar *to remove obstacles; also* = **despejarse** Reg.	hablar	41
despejarse *to clear (weather)* Reg.	hablar	41
despellejar *to skin* Reg.	hablar	41
despenalizar *to decriminalize* Reg.	realizar	65
despeñar *to fling down a precipice* Reg.	hablar	41
despeñarse *to fall down a precipice; to plummet* Reg.	hablar	41
despepitar *to remove the seeds, pips* Reg.	hablar	41
despepitarse *to holler* Reg.	hablar	41
desperdiciar *to waste, squander* Reg.	hablar	41
desperdigar *to scatter* Reg.	pagar	52
desperezarse *to stretch oneself* Reg.	realizar	65
despertar *to wake someone up*	cerrar	18
despertarse *to awake* (intransitive)	cerrar	18
despilfarrar *to squander* Reg.	hablar	41
despintar *to strip the paint off* Reg.	hablar	41
despistar *to throw off the trail or course; to confuse* Reg.	hablar	41

despistarse *to get confused* Reg.	hablar	41
desplacer = **disgustar**	parecer	53
desplazar *to shift something* Reg.	realizar	65
desplazarse *to shift* (intransitive)*; to move; to commute* Reg.	realizar	65
desplegar *to unfold something; to display*	negar	49
desplegarse *to unfold* (intransitive)	negar	49
desplomarse *to tilt over; to collapse* Reg.	hablar	41
desplumar *to pluck* Reg.	hablar	41
despoblar *to depopulate*	contar	24
despojar *to despoil; to deprive of* Reg.	hablar	41
despojarse de *to divest oneself of* Reg.	hablar	41
desportillar *to chip the edge of* Reg.	hablar	41
desposar = **casar** Reg.	hablar	41
desposarse = **casarse** Reg.	hablar	41
desposeer de *to deprive, dispossess of* Reg.	poseer	59
despotricar contra *to rave about/against* Reg.	sacar	74
despreciar *to despise; to scorn* Reg.	hablar	41
desprender *to loosen; to unfasten; to emit* Reg.	comer	22
desprenderse de *to work loose from; to fall off* Reg.	comer	22
despreocuparse de *not to worry about* Reg.	hablar	41
desprestigiar *to discredit; to disparage* Reg.	hablar	41
desprivatizar *to nationalize, de-privatize* Reg.	realizar	65
desproveer de *to deprive of*	proveer	63
despuntar *to blunt; to show (dawn, day)* Reg.	hablar	41
desquiciar *to unhinge* Reg.	hablar	41

desquiciarse *to become unhinged, mad* Reg.	hablar	41
desquitar *to make good (a loss)* Reg.	hablar	41
desquitarse con *to get even with* Reg.	hablar	41
destacar *to make something stand out; to emphasize* Reg.	sacar	74
destacarse *to stand out* Reg.	sacar	74
destapar *to uncover; to open* Reg.	hablar	41
destaparse *to become uncovered; to strip oneself naked* Reg.	hablar	41
destejar *to remove roofing tiles* Reg.	hablar	41
destellar *to twinkle; to flash (lights)* (intransitive) Reg.	hablar	41
destemplar *to put out of tune* Reg.	hablar	41
destemplarse *to get out of tune* Reg.	hablar	41
desteñir *to take the color/(Brit.)colour out of*	reñir	69
desteñirse *to lose color/(Brit.) colour*	reñir	69
desterrar *to exile*	cerrar	18
destetar *to wean* Reg.	hablar	41
destilar *to distill/(Brit.) distil; to drip* Reg.	hablar	41
destinar *to destine; to post (* i.e. *soldiers, officials to a posting)* Reg.	hablar	41
destituir *to dismiss from office*	construir	23
destorcer *to untwist*	cocer	19
destornillar *to unscrew* Reg.	hablar	41
destranquilizar *to make someone worried* Reg.	realizar	65
destranquilizarse *to get worried, upset* Reg.	realizar	65
destripar *to gut; to rip out intestines* Reg.	hablar	41
destroncar *to lop off* Reg.	sacar	74
destronar *to dethrone* Reg.	hablar	41
destrozar *to shatter* Reg.	realizar	65
destruir *to destroy*	construir	23

desvainar *to shell (peas)* Reg.	hablar	41
desvaír *to empty; to vacate*	desvaír	31
desvalijar *to rob; to ransack* Reg.	hablar	41
desvalorar *to devalue* Reg.	hablar	41
desvalorizar = **desvalorar** Reg.	realizar	65
desvanecerse *to vanish*	parecer	53
desvariar *to rave; to talk nonsense*	liar	45
desvelar *to keep someone awake* Reg.	hablar	41
desvelarse *to stay awake; to be sleepless* Reg.	hablar	41
desvencijar *to weaken, wear down* Reg.	hablar	41
desvergonzarse *to speak or act in a shameless manner*	avergonzar	12
desvestir *to undress someone*	pedir	54
desvestirse *to undress oneself*	pedir	54
desviar *to deflect*	liar	45
desviarse *to go awry, off course*	liar	45
desvincular de *to disconnect from* Reg.	hablar	41
desvincularse de *to break off one's connections with* Reg.	hablar	41
desvirtuar *to spoil (quality)*	continuar	25
desvivirse por *to be crazy about; to do one's best for* Reg.	vivir	89
detallar *to detail* Reg.	hablar	41
detectar *to detect* Reg.	hablar	41
detener *to stop (someone); to arrest*	tener	82
detenerse *to stop (= to come to a halt); to pause*	tener	82
detentar *to hold (records, titles)* Reg.	hablar	41
deteriorar *to damage* Reg.	hablar	41
deteriorarse *to deteriorate* Reg.	hablar	41
determinar *to determine; to fix (price, etc.)* Reg.	hablar	41
determinarse a *to make up one's mind to* Reg.	hablar	41
detestar *to detest* Reg.	hablar	41
detonar *to detonate* Reg.	hablar	41

detractar *to detract; to defame* Reg.	hablar	41
detraer *to separate; to defame*	traer	83
devaluar *to devalue*	continuar	25
devanarse (los sesos) *to rack one's brains* Reg.	hablar	41
devanear *to rave* Reg.	hablar	41
devastar *to devastate* Reg.	hablar	41
devengar *to accrue (interest)* Reg.	pagar	52
devenir *to become*	venir	87
devolver *to give back; to vomit*	volver	90
devorar *to devour* Reg.	hablar	41
diagnosticar *to diagnose* Reg.	sacar	74
dialogar *to dialogue* Reg.	pagar	52
dibujar *to draw* Reg.	hablar	41
dibujarse *to be outlined* Reg.	hablar	41
dictaminar en *to pass judgement on* Reg.	hablar	41
dictar *to dictate* Reg.	hablar	41
diezmar *to decimate* Reg.	hablar	41
difamar *to slander, libel* Reg.	hablar	41
diferenciar *to differentiate* Reg.	hablar	41
diferenciarse de *to differ from* Reg.	hablar	41
diferir *to defer;* **d. de** *to differ from*	sentir	78
dificultar *to make difficult; to hinder* Reg.	hablar	41
difuminar *to blur* Reg.	hablar	41
difundir *to diffuse; to broadcast* Reg.	vivir	89
difundirse *to spread (news, etc.)* Reg.	vivir	89
digerir *to digest*	sentir	78
digitalizar *to digitalize* Reg.	realizar	65
dignarse a *to condescend to* Reg.	hablar	41
dignificar *to dignify* Reg.	sacar	74
dignificarse *to become dignified* Reg.	sacar	74
dilapidar *to squander* Reg.	hablar	41
dilatar *to expand (metal); to dilate, enlarge (orifice); to defer (plan, etc.)* (transitive) Reg.	hablar	41

dilatarse *to stretch (space, time); to expand* (intransitive) Reg.	hablar	41
diligenciar *to get busy with; to get something moving* Reg.	hablar	41
dilucidar *to elucidate* Reg.	hablar	41
diluir *to dilute*	construir	23
diluviar *to rain hard; to pour* Reg.	hablar	41
dimanar de *to emanate, flow from* Reg.	hablar	41
dimitir *to resign* Reg.	vivir	89
dinamitar *to dynamite* Reg.	hablar	41
diputar *to delegate* Reg.	hablar	41
dirigir *to steer, direct; to address*	rugir	72
dirigirse a *to proceed towards*	rugir	72
dirimir *to settle (a dispute); to dissolve, annul (a contract)* Reg.	vivir	89
discapacitar *to disable (a person); to handicap* Reg.	hablar	41
discernir *to distinguish; to discern*	discernir	32
disciplinar *to discipline* Reg.	hablar	41
discontinuar *to discontinue*	continuar	25
disconvenir *to disagree*	venir	87
discordar *to disagree; to be out of tune*	contar	24
discrepar de *to dissent from* Reg.	hablar	41
discriminar *to discriminate against* Reg.	hablar	41
disculpar *to excuse, pardon* Reg.	hablar	41
disculparse de *to say sorry for* Reg.	hablar	41
discurrir *to think up, invent (some prank, etc.); to flow (rivers, time)* Reg.	vivir	89
discursear *to make speeches* Reg.	hablar	41
discutir *to have an argument; to discuss* Reg.	vivir	89
disecar *to stuff and mount (a dead animal)* Reg.	sacar	74
diseccionar *to dissect* Reg.	hablar	41
diseminar *to disseminate* Reg.	hablar	41
disentir de *to dissent from*	sentir	78

diseñar *to sketch* Reg.	hablar	41
disertar acerca de *to hold forth about* Reg.	hablar	41
disfrazar *to disguise* (transitive) Reg.	realizar	65
disfrazarse *to disguise oneself* Reg.	realizar	65
disfrutar *to enjoy* Reg.	hablar	41
disgregar *to disintegrate, break up* (transitive) Reg.	pagar	52
disgregarse *to become disintegrated, broken up* Reg.	pagar	52
disgustar *to displease* Reg.	hablar	41
disgustarse *to be displeased* Reg.	hablar	41
disimular *to hide one's feelings; to dissimulate* Reg.	hablar	41
disipar *to dissipate; to disperse something* Reg.	hablar	41
disiparse *to vanish away* Reg.	hablar	41
dislocar *to dislocate* Reg.	sacar	74
disminuir *to diminish* (transitive and intransitive)	construir	23
disonar *to be discordant; to sound unfamiliar*	contar	24
disociar *to disassociate* Reg.	hablar	41
disolver *to dissolve*	volver	90
disonar *to be discordant*	contar	24
disparar *to shoot (a gun)* Reg.	hablar	41
dispararse *to go off (guns, bombs)* Reg.	hablar	41
disparatar *to talk nonsense* Reg.	hablar	41
dispensar *to excuse; to grant (honours, titles)* Reg.	hablar	41
dispersar *to disperse (a group)* Reg.	hablar	41
dispersarse *to scatter* (intransitive) Reg.	hablar	41
displacer = **desplacer**	parecer	53
disponer *to dispose; to order;* **d. de** *to dispose of (= to possess)*	poner	58
disponerse a *to get ready to*	poner	58
disputar *to dispute* Reg.	hablar	41

distanciar *to place at a distance* Reg.	hablar	41
distanciarse de *to distance oneself from* Reg.	hablar	41
distar de *to be far from; to be different from* Reg.	hablar	41
distender *to distend*	perder	55
distinguir *to distinguish* Reg.	distinguir	33
distinguirse por *to distinguish oneself by* Reg.	distinguir	33
distraer *to distract*	traer	83
distraerse *to be distracted*	traer	83
distribuir *to distribute*	construir	23
disturbar *to disturb* Reg.	hablar	41
disuadir de *to dissuade from* Reg.	vivir	89
divagar *to digress, go off the point* Reg.	pagar	52
divergir *to diverge*	rugir	72
diversificar *to diversify* Reg.	sacar	74
divertir *to amuse*	sentir	78
divertirse *to have a good time; to amuse oneself*	sentir	78
dividir *to divide* Reg.	vivir	89
divinizar *to deify* Reg.	realizar	65
divisar *to sight; to make out (in the distance)* Reg.	hablar	41
divorciarse *to get divorced* Reg.	hablar	41
divulgar *to make public* Reg.	pagar	52
divulgarse *to become widespread* Reg.	pagar	52
doblar *to bend something; to fold; to turn (a corner)* Reg.	hablar	41
doblegar *to break (resistance)* Reg.	pagar	52
doblegarse *to submit, knuckle under* Reg.	pagar	52
documentar *to document* Reg.	hablar	41
dogmatizar *to dogmatize* Reg.	realizar	65
doler *to hurt, ache*	mover	48
dolerse de *to suffer because of; to regret*	mover	48
domar *to tame* Reg.	hablar	41

domeñar *to tame; to restrain* Reg.	hablar	41
domesticar *to domesticate* Reg.	sacar	74
domiciliar *to pay by direct billing/ (Brit.) by direct debit* Reg.	hablar	41
domiciliarse *to reside* Reg.	hablar	41
dominar *to dominate; to master* Reg.	hablar	41
dominarse *to control oneself* Reg.	hablar	41
donar *to donate* Reg.	hablar	41
dorar *to gild* Reg.	hablar	41
dormir *to sleep*	dormir	34
dormirse *to fall asleep*	dormir	34
dormitar *to doze* Reg.	hablar	41
dosificar *to measure out (doses)* Reg.	sacar	74
dotar de *to endow with; to equip with* Reg.	hablar	41
dramatizar *to dramatize* Reg.	realizar	65
drenar *to drain* Reg.	hablar	41
driblar *to dribble (soccer)* Reg.	hablar	41
drogar *to drug* Reg.	pagar	52
duchar *to give a shower* Reg.	hablar	41
ducharse *to take a shower* Reg.	hablar	41
dudar *to doubt* Reg.	hablar	41
duplicar *to duplicate* Reg.	sacar	74
durar *to last* Reg.	hablar	41
echar *to throw out; to pour out* (consult dictionary for idiomatic meanings) Reg.	hablar	41
echarse *to throw, move oneself* Reg.	hablar	41
eclipsar *to eclipse something* Reg.	hablar	41
eclipsar *to be eclipsed* Reg.	hablar	41
economizar *to economize on, save (money, fuel, etc.)* Reg.	realizar	65
edificar *to build* Reg.	sacar	74
editar *to publish; to edit* Reg.	hablar	41
educar *to educate; to bring up (children)* Reg.	sacar	74

efectuar *to effect; to carry out*	continuar	25
ejecutar *to execute (plan or criminal); to perform (task)* Reg.	hablar	41
ejemplificar *to exemplify* Reg.	sacar	74
ejercer *to practice/(Brit.) practise (a profession)* Reg.	vencer	86
ejercitar *to exercise* Reg.	hablar	41
elaborar *to manufacture; to work out (a plan)* Reg.	hablar	41
electrificar *to electrify* Reg.	sacar	74
electrizar = **electrificar** Reg.	realizar	65
electrocutar *to electrocute* Reg.	hablar	41
elegir *to elect; to choose*	regir	66
elevar *to elevate* Reg.	hablar	41
elevarse *to rise* Reg.	hablar	41
eliminar *to eliminate* Reg.	hablar	41
elogiar *to praise* Reg.	hablar	41
eludir *to elude* Reg.	vivir	89
emanar *to emanate* Reg.	hablar	41
emancipar *to emancipate* Reg.	hablar	41
emanciparse *to become emancipated* Reg.	hablar	41
embadurnar de *to daub with* Reg.	hablar	41
embaír *to deceive* (archaic = **engañar**)	desvaír	31
embalar *to pack (*e.g. *an article in a crate)*	hablar	41
embalarse *to rush, hurry* Reg.	hablar	41
embalsamar *to embalm* Reg.	hablar	41
embalsar *to dam* Reg.	hablar	41
embarazar *to make pregnant; to get in the way of, hamper* Reg.	realizar	65
embarcar *to embark, go on board* Reg.	sacar	74
embarcarse en *to go on board* Reg.	sacar	74
embargar *to embargo; to distrain* Reg.	pagar	52
embarrancar *to run aground* Reg.	sacar	74
embarrancarse = **embarrancar** Reg.	sacar	74
embarrar *to stain with mud* Reg.	hablar	41

embarullar *to make a mess of; to confuse* Reg.	hablar	41
embarullarse *to get confused* Reg.	hablar	41
embaucar *to bamboozle* Reg.	sacar	74
embeberse en *to get absorbed (in a task)* Reg.	comer	22
embelesar *to charm, captivate* Reg.	hablar	41
embelesarse *to be charmed, captivated* Reg.	hablar	41
embestir *to charge (like a bull)*	pedir	54
emblandecer *to soften*	parecer	53
embobar *to enchant; to fascinate* Reg.	hablar	41
embobarse *to be captivated, spellbound* Reg.	hablar	41
embolsarse *to pocket (money, etc.)* Reg.	hablar	41
emborrachar *to intoxicate* Reg.	hablar	41
emborracharse *to get drunk* Reg.	hablar	41
emborronar *to blot* Reg.	hablar	41
emboscar *to ambush* Reg.	sacar	74
embotar *to dull* Reg.	hablar	41
embotarse *to get sluggish, dull* Reg.	hablar	41
embotellar *to bottle* Reg.	hablar	41
embozarse *to cover one's face with a cloak or muffler* Reg.	realizar	65
embragar *to engage the clutch* Reg.	pagar	52
embravecer *to infuriate*	parecer	53
embravecerse *to get stormy (weather)*	parecer	53
embrear *to cover or soak with tar* Reg.	hablar	41
embriagar *to enrapture* = **emborrachar** Reg.	pagar	52
embriagarse = **emborracharse** Reg.	pagar	52
embrollar *to embroil, entangle* Reg.	hablar	41
embrollarse *to become entangled, embroiled* Reg.	hablar	41
embromar *to tease; to trick* Reg.	hablar	41
embrujar *to bewitch* Reg.	hablar	41

embrutecer *to brutalize*	parecer	53
embutir de *to stuff with* Reg.	vivir	89
emerger *to surface; to come to light* Reg.	proteger	62
emigrar *to emigrate; to migrate* Reg.	hablar	41
emitir *to emit* Reg.	vivir	89
emocionar *to cause emotion; to excite (emotionally)* Reg.	hablar	41
emocionarse *to be excited (emotionally)* Reg.	hablar	41
empacar *to pack* Reg.	sacar	74
empacarse *to become obstinate, dig in one's heels* Reg.	sacar	74
empachar *to cause indigestion* Reg.	hablar	41
empacharse *to have indigestion* Reg.	hablar	41
empadronar *to register (in a census)* Reg.	hablar	41
empalagar: esto me empalaga *I find this sickly* Reg.	pagar	52
empalagarse de *to stuff oneself with* Reg.	pagar	52
empalar *to impale* Reg.	hablar	41
empalizar *to stockade* Reg.	realizar	65
empalmar *to splice together; to connect* Reg.	hablar	41
empanar *to bread* Reg.	hablar	41
empantanar *to swamp* Reg.	hablar	41
empantanarse *to get bogged down* Reg.	hablar	41
empañar *to fog; to tarnish* Reg.	hablar	41
empapar *to soak* Reg.	hablar	41
empaparse *to get soaked* Reg.	hablar	41
empapelar *to wallpaper* Reg.	hablar	41
empaquetar *to pack* Reg.	hablar	41
emparejar *to pair someone off* Reg.	hablar	41
emparentar con *to become related to by marriage* Reg.	hablar	41
empastar *to fill (a tooth)* Reg.	hablar	41

empatar *to tie (in games, etc.)* Reg.	hablar	41
empatarse con *to be dead level with, neck and neck with* Reg.	hablar	41
empecinarse en *to get it into one's head that* Reg.	hablar	41
empedernir *to harden*	abolir	1
empedrar *to pave with stones*	cerrar	18
empeñar *to pawn* Reg.	hablar	41
empeñarse en *to insist on* Reg.	hablar	41
empeorar *to make worse; to get worse* Reg.	hablar	41
empequeñecer *to get smaller*	parecer	53
emperejilarse *to dress up smart* Reg.	hablar	41
emperrarse en *to get stubborn about* Reg.	hablar	41
empezar a *to begin to*	comenzar	21
empinar *to raise (cup, elbow)* Reg.	hablar	41
empinarse *to rise high* Reg.	hablar	41
emplazar *to locate, site (a building)* Reg.	realizar	65
emplear *to employ; to use* Reg.	hablar	41
emplumar *to feather, adorn with feathers* Reg.	hablar	41
empobrecer *to impoverish*	parecer	53
empobrecerse *to become impoverished*	parecer	53
empollar *to hatch (eggs)* Reg.	hablar	41
empolvarse *to get dusty* Reg.	hablar	41
empotrar *to embed, build in (*e.g. **armario empotrado** *built-in cupboard)* Reg.	hablar	41
emprender *to undertake* Reg.	comer	22
empujar *to push* Reg.	hablar	41
empuñar *to brandish (a stick)* Reg.	hablar	41
emular *to emulate* Reg.	hablar	41
enajenar *to alienate; to drive out of one's mind* Reg.	hablar	41

enajenarse *to go mad; to become alienated* Reg.	hablar	41
enaltecer *to exalt*	parecer	53
enaltecerse *to be exalted*	parecer	53
enamorar *to make someone fall in love* Reg.	hablar	41
enamorarse de *to fall in love with* Reg.	hablar	41
enarbolar *to raise, hoist (a banner)* Reg.	hablar	41
enardecerse *to get excited (passions)*	parecer	53
encabezar *to head; to put a heading to* Reg.	realizar	65
encabritarse *to rear (horse)* Reg.	hablar	41
encadenar *to chain* Reg.	hablar	41
encajar en *to fit something to* Reg.	hablar	41
encajarse con *to fit (*i.e. *match)* Reg.	hablar	41
encajonar *to box, crate* Reg.	hablar	41
encalar *to whitewash* Reg.	hablar	41
encallar *to run aground; to get entangled* Reg.	hablar	41
encallecerse *to get callused/(Brit.) calloused, rough (skin)*	parecer	53
encalvecer *to become bald*	parecer	53
encaminar *to channel; to direct* Reg.	hablar	41
encaminarse a *to be on the way to* Reg.	hablar	41
encanecerse *to become gray/(Brit.)grey haired*	parecer	53
encantar *to charm* Reg.	hablar	41
encañonar *to point a gun at* Reg.	hablar	41
encapotarse *to get cloudy* Reg.	hablar	41
encapricharse con *to get a thing about; to get crazy about* Reg.	hablar	41
encaramarse a *to climb up (trees, ladders)* Reg.	hablar	41
encarar *to face up to* Reg.	hablar	41
encararse con *to come face to face with* Reg.	hablar	41

encarcelar *to incarcerate* Reg.	hablar	41
encarecer *to extol; to raise the price of*	parecer	53
encarecerse *to get dearer*	parecer	53
encargar *to order (goods, etc.); to entrust* Reg.	pagar	52
encargarse de *to undertake to* Reg.	pagar	52
encariñarse con *to get fond of* Reg.	hablar	41
encarnar *to embody (qualities); to play (a theatrical role)* Reg.	hablar	41
encarnizarse *to get furious, vicious* Reg.	realizar	65
encarrilar *to put on the right track* Reg.	hablar	41
encarrilarse *to get back on the right track* Reg.	hablar	41
encasillar *to pigeonhole* Reg.	hablar	41
encauzar *to direct; to channel (stream)* Reg.	realizar	65
encauzarse hacia *to be channeled/ (Brit.) channelled towards; to tend to* Reg.	realizar	65
encenagar *to smear with mud* Reg.	pagar	52
encender *to light; to set on fire; to turn on (TV, etc.)*	perder	55
encenderse *to catch fire; to light* (intransitive)	perder	55
encerar *to wax* Reg.	hablar	41
encerrar *to lock up; to contain*	cerrar	18
encharcar *to turn into a puddle; to flood* Reg.	sacar	74
enchufar *to plug in; to switch on* Reg.	hablar	41
encizañar *to sow discord* Reg.	hablar	41
enclaustrarse *to shut oneself away* Reg.	hablar	41
encoger *to shrink* (transitive)*; to shrug* Reg.	proteger	62
encogerse *to shrink* (intransitive) Reg.	proteger	62
encolar *to glue* Reg.	hablar	41
encolerizar *to anger* Reg.	realizar	65
encolerizarse *to become angry* Reg.	realizar	65

encomendar a *to recommend to; to entrust to*	cerrar	18
encomiar *to praise* Reg.	hablar	41
enconar *to inflame (resentment, hatred)* Reg.	hablar	41
enconarse *to become aggravated; to fester* Reg.	hablar	41
encontrar *to find; to meet*	contar	24
encontrarse *to be located; to find by chance;* **e. con** *to come across, meet*	contar	24
encorvarse *to bend over, hunch up* Reg.	hablar	41
encrespar *to ruffle, make curly* Reg.	hablar	41
encresparse *to become choppy; to rise (bad temper)* Reg.	hablar	41
encuadernar *to bind (a book)* Reg.	hablar	41
encuadrar *to frame; to fit; to classify* Reg.	hablar	41
encubrir *to hide; to conceal*	cubrir	26
enderezar *to straighten; to put on the right path* Reg.	realizar	65
enderezarse *to sort oneself out* Reg.	realizar	65
endeudarse *to get into debt* Reg.	hablar	41
endiosar *to deify* Reg.	hablar	41
endiosarse *to be stuck-up* Reg.	hablar	41
endomingarse *to dress up in one's Sunday clothes* Reg.	pagar	52
endosar *to endorse (a cheque)* Reg.	hablar	41
endulzar *to sweeten* Reg.	realizar	65
endurecer *to harden, toughen*	parecer	53
endurecerse *to become hard*	parecer	53
enemistar *to cause enmity between* Reg.	hablar	41
enemistarse con *to fall out with* Reg.	hablar	41
enervar *to get on one's nerves* Reg.	hablar	41
enfadar *to anger* Reg.	hablar	41
enfadarse *to get angry* Reg.	hablar	41
enfatizar *to emphasize* Reg.	realizar	65
enfermar *to become ill* Reg.	hablar	41

enfermarse (Lat. Am.) = **enfermar** Reg.	hablar	41
enfervorizar *to arouse* Reg.	realizar	65
enfervorizarse *to become heated, aroused* Reg.	realizar	65
enfilar *to take (a road, turning)* Reg.	hablar	41
enfocar *to focus* Reg.	sacar	74
enfrascarse en *to become engrossed in* Reg.	sacar	74
enfrentar *to confront* Reg.	hablar	41
enfrentarse con *to meet face to face* Reg.	hablar	41
enfriar *to cool, chill*	liar	45
enfriarse *to grow cool*	liar	45
enfundar *to put in a case* Reg.	hablar	41
enfurecer *to infuriate*	parecer	53
enfurecerse *to become infuriated*	parecer	53
enfurruñarse *to sulk*	hablar	41
enganchar *to hook* Reg.	hablar	41
engancharse *to get hooked (drugs, passions)* Reg.	hablar	41
engañar *to deceive* Reg.	hablar	41
engañarse *to be mistaken* Reg.	hablar	41
engarzar *to set (precious stones)* Reg.	realizar	65
engatusar *to take in (someone gullible)* Reg.	hablar	41
engendrar *to engender* Reg.	hablar	41
englobar *to include; to lump together* Reg.	hablar	41
engolfarse *to become deeply absorbed* Reg.	hablar	41
engomar *to gum* Reg.	hablar	41
engordar *to fatten; to grow fatter* Reg.	hablar	41
engranar *to mesh; to engage (gears)* Reg.	hablar	41
engrandecer *to enlarge; to enhance; to extol*	parecer	53
engrapar *to staple* Reg.	hablar	41

engrasar *to lubricate; to grease* Reg.	hablar	41
engreír *to make vain*	reír	68
engreírse *to become vain*	reír	68
engrosar *to enlarge; to swell (numbers)*	contar	24
engullir *to gulp down*	bullir	15
enhebrar *to thread* Reg.	hablar	41
enjabonar *to soap* Reg.	hablar	41
enjalbegar = **encalar** Reg.	pagar	52
enjambrar *to swarm* Reg.	hablar	41
enjaular *to cage* Reg.	hablar	41
enjuagar *to rinse off* Reg.	pagar	52
enjugar *to dry off, wipe away* Reg.	pagar	52
enjuiciar *to pass judgement on; to indict* Reg.	hablar	41
enlazar *to link* Reg.	realizar	65
enlodar *to muddy* Reg.	hablar	41
enlodarse *to get muddied* Reg.	hablar	41
enloquecer *to madden; to craze*	parecer	53
enloquecerse *to become crazy*	parecer	53
enlosar *to pave with slabs* Reg.	hablar	41
enlutar *to plunge into mourning* Reg.	hablar	41
enmarañar *to entangle; to tangle* Reg.	hablar	41
enmarañarse *to become entangled* Reg.	hablar	41
enmarcar *to frame* Reg.	sacar	74
enmascarar *to mask* Reg.	hablar	41
enmascararse *to put on a mask; to masquerade* Reg.	hablar	41
enmendar *to amend; to emend*	cerrar	18
enmohecerse *to get moldy/(Brit.) mouldy*	parecer	53
enmudecer *to silence*	parecer	53
ennegrecer *to make black*	parecer	53
ennegrecerse *to grow black*	parecer	53
enojar *to anger* Reg.	hablar	41
enojarse *to get angry* Reg.	hablar	41
enorgullecer *to make proud*	parecer	53
enorgullecerse *to be proud*	parecer	53

enraizar *to take root*	arcaizar	8
enredar *to tangle up; to complicate* Reg.	hablar	41
enriquecer *to enrich*	parecer	53
enristrar *to string (onions, etc.)* Reg.	hablar	41
enrojecer *to make red; to turn red*	parecer	53
enrojecerse *to go red*	parecer	53
enrolar *to recruit* Reg.	hablar	41
enrolarse en *to sign up for; to enlist* Reg.	hablar	41
enrollar *to roll up; to coil up* Reg.	hablar	41
enrollarse *to roll up, coil up* (intransitive) Reg.	hablar	41
enronquecer *to make hoarse*	parecer	53
enroscar *to screw in/on (nut, bottle-cap, etc.)* Reg.	sacar	74
enroscarse *to curl up in a ball* Reg.	sacar	74
ensalzar *to extol* Reg.	realizar	65
ensamblar *to assemble (mechanisms, computer programs); to joint* Reg.	hablar	41
ensanchar *to widen* (transitive) Reg.	hablar	41
ensancharse *to get wider* Reg.	hablar	41
ensangrentar *to stain with blood*	cerrar	18
ensangrentarse *to get bloody (wars, etc.)*	cerrar	18
ensañar *to enrage* Reg.	hablar	41
ensañarse con *to act cruelly towards* Reg.	hablar	41
ensartar *to string (beads, etc.); to string together (words)* Reg.	hablar	41
ensayar *to rehearse; to try out* Reg.	hablar	41
enseñar *to teach; to show* Reg.	hablar	41
enseñorearse de *to take possession of* Reg.	hablar	41
ensillar *to saddle* Reg.	hablar	41
ensimismarse *to become absorbed in thought* Reg.	hablar	41
ensombrecer *to make something dark*	parecer	53

ensombrecerse *to become gloomy*	parecer	53
ensordecer *to deafen*	parecer	53
ensuciar *to dirty; to soil* Reg.	hablar	41
ensuciarse *to get dirty* Reg.	hablar	41
entablar *to start (conversation, friendship)* Reg.	hablar	41
entallar *to carve; to engrave* Reg.	hablar	41
entarimar *to floor with boards* Reg.	hablar	41
entender *to understand*	perder	55
entenderse con *to reach an understanding with*	perder	55
entenebrecer *to make dark*	parecer	53
enterar *to inform* Reg.	hablar	41
enterarse de *to find out about* Reg.	hablar	41
enternecer *to move to pity*	parecer	53
enternecerse *to be moved to pity*	parecer	53
enterrar *to bury*	cerrar	18
entibiar *to make lukewarm* Reg.	hablar	41
entibiarse *to cool down; to become lukewarm* Reg.	hablar	41
entoldar *to cover with an awning* Reg.	hablar	41
entonar *to intone; to sing in tune* Reg.	hablar	41
entontecer *to make foolish*	parecer	53
entornar *to half-close (door, eyes)* Reg.	hablar	41
entorpecer *to stupefy; to obstruct (traffic)*	parecer	53
entrampar *to trap; to trick* Reg.	hablar	41
entrañar *to entail* Reg.	hablar	41
entrar en/a *to enter* Reg.	hablar	41
entreabrir *to half-open (door, eyes)*	abrir	2
entregar *to deliver (goods to home, etc.); to hand over* Reg.	pagar	52
entregarse *to surrender* Reg.	pagar	52
entrelazar *to entwine; to interweave* Reg.	realizar	65
entrenar *to train* (transitive and intransitive) Reg.	hablar	41

entrenarse *to train* (intransitive)	hablar	41
entretejer *to weave together* Reg.	comer	22
entretener *to entertain; to delay someone*	tener	82
entrever *to see vaguely; to glimpse*	ver	88
entrevistar *to interview* Reg.	hablar	41
entrevistarse con *to have an interview with* Reg.	hablar	41
entristecer *to sadden*	parecer	53
entristecerse *to grow sad*	parecer	53
entrometerse *to butt in; to intrude* Reg.	comer	22
entroncar con *to be related to; to be connected to* Reg.	sacar	74
entronizar *to enthrone* Reg.	realizar	65
entumecerse *to become numb*	parecer	53
enturbiar *to make cloudy* Reg.	hablar	41
enturbiarse *to become cloudy* Reg.	hablar	41
entusiasmar *to excite; to make enthusiastic* Reg.	hablar	41
entusiasmarse *to get enthusiastic* Reg.	hablar	41
enunciar *to enunciate* Reg.	hablar	41
envainar *to sheathe* Reg.	hablar	41
envalentonar *to make courageous* Reg.	hablar	41
envalentonarse *to get bolder* Reg.	hablar	41
envanecer *to make vain*	parecer	53
envanecerse *to become vain*	parecer	53
envasar *to bottle; to package* Reg.	hablar	41
envejecer *to make old; to make look old; to grow old*	parecer	53
envenenar *to poison* Reg.	hablar	41
enviar *to send*	liar	45
envidiar *to envy* Reg.	hablar	41
envilecer *to vilify*	parecer	53
envilecerse *to debase oneself; to become degraded*	parecer	53
enviudar *to be widowed* Reg.	hablar	41
envolver *to wrap; to imply; to involve*	volver	90

enyesar *to plaster (*e.g. *broken leg)* Reg.	hablar	41
enzarzarse en *to be entangled in difficulties* Reg.	realizar	65
epitomar *to epitomize* Reg.	hablar	41
equilibrar *to balance something* Reg.	hablar	41
equilibrarse *to be balanced* Reg.	hablar	41
equidistar de *to be equidistant from* Reg.	hablar	41
equipar con *to equip with* Reg.	hablar	41
equiparar con *to equate with; to put on the same level as* Reg.	hablar	41
equivaler a *to be equivalent to*	valer	85
equivocar *to make someone make a mistake* Reg.	sacar	74
equivocarse *to make a mistake* Reg.	sacar	74
erguir *to erect; to set up straight; to prick up (ears)*	erguir	35
erguirse *to sit upright; to sit up straight; to rear up (snakes, etc.)*	erguir	35
erigir *to erect*	rugir	72
erigirse en *to set out to be; to set oneself up as*	rugir	72
erizar *to make hair/fur bristle* Reg.	realizar	65
erizarse *to bristle* Reg.	realizar	65
erosionar *to erode* Reg.	hablar	41
erradicar *to eradicate* Reg.	sacar	74
errar *to err; to wander*	errar	36
eructar *to belch* Reg.	hablar	41
esbozar *to sketch* Reg.	realizar	65
escabechar *to pickle* Reg.	hablar	41
escabullirse *to slip away; to skive off*	bullir	15
escalar *to scale (a ladder)* Reg.	hablar	41
escaldar *to scald* Reg.	hablar	41
escalfar *to poach (eggs)* Reg.	hablar	41
escalonar *to stagger (timetable); to scale (wages, figures)* Reg.	hablar	41

escamar *to scale (a fish); to cause suspicion* Reg.	hablar	41
escamotear *to make something disappear by sleight of hand or cunning* Reg.	hablar	41
escampar *to clear up (weather); to stop raining* Reg.	hablar	41
escanciar *to pour wine* Reg.	hablar	41
escandalizar *to scandalize* Reg.	realizar	65
escandalizarse *to be scandalized* Reg.	realizar	65
escapar a *to escape (justice)* Reg.	hablar	41
escaparse de *to escape from (prisoners)* Reg.	hablar	41
escaramuzar *to skirmish* Reg.	realizar	65
escarbar *to scratch about; to pry into* Reg.	hablar	41
escarchar *to frost, crystallize* Reg.	hablar	41
escardar *to weed; to hoe* Reg.	hablar	41
escarmentar *to learn a lesson (through experience)*	cerrar	18
escarnecer *to ridicule*	parecer	53
escasear *to be scarce* Reg.	hablar	41
escatimar *to skimp* Reg.	hablar	41
escayolar *to put in plaster* Reg.	hablar	41
escenificar *to stage (play, etc.)* Reg.	sacar	74
escindirse *to split (into factions,* e.g. *political party)* Reg.	vivir	89
esclarecer *to make clear*	parecer	53
esclavizar *to enslave* Reg.	realizar	65
escocer *to smart, sting*	cocer	19
escoger *to choose, select* Reg.	proteger	62
escolarizar *to educate; to provide schooling for* Reg.	realizar	65
escoltar *to escort* Reg.	hablar	41
esconder *to hide (something)* Reg.	comer	22
esconderse *to hide oneself* Reg.	comer	22

escorar *to heel over; to list (boat)* (intransitive)*; to prop up* (transitive)	hablar	41
escribir *to write*	escribir	37
escrutar *to scrutinize* Reg.	hablar	41
escuchar *to listen to; to heed* Reg.	hablar	41
escudar *to shield* Reg.	hablar	41
escudriñar *to pry into* Reg.	hablar	41
esculpir *to sculpture* Reg.	vivir	89
escupir *to spit* Reg.	vivir	89
escurrir *to drain* (transitive)*; to wring out* Reg.	vivir	89
escurrirse *to drain, drip (dry)* (intransitive)*; to slip away; to skive off* Reg.	vivir	89
esforzar *to encourage; to push (a person into trying harder)*	almorzar	6
esforzarse por *to try hard to*	almorzar	6
esfumar *to tone down* Reg.	hablar	41
esfumarse *to melt away, disappear* Reg.	hablar	41
esgrimir *to brandish; to fence* Reg.	vivir	89
eslabonar *to link together* Reg.	hablar	41
esmaltar *to enamel* Reg.	hablar	41
esmerarse por *to do one's best to; to take pains to* Reg.	hablar	41
espabilar *to wake someone up (figuratively)* Reg.	hablar	41
espabilarse *to wake up (= to get 'clued up')* Reg.	hablar	41
espaciar *to space out* Reg.	hablar	41
espantar *to scare; to frighten away* Reg.	hablar	41
espantarse *to be scared, startled* Reg.	hablar	41
españolizar *to Hispanify, make Spanish* Reg.	realizar	65
esparcir *to scatter* Reg.	zurcir	92
esparcirse por *to be scattered over* Reg.	zurcir	92
especificar *to specify* Reg.	sacar	74
especular *to speculate* Reg.	hablar	41

esperar *to hope; to expect; to wait* Reg.	hablar	41
espesar *to thicken* (transitive and intransitive) Reg.	hablar	41
espetar: espetar una pregunta *to fire/rap out a question*	hablar	41
espiar *to spy*	liar	45
espigar *to form ears (wheat, barley, etc.); to glean* Reg.	pagar	52
espigarse *to grow tall* Reg.	pagar	52
espirar *to exhale* Reg.	hablar	41
espolear *to spur* Reg.	hablar	41
espolvorear *to sprinkle* Reg.	hablar	41
esponjar *to make fluffy* Reg.	hablar	41
esponjarse *to become fluffy* Reg.	hablar	41
esposar *to handcuff* Reg.	hablar	41
espumar *to skim (the foam off)* Reg.	hablar	41
esquematizar *to sketch; to outline* Reg.	realizar	65
esquiar *to ski*	liar	45
esquilar *to shear* Reg.	hablar	41
esquilmar *to exhaust (reserves); to harvest* Reg.	hablar	41
esquivar *to dodge, avoid* Reg.	hablar	41
estabilizar *to stabilize something* Reg.	realizar	65
estabilizarse *to become stable* Reg.	realizar	65
establecer *to establish*	parecer	53
establecerse *to settle in*	parecer	53
estacionar *to park* (transitive) Reg.	hablar	41
estacionarse *to park* (intransitive) Reg.	hablar	41
estafar *to swindle* Reg.	hablar	41
estallar *to explode* Reg.	hablar	41
estampar *to stamp (a sign, seal)* Reg.	hablar	41
estancar *to staunch, dam up* Reg.	sacar	74
estancarse *to stagnate* Reg.	sacar	74
estandarizar *to standardize* Reg.	realizar	65
estañar *to solder* Reg.	hablar	41
estar *to be* (consult a dictionary for idiomatic uses)	estar	38

estarse *to stay*	estar	38
estatuir *to establish, lay down (a law, statute)*	construir	23
estereotipar *to stereotype* Reg.	hablar	41
esterilizar *to sterilize* Reg.	realizar	65
estigmatizar *to stigmatize* Reg.	realizar	65
estilarse *to be in style* Reg.	hablar	41
estilizar *to stylize* Reg.	realizar	65
estimar *to esteem; to estimate* Reg.	hablar	41
estimular *to stimulate* Reg.	hablar	41
estipular *to stipulate* Reg.	hablar	41
estirar *to stretch; to tense* Reg.	hablar	41
estofar *to stew* Reg.	hablar	41
estorbar *to be in the way; to obstruct; to annoy* Reg.	hablar	41
estornudar *to sneeze* Reg.	hablar	41
estrangular *to strangle* Reg.	hablar	41
estratificar *to stratify* Reg.	sacar	74
estrechar *to make narrow, tighter* Reg.	hablar	41
estrecharse *to get narrower, tighter* Reg.	hablar	41
estrellar *to shatter* Reg.	hablar	41
estrellarse *to crash (vehicles)* Reg.	hablar	41
estremecer *to shake something; to shudder*	parecer	53
estremecerse *to tremble*	parecer	53
estrenar *to use, display or wear for the first time* Reg.	hablar	41
estrenarse *to make one's debut* Reg.	hablar	41
estreñir *to constipate*	reñir	69
estreñirse *to become constipated*	reñir	69
estresar *to stress (psychologically)* Reg.	hablar	41
estribar *to be based on (argument, belief)* Reg.	hablar	41
estropear *to spoil* Reg.	hablar	41
estropearse *to break down* Reg.	hablar	41
estructurar *to organize, structure* Reg.	hablar	41
estrujar *to squeeze; to crumple* Reg.	hablar	41

estudiar *to study* Reg.	hablar	41
eternizar *to make endless* Reg.	realizar	65
eternizarse *never to finish; to go on for ever* Reg.	realizar	65
etiquetar *to label* Reg.	hablar	41
europeizar *to Europeanize*	arcaizar	8
evacuar (formerly conjugated like **continuar**) *to evacuate* Reg.	hablar	41
evadir *to evade* Reg.	vivir	89
evadirse *to escape* Reg.	vivir	89
evaluar *to evaluate*	continuar	25
evangelizar *to evangelize* Reg.	realizar	65
evaporar *to evaporate* Reg.	hablar	41
evaporizar *to vaporize* Reg.	realizar	65
evidenciar *to make evident* Reg.	hablar	41
evitar *to avoid* Reg.	hablar	41
evocar *to evoke* Reg.	sacar	74
evolucionar *to evolve* Reg.	hablar	41
exacerbar *to exacerbate* Reg.	hablar	41
exagerar *to exaggerate* Reg.	hablar	41
exaltar *to exalt* Reg.	hablar	41
exaltarse *to become excited* Reg.	hablar	41
examinar *to examine; to inspect* Reg.	hablar	41
examinarse *to take an examination* Reg.	hablar	41
excavar *to excavate* Reg.	hablar	41
exceder *to exceed* Reg.	comer	22
exceptuar *to except*	continuar	25
excitar *to excite* Reg.	hablar	41
excitarse *to become excited* Reg.	hablar	41
exclamar *to exclaim* Reg.	hablar	41
excluir *to exclude*	construir	23
excogitar *to think out; to devise* Reg.	hablar	41
excomulgar *to excommunicate* Reg.	pagar	52
excusar *to excuse; to avoid; to exempt* Reg.	hablar	41
excusarse *to apologize* Reg.	hablar	41

exhalar *to emit; to exhale* Reg.	hablar	41
exhibir *to exhibit* Reg.	vivir	89
exhibirse *to show off* (intransitive) Reg.	vivir	89
exhortar *to exhort* Reg.	hablar	41
exhumar *to exhume* Reg.	hablar	41
exigir *to require; to demand*	rugir	72
eximir *to exempt* Reg.	vivir	89
exonerar *to exonerate* Reg.	hablar	41
exorcizar *to exorcise* Reg.	realizar	65
expansionar *to expand* (transitive) Reg.	hablar	41
expansionarse *to open one's heart* Reg.	hablar	41
expatriar *to expatriate*	liar	45
expedir *to issue*	pedir	54
expeditar *to expedite* Reg.	hablar	41
experimentar *to experience; to experiment* Reg.	hablar	41
expiar *to atone for*	liar	45
expirar *to expire* Reg.	hablar	41
explanar *to level; to explain* Reg.	hablar	41
explayar *to extend* Reg.	hablar	41
explayarse *to discourse at large* Reg.	hablar	41
explicar *to explain* Reg.	sacar	74
explicarse *to make sense of* Reg.	sacar	74
explorar *to explore* Reg.	hablar	41
explosionar *to detonate, fire (explosives); to explode* (transitive and intransitive)	hablar	41
explotar *to exploit; to explode* Reg.	hablar	41
expoliar *to plunder* Reg.	hablar	41
exponer *to expose; to show*	poner	58
exportar *to export* Reg.	hablar	41
expresar *to express* Reg.	hablar	41
exprimir *to squeeze out* Reg.	vivir	89
expropiar *to expropriate* Reg.	hablar	41
expugnar *to take by storm* Reg.	hablar	41
expulsar *to expel* Reg.	hablar	41
expurgar *to expurgate* Reg.	pagar	52

extasiar *to delight*	liar	45
extasiarse *to be in ecstasy*	liar	45
extender *to extend; to draw up (a document)*	perder	55
extenuar *to make exhausted*	continuar	25
exteriorizar *to make manifest* Reg.	realizar	65
exterminar *to exterminate* Reg.	hablar	41
extinguir *to extinguish* Reg.	distinguir	33
extinguirse *to be extinguished* Reg.	distinguir	33
extirpar *to extirpate; to root out* Reg.	hablar	41
extorsionar *to extort* Reg.	hablar	41
extractar *to make a summary of (a text)* Reg.	hablar	41
extradir *to extradite* Reg.	vivir	89
extraditar *to extradite* Reg.	hablar	41
extraer *to extract*	traer	83
extralimitarse *to overstep* Reg.	hablar	41
extranjerizarse *to adopt foreign ways* Reg.	realizar	65
extrañar *to miss (* i.e. *feel longing for)* Reg.	hablar	41
extrañarse de *to be surprised at* Reg.	hablar	41
extrapolar *to extrapolate* Reg.	hablar	41
extraviar *to mislead; to misplace*	liar	45
extraviarse *to get lost*	liar	45
extremar *to carry to an extreme* Reg.	hablar	41
extremarse *to exert oneself to the utmost* Reg.	hablar	41
extrudir *to extrude* Reg.	vivir	89
exultar *to exult* Reg.	hablar	41
eyacular *to ejaculate* Reg.	hablar	41
fabricar *to manufacture* Reg.	sacar	74
facilitar *to make easier* Reg.	hablar	41
facturar *to check baggage (at airport); to invoice* Reg.	hablar	41

facultar para *to authorize someone to* Reg.	hablar	41
faenar *to fish (trawlers)* Reg.	hablar	41
fajar *to girdle; to bind with a bandage or sash* Reg.	hablar	41
fallar *to fail; to make a ruling* Reg.	hablar	41
fallecer *to die*	parecer	53
falsear *to misrepresent* Reg.	hablar	41
falsificar *to falsify; to counterfeit* Reg.	sacar	74
faltar *to be lacking; to be absent* Reg.	hablar	41
familiarizar *to familiarize* Reg.	realizar	65
fanatizar *to make fanatical* Reg.	realizar	65
fanfarronear *to brag* Reg.	hablar	41
fantasear *to daydream; to fantasize* Reg.	hablar	41
farfullar *to jabber; to gabble* Reg.	hablar	41
farolear *to show off* Reg.	hablar	41
fascinar *to fascinate* Reg.	hablar	41
fastidiar *to annoy* Reg.	hablar	41
fatigar *to make tired* Reg.	pagar	52
fatigarse *to get tired* Reg.	pagar	52
favorecer *to favor/(Brit.) favour*	parecer	53
fechar *to date (a document, etc.)* Reg.	hablar	41
fecundar *to inseminate* Reg.	hablar	41
fecundizar *to make fertile* Reg.	realizar	65
felicitar *to congratulate* Reg.	hablar	41
fermentar *to ferment* Reg.	hablar	41
fertilizar *to fertilize* Reg.	realizar	65
festejar *to laugh at (a joke); to celebrate (an occasion)* Reg.	hablar	41
fiar *to sell on credit*	liar	45
fiarse de *to trust*	liar	45
fichar *to put on file* Reg.	hablar	41
figurar *to figure (*e.g. *on a list)* Reg.	hablar	41
figurarse *to imagine* Reg.	hablar	41
fijar *to fix* Reg.	hablar	41
fijarse en *to pay attention to* Reg.	hablar	41

filmar *to film* Reg.	hablar	41
filosofar *to philosophize* Reg.	hablar	41
filtrar *to filter* Reg.	hablar	41
filtrarse *to leak out (information)* Reg.	hablar	41
finalizar *to finalize, finish* (transitive) Reg.	realizar	65
finalizarse *to come to an end* Reg.	realizar	65
financiar *to finance* Reg.	hablar	41
fingir *to pretend*	rugir	72
firmar *to sign* Reg.	hablar	41
fiscalizar *to oversee (*e.g. *expenditure)* Reg.	realizar	65
fisgar *to pry* Reg.	pagar	52
fisgonear *to pry constantly* Reg.	hablar	41
flagelar *to whip* Reg.	hablar	41
flamear *to flame* Reg.	hablar	41
flanquear *to flank* Reg.	hablar	41
flaquear *to grow weak; to falter* Reg.	hablar	41
fletar *to charter (plane, etc.)* Reg.	hablar	41
flexibilizar *to make more flexible* Reg.	realizar	65
flirtear *to flirt* Reg.	hablar	41
flojear *to slacken; to weaken; to go off an idea; to laze around* Reg.	hablar	41
florear *to decorate with flowers* Reg.	hablar	41
florecer *to blossom, flourish*	parecer	53
flotar *to float* Reg.	hablar	41
fluctuar *to fluctuate*	continuar	25
fluir *to flow*	construir	23
fluorizar *to fluoridize* Reg.	realizar	65
fomentar *to promote (idea, campaign, etc.)* Reg.	hablar	41
fondear *to sound (* i.e. *measure the depth of water)* Reg.	hablar	41
forjar *to forge* Reg.	hablar	41
formalizar *to formalize; to formulate,* Reg.	realizar	65
formar *to form, shape* Reg.	hablar	41

formatear *to format (disk, etc.)* Reg.	hablar	41
formular *to formulate* Reg.	hablar	41
fornicar *to fornicate* Reg.	sacar	74
forrar *to line; to cover* Reg.	hablar	41
forrarse *to rake it in (money)* Reg.	hablar	41
fortalecer *to strengthen*	parecer	53
fortificar *to fortify* Reg.	sacar	74
forzar *to force*	almorzar	6
fosilizarse *to fossilize* Reg.	realizar	65
fotograbar *to photoengrave* Reg.	hablar	41
fotografiar *to photograph*	liar	45
fracasar *to fail* (intransitive) Reg.	hablar	41
fraccionar *to divide into fractions, small portions* Reg.	hablar	41
fracturar *to fracture* Reg.	hablar	41
fragmentar *to break something into fragments* Reg.	hablar	41
fragmentarse *to fragment* (intransitive) Reg.	hablar	41
fraguar *to forge; to concoct (a scheme, plot)*	averiguar	13
franquear *to frank (a letter); to exempt* Reg.	hablar	41
fraternizar *to fraternize* Reg.	realizar	65
frecuentar *to frequent* Reg.	hablar	41
fregar *to rub; to scrub; to do the washing up*	negar	49
freír (past participle **frito**) *to fry*	reír	68
frenar *to brake* Reg.	hablar	41
fresar *to mill (engineering)* Reg.	hablar	41
friccionar *to rub; to massage* Reg.	hablar	41
frisar en : frisaba en los sesenta años *he wasn't far off sixty years old* Reg.	hablar	41
frotar *to rub* Reg.	hablar	41
fruncir *to wrinkle (brows)* Reg.	zurcir	92
frustrar *to frustrate* Reg.	hablar	41
fugarse *to run away* Reg.	pagar	52

fulgurar *to flash* Reg.	hablar	41
fulminar *to fulminate* Reg.	hablar	41
fumar *to smoke* Reg.	hablar	41
fumarse (familiar) *to skip (class, seminar)* Reg.	hablar	41
fumigar *to fumigate* Reg.	pagar	52
funcionar *to function; to work (machines)* Reg.	hablar	41
fundamentar *to lay the bases of* Reg.	hablar	41
fundar *to found; to base* Reg.	hablar	41
fundarse en *to be based on* Reg.	hablar	41
fundir *to smelt; to fuse* (transitive) Reg.	vivir	89
fundirse *to melt; to blow (fuse)* (intransitive) Reg.	vivir	89
fusilar *to execute by firing squad* Reg.	hablar	41
fusionar *to merge* Reg.	hablar	41
fustigar *to lash; to censure severely* Reg.	pagar	52
galantear *to flirt with (a woman)* Reg.	hablar	41
galardonar *to reward; to award a prize to (novel, etc.)* Reg.	hablar	41
galopar *to gallop* Reg.	hablar	41
galvanizar *to galvanize, electroplate* Reg.	realizar	65
gallardear *to act dashingly, elegantly* Reg.	hablar	41
ganar *to earn; to gain; to win* Reg.	hablar	41
gandulear *to loaf; to idle* Reg.	hablar	41
gangrenarse *to grow gangrenous* Reg.	hablar	41
garabatear *to scribble* Reg.	hablar	41
garantir = **garantizar**	abolir	1
garantizar *to guarantee* Reg.	realizar	65
gargajear *to spit phlegm* Reg.	hablar	41
gargarear = **gargarizar** Reg.	hablar	41
gargarizar *to gargle* Reg.	realizar	65
garrapatear *to scribble, scrawl* Reg.	hablar	41
garuar = **lloviznar**	continuar	25

gasear *to gas* Reg.	hablar	41
gastar *to spend; to waste; to wear out; to use up* Reg.	hablar	41
gatear *to crawl* Reg.	hablar	41
gemir *to moan; to whine*	pedir	54
generalizar *to generalize* Reg.	realizar	65
generalizarse *to become generalized, widely known* Reg.	realizar	65
generar *to generate* Reg.	hablar	41
germinar *to germinate* Reg.	hablar	41
gestar *to gestate* Reg.	hablar	41
gesticular *to gesture* Reg.	hablar	41
gestionar *to manage* Reg.	hablar	41
gimotear *to whimper* Reg.	hablar	41
girar *to revolve; to spin* Reg.	hablar	41
gloriarse *to boast; to be proud*	liar	45
glorificar *to glorify* Reg.	sacar	74
gobernar *to govern; to steer (boat)*	cerrar	18
golear *to score a goal* (usually **marcar**)	hablar	41
golpear *to beat* Reg.	hablar	41
golpetear *to beat repeatedly; to tap* Reg.	hablar	41
gorjear *to warble* Reg.	hablar	41
gotear *to drip; to sprinkle* Reg.	hablar	41
gozar *to enjoy* Reg.	realizar	65
grabar *to engrave; to record (on tape)* Reg.	hablar	41
graduar *to adjust*	continuar	25
graduarse *to graduate, get a degree*	continuar	25
granar *to seed (plants)* Reg.	hablar	41
granear = **granar** Reg.	hablar	41
granizar *to hail* Reg.	realizar	65
granjear *to win (by one's efforts)* Reg.	hablar	41
granular *to granulate* Reg.	hablar	41
grapar *to staple* Reg.	hablar	41
gratificar *to reward (* i.e. *to give a reward)* Reg.	sacar	74

gratinar *to brown (food, under the grill)* Reg.	hablar	41
gravar *to levy (a tax)* Reg.	hablar	41
gravitar *to gravitate;* **g. sobre** *to weight upon (*e.g. *a burden, responsibility)* Reg.	hablar	41
graznar *to croak; to caw; to quack (ducks)* Reg.	hablar	41
gritar *to shout* Reg.	hablar	41
gruñir *to grunt; to growl; to grumble*	gruñir	39
guadañar *to scythe* Reg.	hablar	41
guardar *to guard; to keep;* Reg.	hablar	41
guardarse *to keep for/to oneself* Reg.	hablar	41
guarecer *to shelter*	parecer	53
guarecerse *to take shelter*	parecer	53
guarnecer de *to garnish with*	parecer	53
guatear *to pad, wad* Reg.	hablar	41
guerrear *to war* Reg.	hablar	41
guerrillear *to wage guerrilla warfare* Reg.	hablar	41
guiar *to guide; to steer*	liar	45
guiarse por *to be guided by*	liar	45
guillotinar *to guillotine* Reg.	hablar	41
guiñar *to wink* (transitive and intransitive) Reg.	hablar	41
guisar *to cook; to stew* Reg.	hablar	41
gustar *to please;* **me gusta** *I like it* Reg.	hablar	41
haber auxiliary verb or *there is/are*	haber	40
habilitar *to equip; to authorize* Reg.	hablar	41
habitar *to inhabit; to live in* Reg.	hablar	41
habituar *to habituate*	continuar	25
habituarse a *to get into the habit of*	continuar	25
hablar *to speak; to talk* Reg.	hablar	41
hacendar *to confer land upon (a knight, etc.)* Reg.	hablar	41
or	perder	55

hacer *to do; to make* (consult a dictionary for idiomatic uses)	hacer	42
hacerse *to become*	hacer	42
hacinar *to jam together; to heap up* (transitive)	hablar	41
hacinarse *to be crowded together*	hablar	41
halagar *to flatter* Reg.	pagar	52
hallar *to find* (**encontrar** is more common) Reg.	hablar	41
hallarse *to find oneself; to be located* Reg.	hablar	41
haraganear *to loaf; to lounge* Reg.	hablar	41
hartar *to satiate; to make fed up* Reg.	hablar	41
hartarse de *to get sick of* Reg.	hablar	41
hastiar *to annoy*	liar	45
hastiarse de *to get sick/tired of*	liar	45
hechizar *to bewitch; to charm* Reg.	realizar	65
heder *to stink*	perder	55
helar *to freeze* (transitive)*; to astonish*	cerrar	18
helarse *to freeze* (intransitive)	cerrar	18
henchir *to fill, swell (*e.g. *a river)*	pedir	54
hender *to cleave*	perder	55
heredar *to inherit* Reg.	hablar	41
herir *to wound; to hurt*	sentir	78
hermanar *to unite (people in a feeling, ideal); to twin (cities)* Reg.	hablar	41
hermosear *to beautify* Reg.	hablar	41
herrar *to shoe (a horse)*	cerrar	18
hervir *to boil*	sentir	78
hibernar *to hibernate* Reg.	hablar	41
hidratar *to moisturize* Reg.	hablar	41
hidrolizar *to hydrolize* Reg.	realizar	65
higienizar *to sanitize* Reg.	realizar	65
hilar *to spin (thread)* Reg.	hablar	41
hilvanar *to baste, tack (sewing); to connect (ideas, phrases)* Reg.	hablar	41

hincar en *to drive, sink into (teeth, stakes)* Reg.	sacar	74
hincarse *to kneel down* Reg.	sacar	74
hinchar *to inflate* Reg.	hablar	41
hincharse *to swell up* Reg.	hablar	41
hipar *to hiccup* Reg.	hablar	41
hipnotizar *to hypnotize* Reg.	realizar	65
hispanizar *to Hispanize* Reg.	realizar	65
historiar *to write the history of* Reg.	hablar	41
hocicar *to nuzzle; to root around* Reg.	sacar	74
hojear *to leaf through (a book, etc.)* Reg.	hablar	41
holgar *to be useless, pointless;* **huelga decir que** *there is no need to say that*	colgar	20
hollar *to tread upon; to trample*	contar	24
homenajear *to pay tribute to (= to praise)* Reg.	hablar	41
homogeneizar *to homogenize*	arcaizar	8
homologar *to make equal; to endorse* Reg.	pagar	52
honrar *to honor/(Brit.) honour* Reg.	hablar	41
horadar *to perforate; to bore/drill through* Reg.	hablar	41
hormiguear *to swarm* Reg.	hablar	41
hornear *to bake* Reg.	hablar	41
horrorizar *to horrify* Reg.	realizar	65
horrorizarse de *to be horrified at* Reg.	realizar	65
hospedar *to lodge, accommodate (people)* Reg.	hablar	41
hospedarse *to stay (in a hotel, etc.)* Reg.	hablar	41
hospitalizar *to hospitalize* Reg.	realizar	65
hostigar *to harass* Reg.	pagar	52
huir *to flee, run away*	construir	23
humanizar *to humanize* Reg.	realizar	65
humedecer *to moisten, wet*	parecer	53
humedecerse *to become moist, damp*	parecer	53

humillar *to humiliate* Reg.	hablar	41
hundir *to sink* (transitive) Reg.	vivir	89
hundirse *to sink* (intransitive) Reg.	vivir	89
hurgar *to poke, rummage* Reg.	pagar	52
hurtar *to steal* (=**robar**) Reg.	hablar	41
husmear *to sniff around* Reg.	hablar	41
idealizar *to idealize* Reg.	realizar	65
idear *to devise (a scheme, plan)* Reg.	hablar	41
identificar *to identify* Reg.	sacar	74
idiotizarse *to become completely stupid* Reg.	realizar	65
idolatrar *to idolize* Reg.	hablar	41
ignorar *not to know; to ignore* Reg.	hablar	41
igualar *to make equal, even, level* Reg.	hablar	41
igualarse con *to be equal to; to match* Reg.	hablar	41
ilegalizar *to make illegal* Reg.	realizar	65
iluminar *to illuminate* Reg.	hablar	41
ilusionar *to fill with excitement (*e.g. *plans, dreams)* Reg.	hablar	41
ilusionarse por *to look forward to; to get excited about* Reg.	hablar	41
ilustrar *to illustrate; to enlighten* Reg.	hablar	41
imaginar *to imagine; to invent* Reg.	hablar	41
imaginarse *to imagine* Reg.	hablar	41
imanar *to magnetize* Reg.	hablar	41
imantar = **imanar** Reg.	hablar	41
imbuir *to imbue*	construir	23
imbuirse de *to become imbued with*	construir	23
imitar *to imitate* Reg.	hablar	41
impacientar *to make impatient* Reg.	hablar	41
impacientarse *to get impatient* Reg.	hablar	41
impactar *to make an impression; to shock* Reg.	hablar	41
impartir *to impart* Reg.	vivir	89
impedir *to prevent*	pedir	54

impeler *to impel* Reg.	comer	22
imperar *to prevail* Reg.	hablar	41
impermeabilizar *to make waterproof* Reg.	realizar	65
implementar *to implement* Reg.	hablar	41
implicar *to imply* Reg.	sacar	74
implicarse *to become implicated* Reg.	sacar	74
implorar *to implore* Reg.	hablar	41
imponer *to impose*	poner	58
imponerse *to prevail; to become established (idea, etc.)*	poner	58
importar *to import; to be worth; to matter* Reg.	hablar	41
importunar *to importune* Reg.	hablar	41
imposibilitar *to make impossible; to prevent* Reg.	hablar	41
imposibilitarse *to become disabled* Reg.	hablar	41
imprecar *to imprecate, curse* Reg.	sacar	74
impregnar *to impregnate, soak* Reg.	hablar	41
impresionar *to impress* Reg.	hablar	41
imprimir *to print* Reg.	vivir	89
improvisar *to improvise* Reg.	hablar	41
impugnar *to impugn; to challenge (an idea, etc.)* Reg.	hablar	41
impulsar *to propel* Reg.	hablar	41
imputar a *to attribute to* Reg.	hablar	41
inactivar *to deactivate* Reg.	hablar	41
inaugurar *to inaugurate* Reg.	hablar	41
incapacitar *to incapacitate; to disqualify* Reg.	hablar	41
incautar *to seize, confiscate* Reg.	hablar	41
incendiar *to set fire to* Reg.	hablar	41
incendiarse *to catch fire* Reg.	hablar	41
incensar *to incense*	cerrar	18
incidir en *to affect, influence; to impinge on* Reg.	vivir	89
incinerar *to incinerate* Reg.	hablar	41

incitar *to incite* Reg.	hablar	41
inclinar *to incline; to tilt* (transitive) Reg.	hablar	41
inclinarse *to lean over; to bow* Reg.	hablar	41
incluir *to include*	construir	23
incoar *to initiate* Reg.	hablar	41
incomodar *to make someone feel awkward* Reg.	hablar	41
incomodarse *to feel embarrassed, awkward* Reg.	hablar	41
incomunicar *to isolate, cut off* Reg.	sacar	74
incordiar (familiar) *to annoy* Reg.	hablar	41
incorporar *to incorporate; to stir in* Reg.	hablar	41
incorporarse a *to sit up; to join (a club, etc.)* Reg.	hablar	41
incrementar *to increase* (transitive) Reg.	hablar	41
incrementarse *to increase* (intransitive) Reg.	hablar	41
increpar *to reprimand* Reg.	hablar	41
incriminar *to incriminate* Reg.	hablar	41
incrustar *to set (a precious stone); to embed* Reg.	hablar	41
incrustarse *to become embedded* Reg.	hablar	41
incubar *to incubate* Reg.	hablar	41
inculcar *to inculcate* Reg.	sacar	74
inculpar *to accuse; to charge (with a crime)* Reg.	hablar	41
incumbir *to concern* (third person only) Reg.	vivir	89
incumplir *to break (promises, laws); to fail to abide by* Reg.	vivir	89
incurrir en *to commit (an error); to incur (expenses)* Reg.	vivir	89
indagar *to investigate, enquire* Reg.	pagar	52
indemnizar *to indemnify* Reg.	realizar	65
independizar *to make independent* Reg.	realizar	65

independizarse *to become independent* Reg.	realizar	65
indexar *to index* Reg.	hablar	41
indicar *to point to; to indicate* Reg.	sacar	74
indiciar = **indexar** Reg.	hablar	41
indigestarse *to cause indigestion;* **se me indigestó** *I couldn't stomach it* Reg.	hablar	41
indignar *to anger, make indignant* Reg.	hablar	41
indignarse *to become angry* Reg.	hablar	41
indisponer *to upset; to indispose*	poner	58
indisponerse *to get upset; to become ill*	poner	58
individualizar *to individualize; to single out by name* Reg.	realizar	65
inducir a *to induce to; to persuade to*	producir	60
indultar *to pardon* Reg.	hablar	41
industrializar *to industrialize* Reg.	realizar	65
industrializarse *to become industrialized* Reg.	realizar	65
infamar *to defame* Reg.	hablar	41
infatuar *to make conceited*	continuar	25
infatuarse *to become conceited*	continuar	25
infectar *to infect* Reg.	hablar	41
infectarse *to become infected* Reg.	hablar	41
inferir de *to infer from*	sentir	78
infestar *to infest* Reg.	hablar	41
infiltrar *to infiltrate* (transitive) Reg.	hablar	41
infiltrarse *to infiltrate* (intransitive)*; to sneak in* Reg.	hablar	41
inflamar *to inflame* Reg.	hablar	41
inflar *to inflate; to exaggerate* Reg.	hablar	41
inflarse *to swell up* Reg.	hablar	41
infligir *to inflict*	rugir	72
influir *to influence*	construir	23
informar *to inform* Reg.	hablar	41
informarse sobre *to find out about* Reg.	hablar	41
infringir *to infringe*	rugir	72

infundir *to infuse; to instill/(Brit.) instil* Reg.	vivir	89
ingeniar *to think up (plan, idea)* Reg.	hablar	41
ingeniarse *to manage* Reg.	hablar	41
ingerir *to ingest*	sentir	78
ingresar *to deposit (money);* **i. en** *to enter (an organization)* Reg.	hablar	41
inhabilitar *to disqualify* Reg.	hablar	41
inhalar *to inhale* Reg.	hablar	41
inhibir *to inhibit* Reg.	vivir	89
inhumar *to inter* (= **enterrar**) Reg.	hablar	41
iniciar *to initiate* Reg.	hablar	41
iniciarse *to begin; to be initiated* Reg.	hablar	41
injerirse en *to interfere*	sentir	78
injertar *to graft (shoots on a plant, etc.)* Reg.	hablar	41
injuriar *to insult; to injure* Reg.	hablar	41
inmergir *to immerse*	rugir	72
inmigrar *to immigrate* Reg.	hablar	41
inmiscuirse en *to interfere in*	construir	23
inmolar *to immolate* (= **sacrificar**) Reg.	hablar	41
inmortalizar *to immortalize* Reg.	realizar	65
inmovilizar *to immobilize* Reg.	realizar	65
inmunizar *to immunize* Reg.	realizar	65
inmutar *to change, perturb* Reg.	hablar	41
innovar *to innovate* Reg.	hablar	41
inocular *to inoculate* Reg.	hablar	41
inquietar *to worry, disturb* Reg.	hablar	41
inquirir sobre *to inquire about*	adquirir	3
inscribir *to enter something in a register*	escribir	37
inscribirse *to enroll/(Brit.) enrol; to register*	escribir	37
inseminar *to inseminate* Reg.	hablar	41
insensibilizar *to desensitize* Reg.	realizar	65
insertar *to insert* Reg.	hablar	41
insidiar *to plot against* Reg.	hablar	41
insinuar *to insinuate, hint*	continuar	25

insinuarse *to show through; to become just visible*	continuar	25
insistir en *to insist on* Reg.	vivir	89
insolentarse *to become insolent* Reg.	hablar	41
insonorizar *to soundproof* Reg.	realizar	65
inspeccionar *to inspect* Reg.	hablar	41
inspirar *to inspire* Reg.	hablar	41
instalar *to install* Reg.	hablar	41
instalarse *to settle in* Reg.	hablar	41
instar a *to urge to* Reg.	hablar	41
instaurar *to establish (regime, etc.)* Reg.	hablar	41
instigar a *to instigate; to incite to* Reg.	pagar	52
instilar *to instill/(Brit.) instil* Reg.	hablar	41
institucionalizar *to institutionalize* Reg.	realizar	65
instituir *to institute*	construir	23
instruir *to instruct*	construir	23
insubordinarse *to rebel* Reg.	hablar	41
insuflar *to breathe into, inspire with (e.g. spirit, enthusiasm)* Reg.	hablar	41
insultar *to insult* Reg.	hablar	41
insumir = **invertir** Reg.	vivir	89
integrar *to make up (numbers);* **i. en** *to incorporate into* Reg.	hablar	41
integrarse en *to become integrated in;* **i. a** *to join (organization)* Reg.	hablar	41
intensificar *to intensify* Reg.	sacar	74
intentar *to try* Reg.	hablar	41
interactuar *to interact*	continuar	25
intercalar en *to insert; to place between; to interpose* Reg.	hablar	41
intercambiar *to exchange* Reg.	hablar	41
interceder *to intercede* Reg.	comer	22
interceptar *to intercept* Reg.	hablar	41
interconectar *to interconnect* (transitive) Reg.	hablar	41
interdecir *to interdict*	decir	28

interesar *to interest* Reg.	hablar	41
interesarse por/en *to be interested in* Reg.	hablar	41
interferir *to interfere*	sentir	78
interiorizar *to internalize* Reg.	realizar	65
interiorizarse sobre *to make oneself familiar with* Reg.	realizar	65
intermediar *to intermediate* Reg.	hablar	41
internacionalizar *to internationalize* Reg.	realizar	65
internar *to intern, put away (*e.g. *in an asylum)* Reg.	hablar	41
internarse en *to penetrate into (territory, etc.)* Reg.	hablar	41
interpelar sobre *to demand explanations about* Reg.	hablar	41
interpolar *to interpolate* Reg.	hablar	41
interponer *to place between, interpose*	poner	58
interponerse *to intervene (*e.g. *between two enemies)*	poner	58
interpretar *to interpret; to play (a film or theatre role)* Reg.	hablar	41
interrogar *to interrogate* Reg.	pagar	52
interrumpir *to interrupt* Reg.	vivir	89
intervenir *to intervene; to take part in (performance, debate, etc.); to tap (phone calls)*	venir	87
intimar con *to be emotionally close to* Reg.	hablar	41
intimidar *to intimidate, threaten* Reg.	hablar	41
intoxicar *to intoxicate, poison* Reg.	sacar	74
intranquilizar *to disquiet; to worry* (transitive) Reg.	realizar	65
intranquilizarse *to be worried* Reg.	realizar	65
intrigar *to intrigue* Reg.	pagar	52
introducir *to introduce (*e.g. *legislation);* **i. en** *to insert in*	producir	60

introducirse *to get in; to gain access*	producir	60
intuir *to know or sense by intuition*	construir	23
inundar *to flood* Reg.	hablar	41
inundarse *to be flooded* Reg.	hablar	41
inutilizar *to make useless* Reg.	realizar	65
inutilizarse *to become useless* Reg.	realizar	65
invadir *to invade* Reg.	vivir	89
invalidar *to invalidate* Reg.	hablar	41
inventar *to invent* Reg.	hablar	41
inventariar *to make an inventory of*	liar	45
invernar *to winter; to hibernate*	cerrar	18
invertir *to invest; to reverse* (transitive)	sentir	78
investigar *to investigate* Reg.	pagar	52
investir *to invest (* i.e. *an official with a title or powers)*	pedir	54
invitar *to invite;* **invito yo** *it's on me/I'm paying* Reg.	hablar	41
invocar *to invoke* Reg.	sacar	74
involucrar *to involve* Reg.	hablar	41
involucrarse en *to be involved in* Reg.	hablar	41
inyectar *to inject* Reg.	hablar	41
ionizar *to ionize* Reg.	realizar	65
ir *to go* (consult a dictionary for idiomatic uses)	ir	43
irse *to go away*	ir	43
irisar *to iridesce; to give off the colors/ (Brit.) colours of the rainbow* Reg.	hablar	41
irradiar *to radiate; to irradiate* Reg.	hablar	41
irrigar *to irrigate* Reg.	pagar	52
irritar *to irritate* Reg.	hablar	41
irritarse *to get irritated* Reg.	hablar	41
irrumpir *to burst in* Reg.	vivir	89
iterar *to iterate, repeat* Reg.	hablar	41
izar *to hoist (flags)* Reg.	realizar	65
jabonar *to soap* Reg.	hablar	41
jactarse de *to boast about* Reg.	hablar	41

jadear *to pant* Reg.	hablar	41
jalar *to pull, haul* (Lat. Am.) Reg.	hablar	41
jalear *to cheer on (performers)* Reg.	hablar	41
jaquear *to put into check (chess)* Reg.	hablar	41
jorobar *to annoy; to bother* Reg.	hablar	41
jubilar *to pension off (an employee)* Reg.	hablar	41
jubilarse *to retire* Reg.	hablar	41
jugar *to play*	jugar	44
jugarse *to risk (*e.g. *one's life)*	jugar	44
juntar *to join together* (transitive) Reg.	hablar	41
juntarse *to join up, unite* (intransitive) Reg.	hablar	41
juramentar *to swear in (*e.g. *a jury)* Reg.	hablar	41
jurar *to swear* Reg.	hablar	41
justificar *to justify* Reg.	sacar	74
juzgar *to judge* Reg.	pagar	52
laborar *to labor/(Brit.) labour* Reg.	hablar	41
laborear *to work the land; also =* **laborar** Reg.	hablar	41
labrar *to carve; to work the land* Reg.	hablar	41
lacerar *to lacerate* Reg.	hablar	41
lactar *to nurse; to feed with milk* Reg.	hablar	41
ladear *to tilt* (transitive) Reg.	hablar	41
ladearse *to tilt over, become crooked* Reg.	hablar	41
ladrar *to bark* Reg.	hablar	41
ladrillar *to pave with bricks* Reg.	hablar	41
ladronear *to go around thieving* Reg.	hablar	41
lagrimar *to weep* Reg.	hablar	41
lagrimear *to water (eyes); to sob* Reg.	hablar	41
laicizar *to secularize* Reg.	realizar	65
lamentar *to regret, deplore* Reg.	hablar	41
lamentarse *to complain* Reg.	hablar	41
lamer *to lick* Reg.	comer	22

laminar *to laminate* Reg.	hablar	41
languidecer *to languish; to flag (= to grow feeble)*	parecer	53
lanzar *to throw; to launch* Reg.	realizar	65
lanzarse *to throw oneself; to leap; to pounce* Reg.	realizar	65
lapidar *to stone* Reg.	hablar	41
laquear *to lacquer* Reg.	hablar	41
largar *to let go; to let out (rope, etc.)* Reg.	pagar	52
largarse *to go away* (familiar) Reg.	pagar	52
lastimar *to hurt* (transitive) Reg.	hablar	41
lastimarse *to hurt oneself* Reg.	hablar	41
latir *to throb; to beat (heart)* Reg.	vivir	89
laurear *to honor/(Brit.) honour with a prize* Reg.	hablar	41
lavar *to wash* (transitive) Reg.	hablar	41
lavarse *to wash oneself* Reg.	hablar	41
lazar *to lasso* Reg.	realizar	65
leer *to read*	poseer	59
legalizar *to legalize* Reg.	realizar	65
legar *to bequeath* Reg.	pagar	52
legislar *to legislate* Reg.	hablar	41
legitimar *to legitimate, authenticate* Reg.	hablar	41
lesionar *to injure* Reg.	hablar	41
lesionarse *to be injured* Reg.	hablar	41
levantar *to raise; to lift* Reg.	hablar	41
levantarse *to stand up; to get up* Reg.	hablar	41
levar *to weigh (anchor)* Reg.	hablar	41
liar *to tie up in a bundle; to embroil*	liar	45
liarse *to get into a mess, jam; to get complicated*	liar	45
liberalizar *to liberalize* Reg.	realizar	65
liberar *to free* Reg.	hablar	41
liberarse de *to free oneself from* Reg.	hablar	41
libertar *to liberate* Reg.	hablar	41

librar de *to free, save from* Reg.	hablar	41
librarse de *to avoid (danger, inconvenience); to save oneself from* Reg.	hablar	41
licenciarse *to graduate (from university)* Reg.	hablar	41
licitar *to put out to tender* Reg.	hablar	41
licuar *to liquidize; to liquefy* (transitive) Reg.	continuar	25
licuarse *to liquefy* (intransitive)	continuar	25
licuefacer *to liquefy* (= **licuar)**	satisfacer	76
lidiar con *to fight, struggle with* Reg.	hablar	41
ligar *to bind, tie* Reg.	pagar	52
ligarse con *to 'pick up' (a person)* Reg.	pagar	52
lijar *to sandpaper* Reg.	hablar	41
limar *to file (*e.g. *nails, metal)* Reg.	hablar	41
limitar *to limit;* **l. con** *to border on* Reg.	hablar	41
limitarse a *to limit oneself to* Reg.	hablar	41
limpiar *to clean* Reg.	hablar	41
lindar con = **limitar con** Reg.	hablar	41
liquidar *to pay off (debt); to sell off (goods); to liquidate* Reg.	hablar	41
lisiar *to cripple* Reg.	hablar	41
lisonjear *to flatter* Reg.	hablar	41
listar *to list* Reg.	hablar	41
litigar *to litigate* Reg.	pagar	52
litografiar *to lithograph*	liar	45
llagar *to wound; to create a sore* Reg.	pagar	52
llamar *to call; to phone* Reg.	hablar	41
llamarse *to be called* Reg.	hablar	41
llamear *to flame* Reg.	hablar	41
llegar *to arrive;* **l. a** *to arrive at/in* Reg.	pagar	52
llenar *to fill* (transitive); *to fulfill/*(Brit.) *fulfil (* i.e. *emotionally, intellectually)* Reg.	hablar	41
llenarse *to fill* (intransitive) Reg.	hablar	41

llevar *to carry; to take* (consult a dictionary for idiomatic meanings) Reg.	hablar	41
llevarse *to take away* Reg.	hablar	41
llorar *to cry; to weep* Reg.	hablar	41
lloriquear *to whine* Reg.	hablar	41
llover *to rain* (usually third person only)	mover	48
lloviznar *to drizzle* (usually third person only) Reg.	hablar	41
loar *to praise* Reg.	hablar	41
lobreguecer *to make gloomy; to grow dark; to make dark*	parecer	53
localizar *to locate* Reg.	realizar	65
localizarse *to be localized* Reg.	realizar	65
lograr *to achieve; to manage to* Reg.	hablar	41
lotear *to divide into lots* Reg.	hablar	41
lozanear *to look fresh and luxuriant* Reg.	hablar	41
lubricar *to lubricate* Reg.	sacar	74
luchar *to fight; to struggle; to wrestle* Reg.	hablar	41
lucir *to shine; to show off* (transitive)	lucir	46
lucirse *to come off well; to excel*	lucir	46
lucrar *to profit* Reg.	hablar	41
lucrarse = **lucrar** Reg.	hablar	41
lustrar *to polish* Reg.	hablar	41
macanear *to joke; to tell lies* (R. Plate region) Reg.	hablar	41
macerar *to marinade, soak* Reg.	hablar	41
machacar *to crush; to nag* Reg.	sacar	74
madrugar *to get up early* Reg.	pagar	52
madurar *to ripen; to mature* Reg.	hablar	41
madurarse = **madurar** Reg.	hablar	41
magnetizar *to magnetize* Reg.	realizar	65
magnificar *to magnify* Reg.	sacar	74
magullar *to bruise* (transitive) Reg.	hablar	41

magullarse *to bruise* (intransitive) Reg.	hablar	41
malbaratar *to squander* Reg.	hablar	41
malcriar *to spoil (a child)*	liar	45
maldecir *to curse*	maldecir	47
malear *to corrupt, pervert* Reg.	hablar	41
malearse *to become corrupted* Reg.	hablar	41
malgastar *to waste, squander* Reg.	hablar	41
malherir *to wound seriously*	sentir	78
maliciar *to suspect* (esp. Lat. Am.) Reg.	hablar	41
maliciarse = **maliciar** Reg.	hablar	41
malograr *to wreck (plans)* Reg.	hablar	41
malograrse *to fail, come to nothing (plans)* Reg.	hablar	41
malquerer *to dislike*	querer	64
malquistarse con *to fall out with* Reg.	hablar	41
maltratar *to mistreat* Reg.	hablar	41
malvender *to sell off at a loss* Reg.	comer	22
malversar *to embezzle* Reg.	hablar	41
mamar *to suckle; to feed at the breast*	hablar	41
mamarse *to get drunk* Reg.	hablar	41
manar *to pour forth* (transitive and intransitive) Reg.	hablar	41
manchar *to stain* Reg.	hablar	41
mancillar *to besmirch* Reg.	hablar	41
mancomunar *to pool (resources)* Reg.	hablar	41
mandar *to command; to send* Reg.	hablar	41
manejar *to handle;* (Lat. Am.) *to drive (cars)* Reg.	hablar	41
manejarse *to cope, manage* (intransitive) Reg.	hablar	41
mangonear *to boss around* Reg.	hablar	41
maniatar *to tie the hands; to shackle* Reg.	hablar	41
manifestar *to declare, state*	cerrar	18
manifestarse *to demonstrate (* i.e. *protest); to become obvious*	cerrar	18

maniobrar *to maneuver/(Brit.) manoeuvre* Reg.	hablar	41
manipular *to manipulate; to handle (goods, etc.)* Reg.	hablar	41
manosear *to handle; to grope* Reg.	hablar	41
manotear *to gesture* Reg.	hablar	41
mantener *to maintain (machinery, etc.); to support (*e.g. *financially)*	tener	82
mantenerse de *to survive on*	tener	82
manufacturar *to manufacture* Reg.	hablar	41
mapear *to map* Reg.	hablar	41
maquinar *to plot; to scheme* Reg.	hablar	41
maravillar *to amaze* Reg.	hablar	41
maravillarse de *to be amazed at* Reg.	hablar	41
marcar *to mark (with a sign); to dial; to score (sport)* Reg.	sacar	74
marchar *to march; to walk; to run (machinery)* Reg.	hablar	41
marcharse *to go away; to leave* Reg.	hablar	41
marchitarse *to wilt; to wither* Reg.	hablar	41
marear *to make someone feel nauseated* Reg.	hablar	41
marearse *to feel nauseated* Reg.	hablar	41
marginar *to marginalize, push to one side* Reg.	hablar	41
marinar *to marinate* Reg.	hablar	41
mariposear *to flutter around* Reg.	hablar	41
martillar *to hammer* Reg.	hablar	41
martillear = **martillar** Reg.	hablar	41
martirizar *to martyrize; to torment* Reg.	realizar	65
mascar *to chew* Reg.	sacar	74
mascullar *to mumble (words)* Reg.	hablar	41
masificarse *to get overcrowded* Reg.	sacar	74
masticar *to chew* Reg.	sacar	74
masturbarse *to masturbate* (intransitive) Reg.	hablar	41
matar *to kill; to butcher* Reg.	hablar	41

materializar *to fulfill/(Brit.) fulfil (a plan, etc.)* Reg.	realizar	65
materializarse *to be fulfilled (plans)* Reg.	realizar	65
matizar *to modify, qualify (a statement)* Reg.	realizar	65
matricular *to register, enroll/(Brit.) enrol* (transitive) Reg.	hablar	41
matricularse *to register, enroll* (intransitive) Reg.	hablar	41
maximizar *to maximize* Reg.	realizar	65
maullar *to meow*	aullar	11
mecanizar *to mechanize* Reg.	realizar	65
mecanografiar *to type*	liar	45
mecer *to rock* (transitive) Reg.	vencer	86
mecerse *to sway* Reg.	vencer	86
mediar *to mediate; to elapse (time); to lie between (space)* Reg.	hablar	41
medir *to measure*	pedir	54
meditar *to meditate* Reg.	hablar	41
medrar *to thrive, prosper* Reg.	hablar	41
mejorar *to improve* (transitive and intransitive) Reg.	hablar	41
mejorarse *to recover (from an illness)* Reg.	hablar	41
mellar *to notch; to nick* Reg.	hablar	41
mencionar *to mention* Reg.	hablar	41
mendigar *to beg (* i.e. *be a beggar)* Reg.	pagar	52
menear *to wag* Reg.	hablar	41
menguar *to diminish* (transitive and intransitive)	averiguar	13
menoscabar *to impair* Reg.	hablar	41
menospreciar *to despise* Reg.	hablar	41
menstruar *to menstruate*	continuar	25
mensurar *to measure* Reg.	hablar	41
mentalizar *to make someone aware* Reg.	realizar	65

mentalizarse *to become aware; to get a clear idea* Reg.	realizar	65
mentar *to mention*	cerrar	18
mentir *to lie*	sentir	78
menudear *to be frequent* Reg.	hablar	41
mercadear *to haggle* Reg.	hablar	41
merecer *to deserve*	parecer	53
merendar *to have an afternoon snack*	cerrar	18
mermar *to decrease* (transitive and intransitive) Reg.	hablar	41
merodear *to prowl* Reg.	hablar	41
metalizarse *to become mercenary* Reg.	realizar	65
meter *to insert* Reg.	comer	22
meterse en *to get involved in* Reg.	comer	22
mezclar *to mix, blend* (transitive) Reg.	hablar	41
mezclarse *to mix, mingle* (intransitive) Reg.	hablar	41
migar *to crumble* Reg.	pagar	52
militar *to be an active member (*e.g. *of a political party)* Reg.	hablar	41
militarizar *to militarize* Reg.	realizar	65
mimar *to pamper; to spoil (a child)* Reg.	hablar	41
minar *to mine; to undermine* Reg.	hablar	41
minimizar *to minimize* Reg.	realizar	65
modelar *to model* Reg.	hablar	41
moderar *to moderate* Reg.	hablar	41
moderarse *to control oneself* Reg.	hablar	41
modernizar *to modernize* Reg.	realizar	65
modificar *to modify* Reg.	sacar	74
modular *to modulate* Reg.	hablar	41
mofarse de *to scoff at* Reg.	hablar	41
mojar *to wet* Reg.	hablar	41
mojarse *to get wet* Reg.	hablar	41
moldear *to shape; to mold/(Brit.) mould* Reg.	hablar	41
moler *to grind*	mover	48

molestar *to disturb; to bother* Reg.	hablar	41
molestarse *to be annoyed; to be bothered* Reg.	hablar	41
momificar *to mummify* Reg.	sacar	74
mondar *to peel* Reg.	hablar	41
monologar *to talk without listening* Reg.	pagar	52
monopolizar *to monopolize* Reg.	realizar	65
montar *to mount* (transitive)*; to set up (organization, etc.)* Reg.	hablar	41
montarse en *to get into/onto (vehicle, horse, etc.)* Reg.	hablar	41
moralizar *to moralize* Reg.	realizar	65
morar *to dwell* (= **habitar**) Reg.	hablar	41
morder *to bite*	mover	48
mordisquear *to nibble* Reg.	hablar	41
morir *to die* (past participle **muerto**)	dormir	34
morirse (past participle **muerto**) = **morir** (familiar or figurative usage)	dormir	34
mortificar *to mortify* Reg.	sacar	74
mosquear *to annoy* (transitive) Reg.	hablar	41
mosquearse *to get annoyed* Reg.	hablar	41
mostrar *to show*	contar	24
motear *to speckle* Reg.	hablar	41
motejar *to call names* Reg.	hablar	41
motivar *to motivate* Reg.	hablar	41
mover *to move* (transitive)	mover	48
moverse *to move* (intransitive)	mover	48
movilizar *to mobilize* Reg.	realizar	65
mudar de *to change (*e.g. *opinion)* (transitive) Reg.	hablar	41
mudarse *to move house; to change clothes* Reg.	hablar	41
mugir *to moo* Reg.	rugir	72
mullir *to fluff up*	bullir	15
multiplicar *to multiply* Reg.	sacar	74
murmurar *to murmur, mutter* Reg.	hablar	41
mutilar *to mutilate* Reg.	hablar	41

mutarse *to mutate* Reg.	hablar	41
nacer *to be born*	parecer	53
nacionalizar *to nationalize; to naturalize* Reg.	realizar	65
naturalizar *to naturalize* Reg.	realizar	65
naufragar *to be shipwrecked; to come to grief (plans)* Reg.	pagar	52
navegar *to navigate* Reg.	pagar	52
necesitar *to need* Reg.	hablar	41
negar *to deny*	negar	49
negarse a *to refuse to*	negar	49
negociar *to negotiate* Reg.	hablar	41
neutralizar *to neutralize* Reg.	realizar	65
nevar *to snow* (usu. third person only)	cerrar	18
neviscar *to snow lightly; to sleet* (usu. third person only) Reg.	sacar	74
nivelar *to level; to even* Reg.	hablar	41
nombrar *to name; to appoint* Reg.	hablar	41
nominar *to nominate* Reg.	hablar	41
normalizar *to normalize* Reg.	realizar	65
notar *to note, notice* Reg.	hablar	41
novelar *to write up in the form of a novel* Reg.	hablar	41
nublar *to cloud, obscure* (transitive) Reg.	hablar	41
nublarse *to become cloudy, misty* Reg.	hablar	41
numerar *to number* (transitive) Reg.	hablar	41
nutrir *to nourish* Reg.	vivir	89
nutrirse de *to feed on* Reg.	vivir	89
obedecer *to obey*	parecer	53
objetar *to object* Reg.	hablar	41
obligar a *to oblige to* Reg.	pagar	52
obligarse a *to make oneself do something* Reg.	hablar	41

obnubilar *to make obscure, befuddled* Reg.	hablar	41
obnubilarse *to become cloudy (mind, ideas)* Reg.	hablar	41
obrar *to act (* i.e. *to work); to perform (* e.g. *miracles)* Reg.	hablar	41
obscurecer = oscurecer	parecer	53
obscurecerse = oscurecerse	parecer	53
obsequiar con *to give something as a present to* Reg.	hablar	41
observar *to observe* Reg.	hablar	41
obsesionar *to obsess* (transitive) Reg.	hablar	41
obsesionarse por *to become obsessed about* Reg.	hablar	41
obstaculizar *to hinder* Reg.	realizar	65
obstar para que *to stand in the way of* Reg.	hablar	41
obstinarse en *to insist obstinately on* Reg.	hablar	41
obstruir *to obstruct*	construir	23
obtener *to obtain*	tener	82
obturar *to stop up, block* Reg.	hablar	41
obviar *to obviate* Reg.	hablar	41
ocasionar *to cause (* e.g. *damage, suffering)* Reg.	hablar	41
ocluir *to occlude*	construir	23
ocultar *to conceal* Reg.	hablar	41
ocultarse *to hide* (intransitive) Reg.	hablar	41
ocupar *to occupy* Reg.	hablar	41
ocuparse de *to look after* Reg.	hablar	41
ocurrir *to happen* Reg.	vivir	89
ocurrirse a *to occur to (* e.g. *idea, thought)* Reg.	vivir	89
odiar *to hate* Reg.	hablar	41
ofender *to offend* Reg.	comer	22
ofenderse *to take offense/(Brit.) offence* Reg.	comer	22

ofertar *to sell as a special offer; to offer (for sale)* Reg.	hablar	41
oficiar *to officiate* Reg.	hablar	41
ofrecer *to offer*	parecer	53
ofrecerse *to present itself (opportunity, etc.)*	parecer	53
ofrendar *to offer up (prayers, sacrifices)* Reg.	hablar	41
ofuscar *to blind (passions, rage)* Reg.	sacar	74
oír *to hear*	oír	50
ojear *to eye* Reg.	hablar	41
oler *to smell*	oler	51
olfatear *to sniff out* Reg.	hablar	41
olvidar *to forget* Reg.	hablar	41
olvidarse de *to forget (unintentionally)* Reg.	hablar	41
omitir *to omit; to neglect* Reg.	vivir	89
ondear *to wave, ripple (*e.g. *flag)* Reg.	hablar	41
operar *to operate* Reg.	hablar	41
opinar *to express/hold an opinion* Reg.	hablar	41
oponer *to set up (*e.g. *a counter-argument, counter-proposal)*	poner	58
oponerse a *to oppose*	poner	58
oprimir *to oppress; to squeeze* Reg.	vivir	89
optar por *to opt;* **o. a** *to apply for* Reg.	hablar	41
optimizar *to optimize* Reg.	realizar	65
ordenar *to put in order; to sort; to ordain; to command* Reg.	hablar	41
ordenarse *to be ordained (priest)* Reg.	hablar	41
ordeñar *to milk* Reg.	hablar	41
organizar *to organize* Reg.	realizar	65
orientar *to orient* Reg.	hablar	41
orientarse *to find one's way around* Reg.	hablar	41
originar *to create, give rise to (*e.g. *conflict)* Reg.	hablar	41
originarse *to arise (problems, etc.)* Reg.	hablar	41

orillar *to skirt round (obstacles, problems)* Reg.	hablar	41
orinar *to urinate* Reg.	hablar	41
orlar *to trim with a fringe* Reg.	hablar	41
ornamentar *to adorn* Reg.	hablar	41
orquestar *to orchestrate* Reg.	hablar	41
osar *to dare* (= **atreverse**) Reg.	hablar	41
oscilar *to oscillate* Reg.	hablar	41
oscurecer *to darken* (transitive and intransitive)	parecer	53
oscurecerse *to darken* (intransitive)	parecer	53
osificarse *to ossify* Reg.	sacar	74
ostentar *to show off* (intransitive)*; to hold (an office); to flaunt (wealth)* Reg.	hablar	41
otear *to scan (with the eyes)* Reg.	hablar	41
otorgar *to grant, award* Reg.	pagar	52
ovillarse *to curl up in a ball* (intransitive) Reg.	hablar	41
oxidarse *to rust* Reg.	hablar	41
oxigenar *to bleach (hair)* Reg.	hablar	41
oxigenarse *to bleach one's (own) hair; to get some fresh air* Reg.	hablar	41
pacer *to pasture; to graze*	parecer	53
pacificar *to pacify* Reg.	sacar	74
pacificarse *to calm down* Reg.	sacar	74
pactar *to agree terms for* Reg.	hablar	41
pactarse *to make a pact* Reg.	hablar	41
padecer *to suffer* (transitive and intransitive)	parecer	53
pagar *to pay; to pay for* Reg.	pagar	52
paladear *to relish* Reg.	hablar	41
palear *to shovel* Reg.	hablar	41
paliar *to palliate; to ease* Reg.	hablar	41
palidecer *to turn pale*	parecer	53
palmear *to slap on the back* Reg.	hablar	41

palmotear *to clap;* also = **palmear** Reg.	hablar	41
palpar *to feel (with the hands)* Reg.	hablar	41
palpitar *to throb* Reg.	hablar	41
papelear *to look through papers* Reg.	hablar	41
parafrasear *to paraphrase* Reg.	hablar	41
paralizar *to paralyze* Reg.	realizar	65
paralizarse *to become paralyzed* Reg.	realizar	65
parangonar *to compare* (= **comparar**) Reg.	hablar	41
parapetarse *to take cover* Reg.	hablar	41
parar *to stop* (transitive and intransitive) Reg.	hablar	41
pararse *to stop* (intransitive); (Lat. Am.) *to stand up* Reg.	hablar	41
parcelar *to parcel out* Reg.	hablar	41
parchar *to patch* Reg.	hablar	41
parear a *to match to* Reg.	hablar	41
parecer *to seem*	parecer	53
parecerse a *resemble*	parecer	53
parir *to give birth* Reg.	vivir	89
parodiar *to parody* Reg.	hablar	41
parpadear *to blink* Reg.	hablar	41
parquear (Lat. Am.) *to park* (= **aparcar**) Reg.	hablar	41
parrandear *to go out on a spree* Reg.	hablar	41
participar *to participate; to notify* Reg.	hablar	41
particularizar *to particularize (= to characterize)* Reg.	realizar	65
partir *to split; to depart* Reg.	vivir	89
partirse *to splinter, break* (intransitive) Reg.	vivir	89
pasar *to pass* (consult a dictionary for idiomatic meanings) Reg.	hablar	41
pasarse *to overdo it; to jump (lights, etc.); to spend (time)* Reg.	hablar	41
pasear *to go for a walk; to take for a walk* Reg.	hablar	41

pasearse *to go for a walk* Reg.	hablar	41
pasmar *to stun* Reg.	hablar	41
pasmarse *to be stunned* Reg.	hablar	41
pastar *to graze* Reg.	hablar	41
pasterizar = **pasteurizar** Reg.	realizar	65
pasteurizar *to pasteurize* Reg.	realizar	65
pastorear *to tend (flocks)* Reg.	hablar	41
patalear *to stamp the feet* Reg.	hablar	41
patear *to kick* Reg.	hablar	41
patentar *to patent* Reg.	hablar	41
patentizar *to make evident; to reveal* Reg.	realizar	65
patinar *to skate; to skid* Reg.	hablar	41
patrocinar *to sponsor* Reg.	hablar	41
patronear *to skipper* Reg.	hablar	41
patrullar *to patrol* Reg.	hablar	41
pavimentar *to pave* Reg.	hablar	41
pavonearse *to strut, swagger* Reg.	hablar	41
pecar *to sin* Reg.	sacar	74
pedalear *to pedal* Reg.	hablar	41
pedantear *to be pedantic* Reg.	hablar	41
pedir *to ask; to ask for*	pedir	54
pegar *to hit; to stick* (transitive and intransitive) Reg.	pagar	52
pegarse *to stick* (intransitive; consult a dictionary for idiomatic meanings) Reg.	pagar	52
peinar *to comb; to do someone's hair* Reg.	hablar	41
peinarse *to get one's hair done; to do one's hair* Reg.	hablar	41
pelar *to peel* (transitive) Reg.	hablar	41
pelarse *to peel* (intransitive) Reg.	hablar	41
pelear *to fight; to quarrel* Reg.	hablar	41
pelearse = **pelear** Reg.	hablar	41
peligrar *to be in danger* Reg.	hablar	41
pellizcar *to pinch* Reg.	sacar	74

penalizar *to penalize* Reg.	realizar	65
pender de *to hang from* (= **colgar**) Reg.	comer	22
penetrar *to penetrate* Reg.	hablar	41
pensar *to think; to intend to*	cerrar	18
pensarse *to think something over*	cerrar	18
percatarse de *to notice, realize* Reg.	hablar	41
percibir *to perceive; to receive (wages, etc.)* Reg.	vivir	89
perder *to lose*	perder	55
perderse *to get lost; to miss (program, appointment, etc.)*	perder	55
perdonar *to pardon* Reg.	hablar	41
perdurar *to last a long time* Reg.	hablar	41
perecer *to perish*	parecer	53
peregrinar *to go on a pilgrimage* Reg.	hablar	41
perfeccionar *to perfect* Reg.	hablar	41
perfilar *to shape* Reg.	hablar	41
perfilarse *to be outlined, silhouetted* Reg.	hablar	41
perforar *to perforate* Reg.	hablar	41
perfumar *to perfume* Reg.	hablar	41
pergeñar (archaic) *to sketch* Reg.	hablar	41
perjudicar *to damage; to be harmful to* Reg.	sacar	74
perjurar *to commit perjury; to swear (an oath)* Reg.	hablar	41
permanecer *to remain; to stay*	parecer	53
permitir *to permit, allow* Reg.	vivir	89
permutar *to barter, exchange* Reg.	hablar	41
pernoctar *to spend the night* Reg.	hablar	41
perorar *to make an impassioned speech; to hold forth* Reg.	hablar	41
perpetrar *to perpetrate* Reg.	hablar	41
perpetuarse *to perpetuate*	continuar	25
perseguir *to persecute; to pursue*	seguir	77
perseverar *to persevere* Reg.	hablar	41
persignarse *to cross oneself* Reg.	hablar	41

persistir *to persist* Reg.	vivir	89
personalizar *to personalize* Reg.	realizar	65
personarse *to appear, show up (persons only)* Reg.	hablar	41
personificar *to personify* Reg.	sacar	74
perspirar *to perspire; to sweat* Reg.	hablar	41
persuadir a *to persuade to* Reg.	vivir	89
persuadirse de *to become convinced of* Reg.	vivir	89
pertenecer a *to belong to*	parecer	53
pertrechar *to equip* Reg.	hablar	41
perturbar *to perturb* Reg.	hablar	41
pervertir *to pervert*	sentir	78
pervertirse *to become perverted*	sentir	78
pesar *to weigh; to weigh down* Reg.	hablar	41
pescar *to fish; to catch* Reg.	sacar	74
pestañear *to blink* Reg.	hablar	41
peticionar *to petition* Reg.	hablar	41
petrificarse *to become petrified* Reg.	sacar	74
piar *to chirp*	liar	45
picar *to itch; to sting* Reg.	sacar	74
picarse *to be irritated; to go rotten* Reg.	sacar	74
picotear *to peck* Reg.	hablar	41
pifiar *to get it wrong* (colloquial) Reg.	hablar	41
pillar *to catch* Reg.	hablar	41
pilotar *to pilot* Reg.	hablar	41
pilotear = **pilotar** Reg.	hablar	41
pinchar *to puncture* Reg.	hablar	41
pincharse *to burst* (intransitive) Reg.	hablar	41
pintar *to paint;* **él no pinta** *he doesn't matter* Reg.	hablar	41
pintarrajear *to daub* Reg.	hablar	41
piratear *to pirate* Reg.	hablar	41
piropear *to compliment (a pretty woman)* Reg.	hablar	41
pisar *to step on* Reg.	hablar	41
pisotear *to trample* Reg.	hablar	41

pitar *to blow a whistle; to whistle* Reg.	hablar	41
placer *to please* (= **gustar)**	placer	56
plagiar *to plagiarize* Reg.	hablar	41
planchar *to iron* Reg.	hablar	41
planear *to plan; to glide* Reg.	hablar	41
planificar *to plan* Reg.	sacar	74
plantar *to plant* Reg.	hablar	41
plantear *to set, pose (a problem)* Reg.	hablar	41
plantearse *to arise (problem); to consider (a problem)* Reg.	hablar	41
plañir (archaic) *to lament*	gruñir	39
plasmar *to give form to (*e.g. *ideas)* Reg.	hablar	41
plasmarse *to be expressed (*e.g. *ideas in a work of art)* Reg.	hablar	41
platear *to plate with silver* Reg.	hablar	41
platicar *to converse* (Lat. Am.) Reg.	sacar	74
plegar *to fold*	negar	49
pleitear *to litigate, go to court* Reg.	hablar	41
pluralizar *to pluralize* Reg.	realizar	65
poblar *to populate*	contar	24
poder *to be able; can; may*	poder	57
podrir = **pudrir** Reg.	vivir	89
poetizar *to poetize* Reg.	realizar	65
polarizar *to polarize* Reg.	realizar	65
polemizar *to start a polemic* Reg.	realizar	65
politiquear *to play politics* Reg.	hablar	41
polvorear *to powder* Reg.	hablar	41
ponderar *to praise* Reg.	hablar	41
poner *to put* (consult a dictionary for idiomatic meanings)	poner	58
ponerse *to become; to put on (clothes)*	poner	58
pontificar *to pontificate* Reg.	sacar	74
popularizar *to popularize* Reg.	realizar	65
porfiar en *to persist in*	liar	45
pormenorizar *to tell in detail; to itemize* Reg.	realizar	65

portar *to carry; to bear* Reg.	hablar	41
portarse *to behave* Reg.	hablar	41
posar *to pose; to place; to perch* Reg.	hablar	41
posarse *to perch; to alight (birds, helicopters)* Reg.	hablar	41
poseer *to possess*	poseer	59
posesionarse de *to take possession of* Reg.	hablar	41
posibilitar *to make possible* Reg.	hablar	41
posponer *to postpone*	poner	58
postergar *to pass over (= disregard seniority); to delay* Reg.	pagar	52
postrar *to prostrate* (transitive) Reg.	hablar	41
postrarse *to be prostrated, laid out (person)* Reg.	hablar	41
postular *to postulate* Reg.	hablar	41
potenciar *to boost* Reg.	hablar	41
practicar *to practice/(Brit.) to practise* Reg.	sacar	74

For the conjugation of unlisted verbs beginning with **pre-** see the root verb

precaverse *to take precautions* Reg.	comer	22
preceder *to precede* Reg.	comer	22
preciarse de *to boast of* Reg.	hablar	41
precintar *to seal* Reg.	hablar	41
precipitar *to precipitate, rush* (transitive) Reg.	hablar	41
precipitarse *to rush* (intransitive) Reg.	hablar	41
precisar *to state precisely; to need* Reg.	hablar	41
preconcebir *to preconceive*	pedir	54
preconizar *to advocate* Reg.	realizar	65
predecir *to predict*	maldecir	47
predestinar *to predestine* Reg.	hablar	41
predicar *to preach* Reg.	sacar	74
predisponer *to predispose*	poner	58
predominar *to predominate* Reg.	hablar	41
prefabricar *to prefabricate* Reg.	sacar	74

preferir *to prefer*	sentir	78
prefijar *to prefix* Reg.	hablar	41
pregonar *to proclaim, make public* Reg.	hablar	41
preguntar *to ask (* i.e. *to ask a question)* Reg.	hablar	41
prejuzgar *to prejudge* Reg.	pagar	52
preludiar *to be a foretaste of* Reg.	hablar	41
premeditar *to premeditate* Reg.	hablar	41
premiar *to reward* Reg.	hablar	41
prendarse *to fall for (a person)* Reg.	hablar	41
prender *to catch; to arrest; to pin on; to switch on* Reg.	comer	22
prenderse *to catch fire* Reg.	comer	22
prensar *to press (* e.g. *grapes, olives)* Reg.	hablar	41
preñar *to make pregnant* (familiar for **dejar embarazada***)* Reg.	hablar	41
preocupar *to preoccupy* Reg.	hablar	41
preocuparse *to be worried* Reg.	hablar	41
preparar *to prepare* Reg.	hablar	41
prepararse *to get ready; to be imminent* Reg.	hablar	41
preponderar *to prevail* Reg.	hablar	41
presagiar *to presage* Reg.	hablar	41
prescindir de *to do without* Reg.	vivir	89
preseleccionar *to shortlist* Reg.	hablar	41
prescribir *to prescribe*	escribir	37
presenciar *to witness (an event)* Reg.	hablar	41
presentar *to present; to introduce* Reg.	hablar	41
presentarse *to appear (= turn up)* Reg.	hablar	41
presentir *to have a presentiment of*	sentir	78
preservar *to preserve (from damage or danger)* Reg.	hablar	41
presidir *to preside over* Reg.	vivir	89
presionar *to pressure* Reg.	hablar	41
prestar *to lend; to pay (attention)* Reg.	hablar	41

prestarse a *to offer or lend oneself to* Reg.	hablar	41
prestigiar *to enhance the prestige of* Reg.	hablar	41
presumir *to boast;* **p. de...** *to boast that one is...* Reg.	vivir	89
presupuestar *to budget for* Reg.	hablar	41
pretender *to claim; to aspire to* Reg.	comer	22
pretextar *to use a pretext* Reg.	hablar	41
prevalecer *to prevail*	parecer	53
prevalerse de *to take advantage of*	valer	85
prevaricar *to pervert (justice); to use corrupt methods* Reg.	sacar	74
prevenir *to prevent*	venir	87
prevenirse contra *to take advance measures against*	venir	87
prever *to foresee*	ver	88
primar *to be foremost* Reg.	hablar	41
principiar *to begin* Reg.	hablar	41
pringar *to cover in grease* Reg.	pagar	52
priorizar *to give priority to* Reg.	realizar	65
privar de *to deprive of; to be foremost (feature)* Reg.	hablar	41
privilegiar *to privilege* Reg.	hablar	41
probar *to test; to try; to prove*	contar	24
probarse *to try on (clothes)*	contar	24
proceder de *to originate from* Reg.	comer	22
procesar *to try (in court); to process* Reg.	hablar	41
proclamar *to proclaim* Reg.	hablar	41
procrastinar *to procrastinate* Reg.	hablar	41
procrear *to breed (*transitive and intransitive*)* Reg.	hablar	41
procurar *to try hard to; to obtain* Reg.	hablar	41
procurarse *to acquire for oneself* Reg.	hablar	41
prodigar *to lavish; to squander* Reg.	pagar	52

prodigarse en *to be generous with (praise, compliments)* Reg.	pagar	52
producir *to produce*	producir	60
producirse *to take place; to occur*	producir	60
profanar *to defile* Reg.	hablar	41
proferir *to utter (insults)*	sentir	78
profesar *to profess* Reg.	hablar	41
profetizar *to prophesy* Reg.	realizar	65
profundizar en *to go into details* Reg.	realizar	65
programar *to program* Reg.	hablar	41
progresar *to progress* Reg.	hablar	41
prohibir *to prohibit; to forbid*	prohibir	61
prohijar *to adopt (child, ideas)*	aislar	5
prologar *to write a preface to* Reg.	pagar	52
prolongar *to prolong* Reg.	pagar	52
prolongarse *to stretch (distance, time)* (intransitive) Reg.	pagar	52
promediar *to average* Reg.	hablar	41
prometer *to promise* Reg.	comer	22
promocionar *to promote (sales)* Reg.	hablar	41
promover *to stimulate, encourage (plan)*	mover	48
pronosticar *to forecast* Reg.	sacar	74
pronunciar *to pronounce* Reg.	hablar	41
propagar *to propagate* Reg.	pagar	52
propagarse *to spread* (intransitive) Reg.	pagar	52
propalar *to divulge* Reg.	hablar	41
propasarse *to go too far* Reg.	hablar	41
propender a *to tend to* Reg.	comer	22
propiciar *to propitiate* Reg.	hablar	41
propinar *to give (a blow)* Reg.	hablar	41
proponer *to propose*	poner	58
proponerse *to resolve; to set out to*	poner	58
proporcionar *to provide* Reg.	hablar	41
propugnar *to advocate* Reg.	hablar	41
propulsar *to propel* Reg.	hablar	41
prorrogar *to defer; to postpone* Reg.	pagar	52

prorrumpir en *to burst out in (applause, etc.)* Reg.	vivir	89
proscribir *to proscribe*	escribir	37
proseguir *to continue; to proceed*	seguir	77
prosperar *to prosper* Reg.	hablar	41
prostituir *to prostitute*	construir	23
protagonizar *to take a leading part in (a performance, etc.)* Reg.	realizar	65
proteger *to protect* Reg.	proteger	62
protestar *to protest* Reg.	hablar	41
proveer *to provide*	proveer	63
proveerse *to get supplies*	proveer	63
provocar *to provoke* Reg.	sacar	74
proyectar *to plan* Reg.	hablar	41
psicoanalizar *to psychoanalyze* Reg.	realizar	65
publicar *to publish* Reg.	sacar	74
pudrir *to rot* (past participle **podrido**) Reg.	vivir	89
pugnar *to strive* Reg.	hablar	41
pujar *to strain (= to push with one's muscles)* Reg.	hablar	41
pulir *to polish* Reg.	vivir	89
pulsar *to press (a button, etc.)* Reg.	hablar	41
pulular *to swarm* Reg.	hablar	41
pulverizar *to pulverize* Reg.	realizar	65
puntualizar *to specify in detail* Reg.	realizar	65
puntuar *to punctuate; to grade/(Brit.) mark (examinations, etc.)*	continuar	25
punzar *to prick; to perforate* Reg.	realizar	65
purgar *to purge; to purify* Reg.	pagar	52
purificar *to purify* Reg.	sacar	74
quebrantar *to break down (morale, health)* (transitive) Reg.	hablar	41
quebrar *to snap, break* (transitive)	cerrar	18
quebrarse *to snap, break* (intransitive)	hablar	41

quedar *to remain; to be left* (consult dictionary for idiomatic uses) Reg.	hablar	41
quedarse *to stay* (consult dictionary for idiomatic uses) Reg.	hablar	41
quejarse *to complain* Reg.	hablar	41
quemar *to burn* (transitive) Reg.	hablar	41
quemarse *to burn* (intransitive) Reg.	hablar	41
querellarse *to take legal action* Reg.	hablar	41
querer *to want; to love*	querer	64
quitar *to remove; to take away* Reg.	hablar	41
quitarse *to take off (clothing)* Reg.	hablar	41
rabiar *to rage* Reg.	hablar	41
racionalizar *to rationalize* Reg.	realizar	65
racionar *to ration* Reg.	hablar	41
radiar *to broadcast* Reg.	hablar	41
radicar en *to stem from* Reg.	sacar	74
radicarse *to settle* Reg.	sacar	74
raer *to scrape* (= **raspar**)	caer	17
rajar *to crack* (transitive) Reg.	hablar	41
rajarse *to crack* (intransitive) Reg.	hablar	41
ralentizar *to slow down* (transitive) Reg.	realizar	65
ralentizarse *to slow down* (intransitive) Reg.	realizar	65
rallar *to grate (*e.g. *cheese)* Reg.	hablar	41
ramificarse *to branch out* Reg.	sacar	74
rapar *to shave* Reg.	hablar	41
raptar *to kidnap* Reg.	hablar	41
rasar *to skim (the surface)* Reg.	hablar	41
rascar *to scratch* Reg.	sacar	74
rasgar *to rip* Reg.	pagar	52
rasguñar *to scratch* (transitive) Reg.	hablar	41
raspar *to scrape* Reg.	hablar	41
rastrear *to track; to trail* Reg.	hablar	41
rastrillar *to rake* Reg.	hablar	41
rasurar *to shave* (Lat. Am.) Reg.	hablar	41
ratificar *to ratify* Reg.	sacar	74

rayar *to scratch, mark;* **r. en** *to border on* Reg.	hablar	41
razonar *to reason* Reg.	hablar	41
For the conjugation of unlisted verbs beginning with **re-**, see the root verb		
reaccionar *to react* Reg.	hablar	41
reacondicionar *to recondition* Reg.	hablar	41
reactivar *to reactivate* Reg.	hablar	41
readaptar *to readapt* Reg.	hablar	41
readmitir *to readmit* Reg.	vivir	89
reafirmar *to reaffirm* Reg.	hablar	41
reajustar *to readjust* Reg.	hablar	41
realinear *to realign* Reg.	hablar	41
realizar *to fulfill/(Brit.) fulfil; to make real; to carry out* Reg.	realizar	65
realzar *to emphasize; to highlight* Reg.	realizar	65
reanimar *to revive; to comfort* Reg.	hablar	41
reanimarse *to be revived* Reg.	hablar	41
reanudar *to renew; to resume* Reg.	hablar	41
reaparecer *to reappear*	parecer	53
rearmar *to rearm* Reg.	hablar	41
reavivar *to revive* Reg.	hablar	41
rebajar *to lower (prices); to humiliate* Reg.	hablar	41
rebajarse a *to lower oneself to* Reg.	hablar	41
rebanar *to slice* Reg.	hablar	41
rebasar *to overflow; to go beyond (limits)* Reg.	hablar	41
rebatir *to refute* Reg.	vivir	89
rebelarse *to rebel* Reg.	hablar	41
reblandecerse *to go soft*	parecer	53
rebobinar *to rewind (tape)* Reg.	hablar	41
rebosar de *to abound in (energy, etc.)* Reg.	hablar	41
rebotar *to rebound* Reg.	hablar	41
rebozar *to cover with batter* Reg.	realizar	65
rebrotar *to sprout* Reg.	hablar	41

rebuscar *to rummage* Reg.	sacar	74
rebuznar *to bray* Reg.	hablar	41
recabar *to gather (information)* Reg.	hablar	41
recaer *to relapse*	caer	17
recalcar *to emphasize* Reg.	sacar	74
recalentar *to reheat; to overheat*	cerrar	18
recalentarse *to become overheated*	cerrar	18
recapacitar *to reconsider* Reg.	hablar	41
recapitular *to recapitulate* Reg.	hablar	41
recargar *to charge extra; to recharge* Reg.	pagar	52
recatarse *to be abashed, ashamed* Reg.	hablar	41
recauchutar *to retread (a tire/(Brit.) tyre)* Reg.	hablar	41
recaudar *to collect (taxes, rent)* Reg.	hablar	41
recelar de *to be suspicious of* Reg.	hablar	41
recetar *to prescribe* Reg.	hablar	41
rechazar *to reject* Reg.	realizar	65
rechinar *to squeak (*e.g. *hinges)* Reg.	hablar	41
rechistar *to winge, complain* Reg.	hablar	41
recibir *to receive* Reg.	vivir	89
recitar *to recite* Reg.	hablar	41
reclamar *to demand (rights, privileges, etc.); to complain* Reg.	hablar	41
reclinar *to rest, lean back* (transitive) Reg.	hablar	41
reclinarse *to lean back* Reg.	hablar	41
recluir *to intern*	construir	23
recluirse *to go into seclusion*	construir	23
reclutar *to recruit* Reg.	hablar	41
recobrar *to recover (*e.g. *health)* Reg.	hablar	41
recobrarse *to recover (from an illness)* Reg.	hablar	41
recoger *to pick up* Reg.	proteger	62
recogerse *to retire (go to bed); to withdraw* (intransitive)*; to roll up (sleeves)* Reg.	proteger	62

recomendar *to recommend*	cerrar	18
recompensar *to reward* Reg.	hablar	41
reconcentrar en *to concentrate on* Reg.	hablar	41
reconciliar *to reconcile* Reg.	hablar	41
reconciliarse con *to be reconciled with* Reg.	hablar	41
reconfortar *to comfort* Reg.	hablar	41
reconocer *to recognize; to admit (truth, fact)*	parecer	53
reconquistar *to reconquer* Reg.	hablar	41
reconsiderar *to reconsider* Reg.	hablar	41
reconstruir *to rebuild*	construir	23
reconvenir *to reproach*	venir	87
recopilar *to compile (anthologies, etc.)* Reg.	hablar	41
recordar *to remember; to remind*	contar	24
recorrer *to travel all over; to tour* Reg.	comer	22
recortar *to cut out (*e.g. *an article from a newspaper); to cut (spending)* Reg.	hablar	41
recortarse *to stand out* Reg.	hablar	41
recostar *to lean* (transitive)	contar	24
recostarse *to lie down; to lie back*	contar	24
recrear *to recreate* Reg.	hablar	41
recrearse *to take pleasure* Reg.	hablar	41
recriminar *to recriminate* Reg.	hablar	41
recrudecerse *to grow more intense*	parecer	53
rectificar *to rectify* Reg.	sacar	74
recubrir de *to cover with (*e.g. *paper, paint)*	cubrir	26
recular *to reverse* (intransitive) Reg.	hablar	41
recuperar *to recover* (transitive) Reg.	hablar	41
recuperarse de *to recover from* (intransitive) Reg.	hablar	41
recurrir *to appeal (a legal decision);* **r. a** *to resort to* Reg.	vivir	89
redactar *to write up (*e.g. *an article)* Reg.	hablar	41

redimir *to redeem* Reg.	vivir	89
redoblar *to redouble* Reg.	hablar	41
redondear *to round off; to make round* Reg.	hablar	41
reducir *to reduce*	producir	60
redundar en *to result in* Reg.	hablar	41
Verbs beginning with **ree-** may be optionally spelt **re-**		
reelegir *to re-elect*	regir	66
reembolsar *to refund* Reg.	hablar	41
reemplazar *to substitute; to replace* Reg.	realizar	65
reencarnarse *to be reincarnated* Reg.	hablar	41
reestructurar *to restructure* Reg.	hablar	41
referir *to tell (story)*	sentir	78
referirse a *to refer to*	sentir	78
refinar *to refine* Reg.	hablar	41
reflejar *to reflect (an image)* Reg.	hablar	41
reflexionar *to reflect (= to think over)* Reg.	hablar	41
reformar *to reform; to renovate (building)* Reg.	hablar	41
reforzar *to reinforce*	almorzar	6
refregar *to scrub hard*	negar	49
refrenar *to restrain; to rein in* Reg.	hablar	41
refrendar *to countersign* Reg.	hablar	41
refrescar *to refresh; to cool* (transitive); *to get cooler (*e.g. *weather)* Reg.	sacar	74
refrigerar *to refrigerate* Reg.	hablar	41
refulgir *to shine brightly* Reg.	rugir	72
refundir *to recast* Reg.	vivir	89
refunfuñar *to grumble* Reg.	hablar	41
refutar *to refute* Reg.	hablar	41
regalar *to give as a present* Reg.	hablar	41
regañar *to scold; to quarrel* Reg.	hablar	41
regar *to water; to irrigate*	negar	49
regatear *to haggle; to bargain* Reg.	hablar	41
regenerar *to regenerate* Reg.	hablar	41

regentar *to manage (a business)* Reg.	hablar	41
regimentar *to regiment*	cerrar	18
regir *to rule; to steer*	regir	66
registrar *to search* (transitive)*; to record* Reg.	hablar	41
regocijarse de *to rejoice at* Reg.	hablar	41
regodearse en/con *to take great pleasure in* Reg.	hablar	41
regresar *to return* Reg.	hablar	41
regular *to regulate* Reg.	hablar	41
regularizar *to regularize* Reg.	realizar	65
regurgitar *to regurgitate* Reg.	hablar	41
rehabilitar *to rehabilitate* Reg.	hablar	41
rehacer *to redo*	hacer	42
rehacerse de *to recover from*	hacer	42
rehilar *to quiver*	aislar	5
rehogar *to toss lightly in oil (cooking)* Reg.	pagar	52
rehuir *to shun, flee from*	rehuir	67
rehusar *to refuse*	aullar	11
reinar *to reign* Reg.	hablar	41
reincidir *to reoffend* Reg.	vivir	89
reincorporarse a *to rejoin (group)* Reg.	hablar	41
reintegrar *to reinstate* Reg.	hablar	41
reintegrarse a *to rejoin; to return to (membership, community)* Reg.	hablar	41
reír = reírse	reír	68
reírse *to laugh*	reír	68
reiterar *to reiterate; to repeat* Reg.	hablar	41
reivindicar *to claim, demand (rights, etc.)* Reg.	sacar	74
reivindicarse *to vindicate oneself* Reg.	sacar	74
rejuvenecer *to reinvigorate*	parecer	53
rejuvenecerse *to become rejuvenated*	parecer	53
relacionar *to relate (= to link together)* Reg.	hablar	41
relajar *to relax* (transitive) Reg.	hablar	41

relajarse *to relax* (intransitive) Reg.	hablar	41
relampaguear *to flash with lightning* Reg.	hablar	41
relatar *to relate (= to narrate)* Reg.	hablar	41
releer *to reread*	poseer	59
relegar *to relegate* Reg.	pagar	52
relevar *to relieve (*e.g. *workmate on shift)* Reg.	hablar	41
relevarse *to take turns; to work in shifts* Reg.	hablar	41
relinchar *to neigh* Reg.	hablar	41
rellenar *to refill; to fill up; to stuff* Reg.	hablar	41
relucir *to shine; to glitter*	lucir	46
relumbrar *to shine* Reg.	hablar	41
remachar *to rivet; to hammer home (a point)* Reg.	hablar	41
remar *to row* Reg.	hablar	41
remarcar *to stress; to mark again* Reg.	sacar	74
rematar *to finish off (job); to auction off* Reg.	hablar	41
remedar *to ape* Reg.	hablar	41
remediar *to remedy* Reg.	hablar	41
rememorar *to recall* Reg.	hablar	41
remendar *to mend; to patch*	cerrar	18
remitir *to remit; to send (letters, etc.)* Reg.	vivir	89
remojar *to soak* (transitive) Reg.	hablar	41
remolcar *to tow* Reg.	sacar	74
remontar *to surmount* Reg.	hablar	41
remorder *to cause remorse*	mover	48
remover *to stir;* (Lat. Am.) *to remove*	mover	48
remozar *to rejuvenate, renovate* Reg.	realizar	65
remunerar *to remunerate* Reg.	hablar	41
renacer *to be born again; to bloom again*	parecer	53
rendir *to produce results/profits* (consult a dictionary for idiomatic uses)	pedir	54

rendirse *to surrender; to give up*	pedir	54
renegar de *to renounce (principles)*	negar	49
renovar *to renovate; to renew*	contar	24
renquear *to limp* Reg.	hablar	41
renunciar a *to renounce; to resign* Reg.	hablar	41
reñir *to scold; to have a quarrel*	reñir	69
reorganizar *to reorganize* Reg.	realizar	65
reorientar *to reorient* Reg.	realizar	65
reparar *to repair;* **r. en** *to notice* Reg.	hablar	41
repartir *to distribute; to share out* Reg.	vivir	89
repasar *to review; to revise* Reg.	hablar	41
repatriar *to repatriate* Reg.	hablar	41
or	liar	45
repeler *to repel* Reg.	comer	22
repetir *to repeat*	pedir	54
repercutir en *to have an impact on* Reg.	vivir	89
repiquetear *to ring out (bells)* Reg.	hablar	41
replantear *to restate (a question)* Reg.	hablar	41
replegar *to fold up; to tuck in*	negar	49
replicar *to answer back* Reg.	sacar	74
repoblar *to repopulate*	contar	24
reponer *to replace*	poner	58
reponerse *to recover* (intransitive)	poner	58
reportar *to bring in (profits, results)* Reg.	hablar	41
reportear (Lat. Am.) *to report (news)* Reg.	hablar	41
reposar *to rest* Reg.	hablar	41
repostar *to refuel*	contar	24
reprender *to scold* Reg.	comer	22
representar *to represent* Reg.	hablar	41
reprimir *to repress* Reg.	vivir	89
reprobar *to reprove*	contar	24
reprochar *to reproach* Reg.	hablar	41
reproducir *to reproduce*	producir	60
reptar *to slither, crawl* Reg.	hablar	41
repudiar *to repudiate* Reg.	hablar	41

repugnar *to disgust* Reg.	hablar	41
repuntar *to recover (prices, economy, etc.)* Reg.	hablar	41
requebrar *to say flattering things to*	cerrar	18
requerir *to require*	sentir	78
requisar *to confiscate* Reg.	hablar	41
resaltar *to stand out* Reg.	hablar	41
resarcir *to compensate; to repay (*e.g. *the effort)* Reg.	zurcir	92
resbalar *to slip* Reg.	hablar	41
resbalarse *to slip (persons)* Reg.	hablar	41
rescatar *to rescue* Reg.	hablar	41
rescindir *to rescind* Reg.	vivir	89
resecar *to dry out* (transitive) Reg.	sacar	74
resecarse *to dry out* (intransitive) Reg.	sacar	74
resentirse de *to be resentful; not to have recovered from*	sentir	78
reseñar *to review (a book, etc.)* Reg.	hablar	41
reservar *to reserve; to put aside* Reg.	hablar	41
resfriarse *to catch cold*	liar	45
resguardar *to protect* Reg.	hablar	41
resguardarse de *to take shelter from* Reg.	hablar	41
residir en *to reside in* Reg.	vivir	89
resignarse a *to resign oneself to* Reg.	hablar	41
resistir *to bear; tolerate; to hold out* Reg.	vivir	89
resistirse a *to resist; to be unwilling to* Reg.	vivir	89
resollar *to breathe hard*	contar	24
resolver *to resolve, solve* (transitive)	volver	90
resolverse a *to make up one's mind to*	volver	90
resonar *to echo*	contar	24
resoplar *to puff* Reg.	hablar	41
respaldar *to back* Reg.	hablar	41
respaldarse *to sit back;* **r. en** *to rely on* Reg.	hablar	41

respectar *to concern* (third person only) Reg.	hablar	41
respetar *to respect* Reg.	hablar	41
respirar *to breathe* Reg.	hablar	41
resplandecer *to shine* (intransitive)	parecer	53
responder *to answer; to respond* Reg.	comer	22
responsabilizar *to hold to account* Reg.	realizar	65
responsabilizarse de *to take responsibility for* Reg.	realizar	65
resquebrajar *to crack; to split* (transitive) Reg.	hablar	41
resquebrajarse *to break up; to split* (intransitive) Reg.	hablar	41
restablecer *to re-establish; to restore*	parecer	53
restablecerse *to recover* (intransitive)	parecer	53
restañar *to staunch (blood)* Reg.	hablar	41
restar *to subtract; to be left* Reg.	hablar	41
restaurar *to restore (order, political regime)* Reg.	hablar	41
restituir a *to return (to the rightful owner)* (transitive)	construir	23
restregar *to rub or scrub hard*	negar	49
restringir *to restrict; to hamper*	rugir	72
resucitar *to bring back to life; to come back to life* Reg.	hablar	41
resultar *to result; to turn out to be* (consult dictionary for idiomatic uses) Reg.	hablar	41
resumir *to summarize* Reg.	vivir	89
resurgir *to resurge; to re-emerge* Reg.	rugir	72
retar *to challenge* Reg.	hablar	41
retardar *to delay; to slow up* (transitive) Reg.	hablar	41
retardarse *to be late* Reg.	hablar	41
retemblar *to shake; to quiver* Reg.	cerrar	18
retener *to keep back; to retain*	tener	82
retenerse *to restrain oneself*	tener	82

retirar *to take away/out; to draw back* (transitive) Reg.	hablar	41
retirarse *to retire; to withdraw* (intransitive) Reg.	hablar	41
retocar *to touch up (painting, photo)* Reg.	sacar	74
retomar *to take up again* Reg.	hablar	41
retoñar *to sprout* Reg.	hablar	41
retorcer *to twist* (transitive)	cocer	19
retorcerse *to twist, writhe* (intransitive)	cocer	19
retornar *to return* (= **volver**, **regresar**) Reg.	hablar	41
retractarse *to go back (on a previous statement)* Reg.	hablar	41
retraer *to bring back; to pull in*	traer	83
retraerse *to withdraw* (intransitive)	traer	83
retransmitir *to repeat (a radio or TV program)* Reg.	vivir	89
retrasar *to delay* (transitive) Reg.	hablar	41
retrasarse *to be late; to fall behind* Reg.	hablar	41
retratar *to photograph; to make a painting of* Reg.	hablar	41
retribuir *to reward (financially, for one's efforts)*	construir	23
retroceder *to back away; to move back* (intransitive) Reg.	comer	22
retumbar *to rumble* Reg.	hablar	41
reunir *to join together, assemble* (transitive)	reunir	70
reunirse *to gather (*e.g. *for a meeting)* (intransitive)	reunir	70
revalorar = **revalorizar** Reg.	hablar	41
revalorizar *to revalue* Reg.	realizar	65
revelar *to reveal; to develop (a photo)* Reg.	hablar	41
revelarse *to reveal oneself* Reg.	hablar	41
revender *to resell* Reg.	comer	22

reventar *to burst* (transitive and intransitive)	cerrar	18
reverberar *to twinkle, glimmer* Reg.	hablar	41
reverdecer *to grow green again*	parecer	53
reverter *to overflow*	perder	55
revertir a *to revert to*	sentir	78
revestir de *to coat, cover with (a substance)*	pedir	54
revestirse de *to arm oneself with (*e.g. *courage)*	pedir	54
revisar *to review* Reg.	hablar	41
revitalizar *to revitalize* Reg.	realizar	65
revivir *to revive* (intransitive)*; to relive (past experience)* Reg.	vivir	89
revocar *to revoke; to plaster* Reg.	sacar	74
revolcar *to knock to the ground*	trocar	84
revolcarse *to wallow; to roll around* (intransitive)	trocar	84
revolotear *to flutter around* Reg.	hablar	41
revolucionar *to revolutionize* Reg.	hablar	41
revolucionarse *to revolt; to get excited* Reg.	hablar	41
revolver *to stir up; to disorder*	volver	90
revolverse *to twist and turn* (intransitive)	volver	90
rezagarse *to fall behind* Reg.	pagar	52
rezar *to pray* Reg.	realizar	65
rezongar *to grumble* Reg.	pagar	52
rezumar *to ooze* (transitive and intransitive) Reg.	hablar	41
ridiculizar *to ridicule* Reg.	realizar	65
rielar *to twinkle, glisten* Reg.	hablar	41
rifar *to raffle* Reg.	hablar	41
rimar *to rhyme* Reg.	hablar	41
rivalizar en *to compete; to vie in* Reg.	realizar	65
rizar *to curl* (transitive) Reg.	realizar	65
rizarse *to curl* (intransitive) Reg.	realizar	65

robar *to steal* Reg.	hablar	41
robustecer *to strengthen*	parecer	53
robustecerse *to become strong*	parecer	53
rociar *to sprinkle (with liquid)*	liar	45
rodar *to roll* (intransitive)*; to film; to travel (cars, etc.)*	contar	24
rodear *to surround* Reg.	hablar	41
rodearse de *to surround oneself with* Reg.	hablar	41
rodrigar *to prop; to prop up (plants)* Reg.	pagar	52
roer *to gnaw*	roer	71
rogar *to beg*	colgar	20
romper (past participle **roto**) *to break* (transitive)*; to tear up* Reg.	comer	22
romperse (past participle **roto**) *to break* (intransitive) Reg.	comer	22
roncar *to snore* Reg.	sacar	74
rondar *to hover around; to patrol; to lurk* Reg.	hablar	41
ronronear *to purr* Reg.	hablar	41
rotar *to rotate* (transitive and intransitive) Reg.	hablar	41
rotarse *to take turns (according to a rota)* Reg.	hablar	41
rotular *to label* Reg.	hablar	41
rozar *to brush (= to touch lightly)* Reg.	realizar	65
rubicar *to add one's flourish (to a signature)* Reg.	sacar	74
rugir *to bellow; to rumble*	rugir	72
rumiar *to ruminate; to chew the cud* Reg.	hablar	41
rumorear *to rumor/(Brit.) rumour; to spread by rumor* Reg.	hablar	41
runrunear *to purr* Reg.	hablar	41
rutilar *to sparkle; to shine* Reg.	hablar	41

saber *to know; to know how to;* **s. a** *to taste of*	saber	73
saborear *to relish, savor/(Brit.) savour* Reg.	hablar	41
sabotear *to sabotage* Reg.	hablar	41
sacar *to draw out; to pull out* (consult dictionary for idiomatic meanings) Reg.	sacar	74
saciar *to satiate* Reg.	hablar	41
saciarse de *to eat one's fill of* Reg.	hablar	41
sacrificar *to sacrifice* Reg.	sacar	74
sacrificarse *to make a sacrifice (of oneself)* Reg.	sacar	74
sacudir *to jolt, shake* (transitive) Reg.	vivir	89
sacudirse *to shrug off (problem, etc.)* Reg.	vivir	89
sahumar *to perfume with incense*	aislar	5
sajar *to make an incision in; to cut open* Reg.	hablar	41
salar *to salt* Reg.	hablar	41
salir *to leave; to go out; to come out*	salir	75
salirse *to leak (liquids, etc.); to walk out (of meetings, etc.)*	salir	75
salivar *to salivate* Reg.	hablar	41
salmodiar *to sing in a monotone; to sing psalms* Reg.	hablar	41
salpicar de *to splash with* Reg.	sacar	74
salpimentar *to season (*e.g. *with salt and pepper)*	cerrar	18
saltar *to jump* (transitive and intransitive) Reg.	hablar	41
saltarse *to jump (traffic lights); to skip (* i.e. *to miss out)* Reg.	hablar	41
saltear *to sauté; to hold up (* i.e. *to rob)* Reg.	hablar	41
saludar *to greet; to salute* Reg.	hablar	41

salvar *to save (* i.e. *from danger); to salvage* Reg.	hablar	41
salvarse de *to avoid (death, ignominy, etc.)* Reg.	hablar	41
sanar *to recover; to heal* Reg.	hablar	41
sancionar *to fine; to sanction* Reg.	hablar	41
sanear *to clean up* Reg.	hablar	41
sangrar *to bleed* (transitive and intransitive)*; to indent (paragraph)* Reg.	hablar	41
santificar *to sanctify* Reg.	sacar	74
santiguarse *to make the sign of the cross*	averiguar	13
saquear *to loot, pillage* Reg.	hablar	41
satirizar *to satirize* Reg.	realizar	65
satisfacer *to satisfy*	satisfacer	76
satisfacerse *to take satisfaction; to be satisfied*	satisfacer	76
saturar *to saturate* Reg.	hablar	41
sazonar *to season* Reg.	hablar	41
secar *to dry* (transitive) Reg.	sacar	74
secarse *to dry* (intransitive) Reg.	sacar	74
seccionar *to section* Reg.	hablar	41
secretar *to secrete* Reg.	hablar	41
secuestrar *to kidnap* Reg.	hablar	41
secularizar *to secularize* Reg.	realizar	65
secundar *to support (= to back up)* Reg.	hablar	41
sedar *to sedate* Reg.	hablar	41
sedimentarse *to settle (=form a sediment)* Reg.	hablar	41
seducir *to seduce; to charm*	producir	60
segar *to reap*	negar	49
segregar *to segregate; to secrete* Reg.	pagar	52
seguir *to follow;* + gerund *to continue to*	seguir	77
seguirse de *to follow on from*	seguir	77
sellar *to seal; to stamp* Reg.	hablar	41
sembrar *to sow*	cerrar	18
semejar *to resemble* Reg.	hablar	41

sensacionalizar *to sensationalize* Reg.	realizar	65
sensibilizar *to sensitize* Reg.	realizar	65
sentar *to seat; to suit*	cerrar	18
sentarse *to sit down*	cerrar	18
sentenciar *to sentence* Reg.	hablar	41
sentir *to feel; to regret*	sentir	78
sentirse *to feel*	sentir	78
señalar *to indicate; to point out; to signal* Reg.	hablar	41
señalarse por *to be distinguished by* Reg.	hablar	41
separar *to separate* (transitive) Reg.	hablar	41
separarse *to separate* (intransitive) Reg.	hablar	41
sepultar *to bury* Reg.	hablar	41
ser *to be*	ser	79
serenar *to calm* Reg.	hablar	41
serenarse *to grow calm* Reg.	hablar	41
sermonear *to lecture (= to reprimand)* Reg.	hablar	41
serpentear *to meander* Reg.	hablar	41
serrar *to saw*	cerrar	18
servir *to serve; to be useful*	pedir	54
servirse *to help oneself to*	pedir	54
sesear *to pronounce Spanish c before e or i, and also z, like s* Reg.	hablar	41
sesgar *to bias (data)* Reg.	pagar	52
sicoanalizar = psicoanalizar Reg.	realizar	65
signar *to put a mark on; to sign* Reg.	hablar	41
significar *to mean; to signify* Reg.	sacar	74
significarse *to distinguish oneself* Reg.	sacar	74
silbar *to whistle* Reg.	hablar	41
silenciar *to silence* Reg.	hablar	41
simbolizar *to symbolize* Reg.	realizar	65
simpatizar *to get on well (with others); to be sympathetic to (ideas)* Reg.	realizar	65
simplificar *to simplify* Reg.	sacar	74
simular *to simulate* Reg.	hablar	41

simultanear con *to carry on simultaneously with* (transitive) Reg.	hablar	41
sincerarse *to tell the whole truth* Reg.	hablar	41
sincronizar *to synchronize* Reg.	realizar	65
sindicalizarse *to join a union* Reg.	realizar	65
singularizar *to single out* Reg.	realizar	65
singularizarse por *to stand out because of* Reg.	realizar	65
sintonizar *to tune (a radio)* Reg.	realizar	65
sirgar *to tow (a boat)* Reg.	pagar	52
sistematizar *to systematize* Reg.	realizar	65
sitiar *to besiege* Reg.	hablar	41
situar *to situate; to locate*	continuar	25
situarse *to be located*	continuar	25
sobar *to grope* Reg.	hablar	41
sobornar *to bribe* Reg.	hablar	41
sobrar *to be more than enough; to be left over* Reg.	hablar	41

For the conjugation of unlisted verbs beginning with **sobre-**, see the root verb

sobreactuar *to overact*	continuar	25
sobrecalentar *to overheat*	cerrar	18
sobrecargar *to overload; to overcharge* Reg.	pagar	52
sobrecoger *to frighten; to overcome with emotion* Reg.	proteger	62
sobrecogerse *to be overcome with emotion* Reg.	proteger	62
sobrecompensar *to overcompensate* Reg.	hablar	41
sobreentender *to understand (something not made explicit)*	perder	55
sobreexcitar *to overexcite* Reg.	hablar	41
sobreexponer *to overexpose*	poner	58
sobrehilar *to overcast (sewing)*	aislar	5
sobrellenar *to overfill* Reg.	hablar	41
sobrellevar *to endure; to suffer* Reg.	hablar	41

sobrepasar *to surpass; to exceed* Reg.	hablar	41
sobrepasarse *to go too far* Reg.	hablar	41
sobreponer *to superimpose*	poner	58
sobreponerse *to get a grip on oneself*	poner	58
sobresalir *to stand out; to excel*	salir	75
sobresaltar *to frighten* Reg.	hablar	41
sobresaltarse *to jump (with fright)* Reg.	hablar	41
sobreseer *to dismiss* (= **despedir**)	poseer	59
sobrevenir *to happen; to take place (usually tragedies, etc.)*	venir	87
sobrevivir *to survive* Reg.	vivir	89
sobrevolar *to fly over; to overfly*	contar	24
socarrar *to singe; to scorch* (transitive) Reg.	hablar	41
socavar *to undermine* Reg.	hablar	41
socializar *to socialize* Reg.	realizar	65
socorrer *to assist; to aid* Reg.	comer	22
sofocar *to suffocate* (transitive) Reg.	sacar	74
sofocarse *to get intensely upset* Reg.	sacar	74
sofreír *to sauté*	reír	68
sofrenar *to restrain* Reg.	hablar	41
solaparse *to overlap* Reg.	hablar	41
solazar *to solace; to console* Reg.	realizar	65
solazarse *to take one's ease* Reg.	realizar	65
soldar *to solder; to weld*	contar	24
soldarse *to fuse together* (intransitive)	contar	24
solear *to sun* Reg.	hablar	41
solemnizar *to solemnize* Reg.	realizar	65
soler *to be accustomed to; to be used to*	soler	80
solicitar *to apply for* Reg.	hablar	41
solidarizar con *to make common cause with* Reg.	realizar	65
solidarizarse con = **solidarizar** Reg.	realizar	65
solidificarse *to solidify* Reg.	sacar	74
soliviantar *to rouse; to incite* Reg.	hablar	41
soliviantarse *to mutiny* Reg.	hablar	41
sollozar *to sob* Reg.	realizar	65

soltar *to untie; to unfasten; to set free; to release*	contar	24
soltarse *to become loose; to loosen up*	contar	24
solucionar *to solve* Reg.	hablar	41
solventar *to settle (accounts); to resolve (a matter)* Reg.	hablar	41
sombrear *to shade* Reg.	hablar	41
someter *to subdue; to submit* Reg.	comer	22
someterse a *to submit to* Reg.	comer	22
sonar *to sound; to ring*	contar	24
sonarse *to blow one's nose*	contar	24
sondear *to sound; to poll (opinion)* Reg.	hablar	41
sonorizar *to add the sound track (to a film)* Reg.	realizar	65
sonreír = **sonreírse**	reír	68
sonreírse *to smile*	reír	68
sonrojarse *to flush; to blush* Reg.	hablar	41
sonsacar *to draw out (a secret)* Reg.	sacar	74
soñar *to dream*	contar	24
sopesar *to weigh up* Reg.	hablar	41
soplar *to blow (wind, etc.); to whisper* Reg.	hablar	41
soportar *to endure; to put up with* Reg.	hablar	41
sorber *to sip* Reg.	comer	22
sorprender *to surprise* Reg.	comer	22
sorprenderse de *to be surprised at* Reg.	comer	22
sortear *to draw lots for; to raffle; to get round (a problem)* Reg.	hablar	41
sosegar *to calm*	negar	49
sosegarse *to calm down*	negar	49
soslayar *to dodge, get round (a problem)* Reg.	hablar	41
sospechar *to suspect* Reg.	hablar	41
sostener *to support (*e.g.* weight); to maintain (an opinion)*	tener	82
soterrar *to bury*	cerrar	18
suavizar *to smooth; to tone down* Reg.	realizar	65

subarrendar *to sublet*	cerrar	18
subastar *to auction* Reg.	hablar	41
subcontratar *to subcontract* Reg.	hablar	41
subdividir *to subdivide* Reg.	vivir	89
subir *to go up; to come up; to raise; to lift; to increase* (transitive and intransitive) Reg.	vivir	89
subirse *to get on (vehicles); to climb* Reg.	vivir	89
sublevar *to incite to rebellion* Reg.	hablar	41
sublevarse *to revolt* Reg.	hablar	41
sublimar *to sublimate* Reg.	hablar	41
subordinar *to subordinate* Reg.	hablar	41
subrayar *to underline; to emphasize* Reg.	hablar	41
subrogar *to subrogate; to substitute* Reg.	pagar	52
subsanar *to correct (an error)* Reg.	hablar	41
subscribir *to subscribe; to endorse; to sign*	escribir	37
subsidiar *to subsidize* Reg.	hablar	41
subsistir *to subsist* Reg.	vivir	89
subtitular *to subtitle* Reg.	hablar	41
subvencionar *to subsidize* Reg.	hablar	41
subvertir *to subvert*	sentir	78
subyacer *to underlie*	yacer	91
subyugar *to subjugate* Reg.	pagar	52
succionar *to suck* Reg.	hablar	41
suceder *to happen* Reg.	comer	22
sucederse *to follow one after the other* Reg.	comer	22
sucumbir *to succumb* Reg.	vivir	89
sudar *to sweat* Reg.	hablar	41
sufragar *to defray (costs)* Reg.	pagar	52
sufrir *to suffer; to undergo* Reg.	vivir	89
sugerir *to suggest*	sentir	78
sugestionar *to put an idea into someone's head* Reg.	hablar	41

sujetar *to fasten; to subject* Reg.	hablar	41
sujetarse a *to hold tight to; to submit to* Reg.	hablar	41
sumar *to add* Reg.	hablar	41
sumarse a *to be additional to* Reg.	hablar	41
sumergir *to submerge* (transitive)	rugir	72
sumergirse *to submerge* (intransitive)	rugir	72
suministrar *to supply* Reg.	hablar	41
sumir en *to plunge into (doubt, despair)* (transitive) Reg.	vivir	89
sumirse en *to be plunged into* Reg.	vivir	89
supeditar a *to subordinate to* Reg.	hablar	41
superar *to surpass* Reg.	hablar	41
superponer *to superimpose*	poner	58
suplantar *to supplant* Reg.	hablar	41
suplementar *to supplement* Reg.	hablar	41
suplir *to substitute; to make up for* Reg.	vivir	89
suponer *to suppose; to presuppose*	poner	58
suprimir *to suppress; to do away with; to withdraw (bus, train services, etc.)* Reg.	vivir	89
supurar *to fester* Reg.	hablar	41
surgir *to arise (problem); to spurt out*	rugir	72
surtir *to produce (success)* Reg.	vivir	89
suscitar *to arouse* Reg.	hablar	41
suscribir = subscribir	escribir	37
suspender *to suspend; to fail (examination)* (transitive and intransitive) Reg.	comer	22
suspirar *to sigh* Reg.	hablar	41
sustanciar *to substantiate* Reg.	hablar	41
sustentar *to maintain (an opinion); to support (financially)* Reg.	hablar	41
sustituir *to replace, substitute*	construir	23
sustraer *to subtract; to steal*	traer	83
sustraerse a *to get out of (a duty, chore)*	traer	83

tabalear *to drum with the fingers* Reg.	hablar	41
tabicar *to wall up* Reg.	sacar	74
tabletear *to rattle* Reg.	hablar	41
tabular *to tabulate* Reg.	hablar	41
tachar *to cross out;* **t. de** *to label someone (*e.g. *as a liar)* Reg.	hablar	41
taconear *to walk noisily (*e.g. *wearing high heels)* Reg.	hablar	41
taladrar *to drill* Reg.	hablar	41
talar *to fell (trees)* Reg.	hablar	41
tallar *to carve* Reg.	hablar	41
tambalearse *to stagger* Reg.	hablar	41
tamizar *to sieve, sift* Reg.	realizar	65
tantear *to feel (with the hands)* (transitive)*; to grope* Reg.	hablar	41
tañer *to play (musical instrument); to chime*	tañer	81
tapar *to cover up* Reg.	hablar	41
tapiar *to wall in* Reg.	hablar	41
tapizar *to line (sewing)* Reg.	realizar	65
taponar *to plug* Reg.	hablar	41
taponarse *to get blocked* Reg.	hablar	41
taquigrafiar *to take down in shorthand*	liar	45
tararear *to hum* Reg.	hablar	41
tardar *to be late; to take (time)* Reg.	hablar	41
tartajear *to stutter* Reg.	hablar	41
tartamudear *to stutter* Reg.	hablar	41
tasar *to evaluate; to tax* Reg.	hablar	41
tatuar *to tattoo*	continuar	25
techar *to roof* Reg.	hablar	41
teclear *to type (on a keyboard); to key in* Reg.	hablar	41
tejar *to roof with tiles* Reg.	hablar	41
tejer *to weave* Reg.	comer	22
telefonear *to telephone* Reg.	hablar	41
televisar *to televise* Reg.	hablar	41
temblar *to tremble*	cerrar	18

temer *to fear* Reg.	comer	22
temerse *to fear (= to regret that)* Reg.	comer	22
temperar *to temper* Reg.	hablar	41
templar *to tune; to grow more moderate (temperature)* Reg.	hablar	41
templarse *to grow moderate (temperature)* Reg.	hablar	41
tender *to spread out; to reach out;* **t. a** *to tend to*	perder	55
tenderse *to lie down*	perder	55
tener *to have* (consult a dictionary for idiomatic meanings)	tener	82
tensar *to tense* Reg.	hablar	41
tentar *to tempt; to feel (with the hands)*	cerrar	18
teñir *to dye*	reñir	69
teorizar *to theorize* Reg.	realizar	65
terciar *to mediate* Reg.	hablar	41
terciarse *to crop up (subject)* Reg.	hablar	41
tergiversar *to twist (facts, etc.)* Reg.	hablar	41
terminar *to end; to finish* (transitive and intransitive) Reg.	hablar	41
terminarse *to run out (* i.e. *become exhausted)* Reg.	hablar	41
terraplenar *to bank; to fill (with dirt)* Reg.	hablar	41
tertuliar *to sit around and talk* Reg.	hablar	41
testar *to make a testament or will* Reg.	hablar	41
testimoniar *to testify* Reg.	hablar	41
tildar de *to brand/label as (* e.g. *liar, etc.)* Reg.	hablar	41
timar *to swindle* Reg.	hablar	41
timbrar *to stamp (* e.g. *document)* Reg.	hablar	41
timonear *to steer (boat)* Reg.	hablar	41
tintar *to tint* Reg.	hablar	41
tintinear *to jingle* Reg.	hablar	41
tirar *to pull; to throw away* Reg.	hablar	41
tirarse *to dive; to throw oneself* Reg.	hablar	41

tiritar *to shiver* Reg.	hablar	41
tirotear *to shoot at random* Reg.	hablar	41
titilar *to twinkle* Reg.	hablar	41
titiritar *to shiver* Reg.	hablar	41
titubear *to hesitate; to stutter* Reg.	hablar	41
titular *to give a title to* Reg.	hablar	41
titularse *to be called (books, films)* Reg.	hablar	41
tiznar *to smudge with soot* Reg.	hablar	41
tocar *to touch; to play (musical instrument)* Reg.	sacar	74
tolerar *to tolerate* Reg.	hablar	41
tomar *to take;* (Lat. Am.) *to drink* Reg.	hablar	41
tonificar *to invigorate* Reg.	sacar	74
tontear *to talk or act foolishly* Reg.	hablar	41
toparse con *to run into (* i.e. *to meet by chance)* Reg.	hablar	41
topetar = topetear	hablar	41
topetear *to bump into* Reg.	hablar	41
torcer *to twist; to bend* (transitive)	cocer	19
torcerse *to become twisted*	cocer	19
torear *to fight bulls* Reg.	hablar	41
tornar *to return* (= **volver**) Reg.	hablar	41
tornear *to turn (on a lathe)* Reg.	hablar	41
torpedear *to torpedo* Reg.	hablar	41
torrar *to toast, brown* Reg.	hablar	41
torturar *to torture* Reg.	hablar	41
toser *to cough* Reg.	comer	22
tostar *to toast*	contar	24
totalizar *to totalize* Reg.	realizar	65
trabajar *to work* Reg.	hablar	41
trabar *to clasp together; to join; to strike up (* e.g. *friendship)* Reg.	hablar	41
trabarse *to get stuck* Reg.	hablar	41
trabucarse *to become confused; to be mixed up* Reg.	sacar	74
traducir *to translate*	producir	60

traer *to bring*	traer	83
traficar *to trade; to traffic* Reg.	sacar	74
tragar *to swallow* Reg.	pagar	52
tramar *to plot; to devise (a scheme)* Reg.	hablar	41
tramitar *to deal with (formalities)* Reg.	hablar	41
trampear *to cheat* Reg.	hablar	41
tranquilizar *to tranquilize/(Brit.) tranquillize* Reg.	realizar	65
Verbs beginning with **trans-** not listed here may be found under the spelling **tras-**		
transbordar *to transfer; to change trains* Reg.	hablar	41
transcender = trascender	perder	55
transcribir *to transcribe*	escribir	37
transcurrir *to elapse; to pass (time;* intransitive*)* Reg.	vivir	89
transferir *to transfer*	sentir	78
transfigurar *to transfigure* Reg.	hablar	41
transformar *to transform* Reg.	hablar	41
transfundir *to transfuse* Reg.	vivir	89
transgredir *to transgress*	abolir	1
transigir *to compromise; to give in*	rugir	72
transitar *to travel around* Reg.	hablar	41
translucirse = traslucirse	lucir	46
transmitir *to transmit* Reg.	lucir	46
transpirar *to sweat* Reg.	hablar	41
transponer = trasponer	poner	58
transvasar = trasvasar Reg.	hablar	41
trapichear *to fence (stolen goods)* Reg.	hablar	41
traquetear *to rattle* Reg.	hablar	41
trascender *to come to light; to transcend*	perder	55
trascribir = transcribir	escribir	37
trascurrir = transcurrir	vivir	89
trasegar *to shuffle; to decant*	negar	49
trasfundir = transfundir	vivir	89
trasgredir = transgredir	abolir	1

trashumar *to move to new pastures (seasonally)* Reg.	abolir	1
trasladar *to transfer* (transitive) Reg.	hablar	41
trasladarse *to move (to new premises)* Reg.	hablar	41
traslucirse *to show through (emotions)*	lucir	46
trasnochar *to stay up all night* Reg.	hablar	41
traspapelar *to mislay among other papers* Reg.	hablar	41
traspapelarse *to be mislaid among other papers* Reg.	hablar	41
traspasar *to pierce through; to go beyond; to sell (lease on a property)* Reg.	hablar	41
trasplantar *to transplant* Reg.	hablar	41
trasponer *to surpass; to transpose*	poner	58
trasquilar *to shear* Reg.	hablar	41
trastear *to rummage* Reg.	hablar	41
trastocar *to disorder, shuffle (papers)* Reg.	sacar	74
trastornar *to upset* Reg.	hablar	41
trastornarse *to be upset* Reg.	hablar	41
trastrocar *to alter*	trocar	84
trastrocarse *to become shuffled, disordered*	trocar	84
trasvasar *to decant* Reg.	hablar	41
tratar *to deal with; to treat; to handle;* **t. de** *to try to* Reg.	hablar	41
tratarse de *to be a question of* Reg.	hablar	41
traumatizar *to traumatize* Reg.	realizar	65
trazar *to trace* Reg.	realizar	65
trenzar *to braid* Reg.	realizar	65
trepar *to clamber; to climb* Reg.	hablar	41
treparse a *to climb onto* Reg.	hablar	41
trepidar *to vibrate* Reg.	hablar	41
tributar *to pay (homage, admiration, etc.); to pay taxes* Reg.	hablar	41

trillar *to thresh* Reg.	hablar	41
trinar *to warble* Reg.	hablar	41
triplicar *to triple* (transitive) Reg.	sacar	74
triplicarse *to triple* (intransitive) Reg.	sacar	74
tripular *to man (ships, planes, etc.)* Reg.	hablar	41
triturar *to pulverize; to crush* Reg.	hablar	41
triunfar *to triumph* Reg.	hablar	41
trizarse *to break into pieces* (intransitive) Reg.	realizar	65
trocar *to exchange, barter*	trocar	84
trocarse en = **convertirse en**	trocar	84
trompicar *to stumble* Reg.	sacar	74
tronar *to thunder*	contar	24
tronchar *to snap* (transitive) Reg.	hablar	41
troncharse *to snap* (intransitive) Reg.	hablar	41
tropezar *to stumble*	comenzar	21
troquelar *to strike, mint (* i.e. *a coin)* Reg.	hablar	41
trozar *to break to pieces; to cut into pieces* Reg.	realizar	65
truhanear *to act like a rascal* Reg.	hablar	41
truncar *to truncate, cut short* Reg.	sacar	74
tumbar *to knock down* Reg.	hablar	41
tumbarse *to lie down* Reg.	hablar	41
turbar *to disturb* Reg.	hablar	41
turbarse *to be disturbed, embarrassed* Reg.	hablar	41
turnarse *to take turns* Reg.	hablar	41
tutear *to address someone using the familiar pronoun* **tú** Reg.	hablar	41
ubicar *to place; to locate* (esp. Lat. Am.) Reg.	sacar	74
ufanarse de *to boast about* Reg.	hablar	41
ultimar *to finalize* Reg.	hablar	41
ultrajar *to offend; to insult* Reg.	hablar	41

ulular *to hoot* Reg.	hablar	41
uncir *to yoke* Reg.	zurcir	92
ungir *to anoint*	rugir	72
unificar *to unify* Reg.	sacar	74
unificarse *to become unified* Reg.	sacar	74
unir *to join together* (transitive) Reg.	vivir	89
unirse *to join together* (intransitive) Reg.	hablar	41
untar de *to smear with* Reg.	hablar	41
untarse *to become smeared* Reg.	hablar	41
urbanizar *to develop (land)* Reg.	realizar	65
urdir *to plot; to scheme* Reg.	vivir	89
urgir *to be urgent; to drive on (*e.g. *ambition)*	rugir	72
usar *to use* Reg.	hablar	41
usurpar *to usurp* Reg.	hablar	41
utilizar *to utilize* Reg.	realizar	65
vacar *to be vacant; to be idle* Reg.	sacar	74
vaciar *to empty* (transitive)	liar	45
vaciarse *to empty* (intransitive)	liar	45
vacilar *to vacillate* Reg.	hablar	41
vacunar *to vaccinate* Reg.	hablar	41
vadear *to ford; to overcome* Reg.	hablar	41
vagabundear *to loaf around* Reg.	hablar	41
vagar *to wander; to drift* Reg.	pagar	52
vaguear *to loaf, laze about* Reg.	hablar	41
valer *to be worth; to be valid*	valer	85
valerse de *to take advantage of; to use*	valer	85
vallar *to fence* Reg.	hablar	41
valorar en *to value at (amount)* Reg.	hablar	41
valorizar = **valorar** Reg.	realizar	65
valorizarse *to appreciate (in value)* Reg.	realizar	65
vanagloriarse *to boast* Reg.	hablar	41
vaporizar *to vaporize; to atomize* Reg.	realizar	65
vapulear *to beat, whip* Reg.	hablar	41

varar *to beach (a boat)* Reg.	hablar	41
varear *to knock down (olives, nuts)* Reg.	hablar	41
variar *to vary*	liar	45
vaticinar *to forecast* Reg.	hablar	41
vedar *to prohibit* (= **prohibir**) Reg.	hablar	41
vegetar *to vegetate* Reg.	hablar	41
vejar *to vex; to treat badly* Reg.	hablar	41
velar *to keep a vigil; to stay up all night;* **v. por** *to care for* Reg.	hablar	41
vencer *to defeat* Reg.	vencer	86
vendar *to bandage* Reg.	hablar	41
vender *to sell* Reg.	comer	22
vendimiar *to harvest* Reg.	hablar	41
venerar *to revere; to worship* Reg.	hablar	41
vengar *to avenge* Reg.	pagar	52
vengarse de *to take revenge for* Reg.	pagar	52
venir *to come* (consult a dictionary for idiomatic meanings)	venir	87
venirse de *to come away from, leave a place*	venir	87
ventilar *to ventilate* Reg.	hablar	41
ventiscar *to drift (snow); to blow a blizzard* Reg.	sacar	74
ver *to see*	ver	88
verse *to see oneself; to be seen* (consult a dictionary for idiomatic meanings)	ver	88
veranear *to summer* Reg.	hablar	41
verdear *to turn green; to show its greenness* Reg.	hablar	41
verificar *to verify; to check; to carry out* Reg.	sacar	74
verificarse *to take place; to occur* Reg.	sacar	74
versar sobre *to deal with (* as in *this book 'deals with'...)* Reg.	hablar	41
versificar *to versify* Reg.	sacar	74
verter *to pour out*	perder	55

vestir *to dress; to wear*	pedir	54
vestirse *to get dressed*	pedir	54
vetar *to veto* Reg.	hablar	41
viajar *to travel* Reg.	hablar	41
vibrar *to vibrate* Reg.	hablar	41
viciar *to vitiate; to become degenerate (person)* Reg.	hablar	41
viciarse *to get into bad habits*	hablar	41
vidriar *to glaze* Reg.	hablar	41
vigorizar *to invigorate* Reg.	realizar	65
vilipendiar *to vilify* Reg.	hablar	41
vincular *to link* Reg.	hablar	41
vindicar *to vindicate* Reg.	sacar	74
violar *to violate; to rape* Reg.	hablar	41
violentar *to do violence to; to force (doors, etc.)* Reg.	hablar	41
virar *to veer* Reg.	hablar	41
visar *to grant a visa; to endorse* Reg.	hablar	41
visitar *to visit* Reg.	hablar	41
vislumbrar *to glimpse* Reg.	hablar	41
visualizar *to visualize; to display (*e.g. *on computer screen)* Reg.	realizar	65
vitalizar *to vitalize* Reg.	realizar	65
vituperar *to vituperate* Reg.	hablar	41
vivaquear *to bivouac* Reg.	hablar	41
vivir *to live* Reg.	vivir	89
vocalizar *to vocalize* Reg.	realizar	65
vocear *to shout* Reg.	hablar	41
vociferar *to shout; to announce boastfully* Reg.	hablar	41
volar *to fly; to blow up (* i.e. *with explosives)*	contar	24
volatilizar *to make volatile* Reg.	realizar	65
volatilizarse *to vanish into thin air* Reg.	realizar	65
volcar *to tip over; to overturn*	trocar	84
volcarse *to be knocked over; to overturn* (intransitive)	trocar	84

voltear *to turn over* (transitive) Reg.	hablar	41
volver *to return* (intransitive)*; to turn over* (transitive)	volver	90
volverse *to become; to turn round* (intransitive)*; to turn back* (intransitive)	volver	90
vomitar *to vomit* Reg.	hablar	41
votar *to vote* Reg.	hablar	41
vulcanizar *to vulcanize* Reg.	realizar	65
vulgarizar *to popularize* Reg.	realizar	65
vulnerar *to wound* Reg.	hablar	41
yacer *to lie (* i.e. *be lying down)*	yacer	91
yuxtaponer *to juxtapose*	poner	58
zafarse de *to get out of (an obligation)* Reg.	hablar	41
zaherir *to wound (emotionally)*	sentir	78
zambullirse *to dive* (= **tirarse al agua**)	bullir	15
zamparse *to gobble down (food)* Reg.	hablar	41
zanganear *to loaf; to idle* Reg.	hablar	41
zangolotear *to jiggle* (transitive) Reg.	hablar	41
zangolotearse *to jiggle or shake about* (intransitive) Reg.	hablar	41
zanjar *to settle (a problem, debt)* Reg.	hablar	41
zapatear *to tap with the feet; to tap dance* Reg.	hablar	41
zarandear *to shake hard* Reg.	hablar	41
zarandearse *to be shaken about* Reg.	hablar	41
zarpar *to set sail* Reg.	hablar	41
zigzaguear *to zigzag* Reg.	hablar	41
zozobrar *to founder* Reg.	hablar	41
zumbar *to buzz* (intransitive)*; to thrash* Reg.	hablar	41
zurcir *to darn* Reg.	zurcir	92
zurrar *to spank* Reg.	hablar	41
zurriagar *to whip* Reg.	pagar	52

TABLES OF MODEL VERBS

The following three sets of forms are not shown in the tables

(1) Compound Tenses, since they all formed the same way in Spanish, i.e. by adding the past participle (shown in the tables) to the appropriate tense of the verb **haber** (no. 40). There are no exceptions: unlike French, Italian and German, Spanish has no compound tenses conjugated with the verb *to be*.

The compound tenses include:

- Perfect Indicative, corresponding roughly to the English *I have done, I have seen.* It is formed from the present indicative of **haber** plus the past participle, e.g. from **hablar**:

he hablado *I have spoken*	**hemos hablado**
has hablado *you have spoken*	**habéis hablado**
ha hablado *etc.*	**han hablado**

- The Pluperfect, a common tense corresponding to the English *I had done, I had said, I had gone,* etc. It is formed from the imperfect indicative of **haber** plus the past participle, e.g.

había hablado *I had spoken*	**habíamos hablado**
habías hablado *you had spoken*	**habíais hablado**
había hablado *etc.*	**habían hablado**

- The Conditional Perfect, commonly found in conditional tenses like **si hubieras tenido más dinero,** ***lo habrías comprado*** *if you'd had more money,* ***you would have bought it***. It therefore corresponds to the English *I would have done, I would have said, he would have gone,* etc. It is formed from the imperfect indicative or, optionally, the **-ra** subjunctive of **haber** plus the past participle, e.g.

  habría/hubiera hablado *I would have spoken*
  habrías/hubieras hablado *you would have spoken*

habría/hubiera hablado *etc.*
habríamos/hubiéramos hablado
habríais/hubierais hablado
habrían/hubieran hablado

- The Perfect Subjunctive, a fairly common form which has no exact English translation. It is the subjunctive form of the perfect indicative, and occurs in phrases like **no creo que lo haya hecho** *I don't think that he did it*, **sin que te hayamos visto** *without us seeing you*. It is formed from the present subjunctive of **haber** plus the past participle, e.g.

haya hablado	**hayamos hablado**
hayas hablado	**hayáis hablado**
haya hablado	**hayan hablado**

- The Pluperfect Subjunctive, which has no exact English equivalent. It is found in phrases like **antes de que hubieran llegado** *before they had arrived*, **era poco probable que se hubiera dado cuenta** *it was unlikely that he had realized*. It is formed from the imperfect subjunctive, **-ra** or **-se** form, of **haber** plus the past participle, e.g.

hubiera/hubiese hablado
hubieras/hubieses hablado
hubiera/hubiese hablado
hubiéramos/hubiésemos hablado
hubierais/hubieseis hablado
hubieran/hubiesen hablado

- The Anterior Preterit (**pretérito anterior**). This tense is virtually extinct in spoken Spanish and is unusual in written language. It means the same as the pluperfect indicative, i.e. *I had seen, etc.* and is usually replaced by the preterit tense, e.g. **cuando hubo terminado** is normally said **cuando terminó** *when he finished*. It is formed from the preterit of **haber** plus the past participle:

hube hablado	**hubimos hablado**
hubiste hablado	**hubisteis hablado**
hubo hablado	**hubieran hablado**

(2) The Future Subjunctive. This is obsolete and is only found nowadays in legal or other very formal documents. In ordinary language the imperfect subjunctive replaces it. It is formed by replacing the last **a** in the **-ra** imperfect subjunctive by an **e**, e.g.

hablare	**habláremos**
hablares	**hablareis**
hablare	**hablaren**

(3) Continuous forms, e.g. **estoy hablando** *I am speaking,* **estamos poniendo** *we are putting,* etc. These are always formed by combining the correct form of **estar** (no.38) with the gerund, which is shown in the verb tables. The following forms are possible.

Indicative

Present	**estoy hablando**, etc.	*I am speaking*
Imperfect	**estaba hablando**, etc.	*I was speaking*
Preterit	**estuve hablando**, etc.	*I spoke (for a certain time)*
Perfect	**he estado**, etc. **hablando**	*I have been speaking*
Pluperfect	**había estado**, etc. **hablando**	*I had been speaking*
Future	**estaré hablando**, etc.	*I will be speaking*
Conditional	**estaria hablando**, etc.	*I would be speaking*
Future Perfect	**habré estado**, etc. **hablando**	*I will have been speaking*
Conditional Perfect	**habría estado**, etc. **hablando**	*I would have been speaking*

Subjunctive (no exact English translations)

Present	**esté hablando**, etc.
Imperfect	**estuviera/estuviese hablando**, etc.

Perfect	**haya estado hablando**, etc.
Future Perfect	**hubiera/hubiese estado hablando**, etc.

Note: The meaning of these various continuous tenses is usually self-evident to English-speakers, with the following two exceptions:

The present continuous can never refer to the future in Spanish: *I am going to Florida tomorrow* is **mañana voy a Florida**, never *'mañana estoy yendo'*.

The preterit continuous has no clear English equivalent. It refers to an action that went on for a certain time in the past, and then finished. Compare **hablé con ella** *I talked to her* and **estuve hablando con ella** *I spent a certain time talking to her, I had a talk with her.*

1 **Abolir** *to abolish*

Gerund **aboliendo** *Past Participle* **abolido**

Imperative (*the* **tú** *form is not used)* **abolid**
(*the* **ustedes** *forms are not used)*

PRESENT *not used, not used, not used,* **abolimos, abolís,** *not used*

PRETERIT **abolí, aboliste, abolió, abolimos, abolisteis, abolieron**

IMPERFECT **abolía, abolías, abolía, abolíamos, abolíais, abolían**

FUTURE **aboliré, abolirás, abolirá, aboliremos, aboliréis, abolirán**

CONDITIONAL **aboliría, abolirías, aboliría, aboliríamos, aboliríais, abolirían**

PRESENT SUBJUNCTIVE *not used*

IMPERFECT SUBJUNCTIVE **(-ra) aboliera, abolieras, aboliera, aboliéramos, abolierais, abolieran**

IMPERFECT SUBJUNCTIVE **(-se) aboliese, abolieses, aboliese, aboliésemos, abolieseis, aboliesen**

This is a so-called 'defective' verb. These verbs have the peculiarity that the only forms allowed are those whose ending begins with **i**. There is only one other defective verb in common use, **agredir** *to assault*, although **garantir** is sometimes still used in Latin America for **garantizar** *to guarantee*. There is a tendency nowadays also to use forms of these verbs whose ending begins with **e**, e.g. **abole** *he abolishes*.

The other verbs of this type listed in this book are virtually unused nowadays, only their past participle being found (e.g. **aguerrido** *battle-hardened*).

2 Abrir *to open*

Gerund **abriendo** *Past Participle* **abierto**

Imperative **abre abrid**
abra abran

PRESENT **abro**, **abres**, **abre**, **abrimos**, **abrís**, **abren**
PRETERIT **abrí**, **abriste**, **abrió**, **abrimos**, **abristeis**, **abrieron**
IMPERFECT **abría**, **abrías**, **abría**, **abríamos**, **abríais**, **abrían**
FUTURE **abriré**, **abrirás**, **abrirá**, **abriremos**, **abriréis**, **abrirán**
CONDITIONAL **abriría**, **abrirías**, **abriría**, **abriríamos**, **abriríais**, **abrirían**
PRESENT SUBJUNCTIVE **abra**, **abras**, **abra**, **abramos**, **abráis**, **abran**
IMPERFECT SUBJUNCTIVE **(-ra) abriera**, **abrieras**, **abriera**, **abriéramos**, **abrierais**, **abrieran**
IMPERFECT SUBJUNCTIVE **(-se) abriese**, **abrieses**, **abriese**, **abriésemos**, **abrieseis**, **abriesen**

This is a regular **-ir** verb except for the irregular past participle **abierto**. **Reabrir** *to reopen* and **entreabrir** *to half-open* are conjugated the same way.

3 Adquirir *to acquire*

Gerund **adquiriendo** *Past Participle* **adquirido**

Imperative **adquiere adquirid**
adquiera adquieran

PRESENT **adquiero**, **adquieres**, **adquiere**, **adquirimos**, **adquirís**, **adquieren**

PRETERIT **adquirí**, **adquiriste**, **adquirió**, **adquirimos**, **adquiristeis**, **adquirieron**

IMPERFECT **adquiría**, **adquirías**, **adquiría**, **adquiríamos**, **adquiríais**, **adquirían**

FUTURE **adquiriré**, **adquirirás**, **adquirirá**, **adquiriremos**, **adquiriréis**, **adquirirán**

CONDITIONAL **adquiriría**, **adquirirías**, **adquiriría**, **adquiriríamos**, **adquiriríais**, **adquirirían**

PRESENT SUBJUNCTIVE **adquiera**, **adquieras**, **adquiera**, **adquiramos**, **adquiráis**, **adquieran**

IMPERFECT SUBJUNCTIVE (**-ra**) **adquiriera**, **adquirieras**, **adquiriera**, **adquiriéramos**, **adquirierais**, **adquirieran**

IMPERFECT SUBJUNCTIVE (**-se**) **adquiriese**, **adquirieses**, **adquiriese**, **adquiriésemos**, **adquirieseis**, **adquiriesen**

In older Spanish this verb was **adquerir**, which explains the unusual change **i** > **ie** when stressed. The only other verb conjugated like it is the rare and literary **inquirir** *to enquire*.

4 Agorar *to prophesy*

Gerund **agorando** *Past Participle* **agorado**

Imperative **agüera agorad**
agüere agüeren

PRESENT **agüero, agüeras, agüera, agoramos, agoráis, agüeran**

PRETERIT **agoré, agoraste, agoró, agoramos, agorasteis, agoraron**

IMPERFECT **agoraba, agorabas, agoraba, agorábamos, agorabais, agoraban**

FUTURE **agoraré, agorarás, agorará, agoraremos, agoraréis, agorarán**

CONDITIONAL **agoraría, agorarías, agoraría, agoraríamos, agoraríais, agorarían**

PRESENT SUBJUNCTIVE **agüere, agüeres, agüere, agoremos, agoréis, agüeren**

IMPERFECT SUBJUNCTIVE **(-ra) agorara, agoraras, agorara, agoráramos, agorarais, agoraran**

IMPERFECT SUBJUNCTIVE **(-se) agorase, agorases, agorase, agorásemos, agoraseis, agorasen**

An archaic verb, **augurar** being the normal ways of expressing *to prophesy*. It is a radical-changing verb conjugated exactly like **contar** (no. 24) save for the dieresis over the **u** to show that this vowel is not silent.

5 Aislar *to isolate; to insulate*

Gerund **aislando** *Past Participle* **aislado**

Imperative **aísla aislad**
aísle aíslen

PRESENT **aíslo, aíslas, aísla, aislamos, aisláis, aíslan**
PRETERIT **aislé, aislaste, aisló, aislamos, aislasteis, aislaron**
IMPERFECT **aislaba, aislabas, aislaba, aislábamos, aislabais, aislaban**
FUTURE **aislaré, aislarás, aislará, aislaremos, aislaréis, aislarán**
CONDITIONAL **aislaría, aislarías, aislaría, aislaríamos, aislaríais, aislarían**
PRESENT SUBJUNCTIVE **aísle, aísles, aísle, aislemos, aisléis, aíslen**
IMPERFECT SUBJUNCTIVE **(-ra) aislara, aislaras, aislara, aisláramos, aislarais, aislaran**
IMPERFECT SUBJUNCTIVE **(-se) aislase, aislases, aislase, aislásemos, aislaseis, aislasen**

This is a regular **-ar** verb except for the accent written on **i** when the latter is stressed. This accent was introduced by the spelling reforms of 1959 and even today many people omit it. There are a few other verbs similarly affected; an **h** between the vowel and the **i** does not make the accent unnecessary. The following are occasionally found:

ahitarse de *to gorge on, to stuff oneself* (i.e. **atiborrarse de**)
amohinarse *to sulk* (i.e. **enfurruñarse**)
rehilar *to quiver* (i.e. **temblar**) accented form **rehílo,** etc.

6 Almorzar *to have lunch*

Gerund **almorzando** *Past Participle* **almorzado**

Imperative **almuerza almorzad**
almuerce almuercen

PRESENT **almuerzo, almuerzas, almuerza, almorzamos, almorzáis, almuerzan**

PRETERIT **almorcé, almorzaste, almorzó, almorzamos, almorzasteis, almorzaron**

IMPERFECT **almorzaba, almorzabas, almorzaba, almorzábamos, almorzabais, almorzaban**

FUTURE **almorzaré, almorzarás, almorzará, almorzaremos, almorzaréis, almorzarán**

CONDITIONAL **almorzaría, almorzarías, almorzaría, almorzaríamos, almorzaríais, almorzarían**

PRESENT SUBJUNCTIVE **almuerce, almuerces, almuerce, almorcemos, almorcéis, almuercen**

IMPERFECT SUBJUNCTIVE **(-ra) almorzara, almorzaras, almorzara, almorzáramos, almorzarais, almorzaran**

IMPERFECT SUBJUNCTIVE **(-se) almorzase, almorzases, almorzase, almorzásemos, almorzaseis, almorzasen**

A radical-changing verb conjugated like **contar** (no. 24) except for the predictable **z** > **c** before **e.** Other common verbs conjugated in the same way are:

esforzar *to encourage; to push (a person into trying harder)*
esforzarse por *to try hard to*
forzar *to force*
reforzar *to strengthen*

7 Andar *to walk; to go about*

Gerund **andando** *Past Participle* **andado**

Imperative **anda andad**
ande anden

PRESENT **ando, andas, anda, andamos, andáis, andan**
PRETERIT **anduve, anduviste, anduvo, anduvimos, anduvisteis, anduvieron**
IMPERFECT **andaba, andabas, andaba, andábamos, andabais, andaban**
FUTURE **andaré, andarás, andará, andaremos, andaréis, andarán**
CONDITIONAL **andaría, andarías, andaría, andaríamos, andaríais, andarían**
PRESENT SUBJUNCTIVE **ande, andes, ande, andemos, andéis, anden**
IMPERFECT SUBJUNCTIVE (**-ra**) **anduviera, anduvieras, anduviera, anduviéramos, anduvierais, anduvieran**
IMPERFECT SUBJUNCTIVE (**-se**) **anduviese, anduvieses, anduviese, anduviésemos, anduvieseis, anduviesen**

Irregular verb in constant use. It is in fact a regular **-ar** verb except for the preterit and imperfect subjunctive forms in **-uv-**. The preterit uses the irregular preterit endings and is completely unexpected: Spanish-speaking children have to be reminded to say **anduve** and not 'andé'. **Andar** has numerous other meanings and idiomatic uses that should be sought in a dictionary.

The only other verb conjugated like it is **desandar** *to retrace steps*, which is rarely seen and then usually only in the infinitive form.

8 Arcaizar *to make archaic*

Gerund **arcaizando** *Past Participle* **arcaizado**

Imperative **arcaíza arcaizad**
arcaíce arcaícen

PRESENT **arcaízo, arcaízas, arcaíza, arcaizamos, arcaizáis, arcaízan**

PRETERIT **arcaicé, arcaizaste, arcaizó, arcaizamos, arcaizasteis, arcaizaron**

IMPERFECT **arcaizaba, arcaizabas, arcaizaba, arcaizábamos, arcaizabais, arcaizaban**

FUTURE **arcaizaré, arcaizarás, arcaizará, arcaizaremos, arcaizaréis, arcaizarán**

CONDITIONAL **arcaizaría, arcaizarías, arcaizaría, arcaizaríamos, arcaizaríais, arcaizarían**

PRESENT SUBJUNCTIVE **arcaíce, arcaíces, arcaíce, arcaicemos, arcaicéis, arcaícen**

IMPERFECT SUBJUNCTIVE **(-ra) arcaizara, arcaizaras, arcaizara, arcaizáramos, arcaizarais, arcaizaran**

IMPERFECT SUBJUNCTIVE **(-se) arcaizase, arcaizases, arcaizase, arcaizásemos, arcaizaseis, arcaizasen**

This verb is conjugated exactly like **aislar** (no. 5), and is therefore a regular **-ar** verb except for the spelling change **z** > **c** before **e** and the accent on the stressed **í** (introduced in 1959). It is a rare verb, and verbs conjugated like it are not very common, e.g.

enraizar *to take root* (i.e. **echar raíces)**
europeizar *to Europeanise*, stressed form **europeíza**, etc.
homogeneizar *to homogenise*
judaizar *to Judaise*

9 Argüir *to argue a point*

Gerund **arguyendo** *Past Participle* **argüido**

Imperative **arguye argüid**
arguya arguyan

PRESENT **arguyo, arguyes, arguye, argüimos, argüís, arguyen**

PRETERIT **argüí, argüiste, arguyó, argüimos, argüisteis, arguyeron**

IMPERFECT **argüía, argüías, argüía, argüíamos, argüíais, argüían**

FUTURE **argüiré, argüirás, argüirá, argüiremos, argüiréis, argüirán**

CONDITIONAL **argüiría, argüirías, argüiría, argüiríamos, argüiríais, argüirían**

PRESENT SUBJUNCTIVE **arguya, arguyas, arguya, arguyamos, arguyáis, arguyan**

IMPERFECT SUBJUNCTIVE **(-ra) arguyera, arguyeras, arguyera, arguyéramos, arguyerais, arguyeran**

IMPERFECT SUBJUNCTIVE **(-se) arguyese, arguyeses, arguyese, arguyésemos, arguyeseis, arguyesen**

This verb is conjugated exactly like **construir** (no. 23), except that a dieresis appears in the combination **üi** to show that the **u** is not silent. The regular verb **argumentar** has almost the same meaning and is increasingly common. Both verbs mean *to argue* ***that***. *To have an argument* is **discutir**.

No other verbs are conjugated like **argüir**, but many are conjugated like **construir**.

10 Asir *to grasp/seize*

Gerund **asiendo** *Past Participle* **asido**

Imperative **ase asid**
(asga asgan)

PRESENT **(asgo), ases, ase, asimos, asís, asen**
PRETERIT **así, asiste, asió, asimos, asisteis, asieron**
IMPERFECT **asía, asías, asía, asíamos, asíais, asían**
FUTURE **asiré, asirás, asirá, asiremos, asiréis, asirán**
CONDITIONAL **asiría, asirías, asiría, asiríamos, asiríais, asirían**
PRESENT SUBJUNCTIVE **(asga), (asgas), (asga), (asgamos), (asgáis), (asgan)**
IMPERFECT SUBJUNCTIVE **(-ra) asiera, asieras, asiera, asiéramos, asierais, asieran**
IMPERFECT SUBJUNCTIVE **(-se) asiese, asieses, asiese, asiésemos, asieseis, asiesen**

This verb rarely used and the forms containing a **g** are always avoided. The idea of *seize*, *grasp* is nowadays usually expressed by the regular verb **agarrar**.

Desasirse de *to free oneself from someone's clutches* is conjugated in the same way, but it is also rare; **librarse de** (regular) expresses the same idea.

11 Aullar *to howl*

Gerund **aullando** *Past Participle* **aullado**

Imperative **aúlla aullad**

aúlle aúllen

Present **aúllo, aúllas, aúlla, aullamos, aulláis, aúllan**

PRETERIT **aullé, aullaste, aulló, aullamos, aullasteis, aullaron**

IMPERFECT **aullaba, aullabas, aullaba, aullábamos, aullabais, aullaban**

FUTURE **aullaré, aullarás, aullará, aullaremos, aullaréis, aullarán**

CONDITIONAL **aullaría, aullarías, aullaría, aullaríamos, aullaríais, aullarían**

PRESENT *Subjunctive* **aúlle, aúlles, aúlle, aullemos, aulléis, aúllen**

IMPERFECT SUBJUNCTIVE **(-ra) aullara, aullaras, aullara, aulláramos, aullarais, aullaran**

IMPERFECT SUBJUNCTIVE **(-se) aullase, aullases, aullase, aullásemos, aullaseis, aullasen**

A regular **-ar** verb except for the accent on the stressed **ú**. This accent has been required since the spelling reforms of 1959. A few other verbs are similarly affected, of which the only ones likely to be occasionally encountered are:

ahumar *to smoke (meat,* etc.*)*, stressed form **ahúmo**, etc. To smoke a cigarette is **fumar**.

desahuciar *to evict* (usually **desalojar**), stressed form **desahúcio**, etc.

rehusar *to refuse* (transitive, usually **rechazar**), stressed form **rehúso**, etc.

12 Avergonzar *to shame*

Gerund **avergonzando** *Past Participle* **avergonzado**

Imperative **avergüenza avergonzad**
avergüence avergüencen

PRESENT **avergüenzo, avergüenzas, avergüenza, avergonzamos, avergonzáis, avergüenzan**

PRETERIT **avergoncé, avergonzaste, avergonzó, avergonzamos, avergonzasteis, avergonzaron**

IMPERFECT **avergonzaba, avergonzabas, avergonzaba, avergonzábamos, avergonzabais, avergonzaban**

FUTURE **avergonzaré, avergonzarás, avergonzará, avergonzaremos, avergonzaréis, avergonzarán**

CONDITIONAL **avergonzaría, avergonzarías, avergonzaría, avergonzaríamos, avergonzaríais, avergonzarían**

PRESENT SUBJUNCTIVE **avergüence, avergüences, avergüence, avergoncemos, avergoncéis, avergüencen**

IMPERFECT SUBJUNCTIVE **(-ra) avergonzara, avergonzaras, avergonzara, avergonzáramos, avergonzarais, avergonzaran**

IMPERFECT SUBJUNCTIVE **(-se) avergonzase, avergonzases, avergonzase, avergonzásemos, avergonzaseis, avergonzasen**

Conjugated like **almorzar** (no. 6), except for the dieresis on the **üe** to show that the **u** is not silent. Note the regular spelling change **z** > **c** before **e**. **Avergonzarse** *to be ashamed* is conjugated in the same way. So is **desvergonzarse** *to act in a shameless manner*, but it is rare.

13 Averiguar *to ascertain*

Gerund **averiguando** *Past Participle* **averiguado**

Imperative **averigua averiguad**
averigüe averigüen

PRESENT **averiguo, averiguas, averigua, averiguamos, averiguáis, averiguan**

PRETERIT **averigüé, averiguaste, averiguó, averiguamos, averiguasteis, averiguaron**

IMPERFECT **averiguaba, averiguabas, averiguaba, averiguábamos, averiguabais, averiguaban**

FUTURE **averiguaré, averiguarás, averiguará, averiguaremos, averiguaréis, averiguarán**

CONDITIONAL **averiguaría, averiguarías, averiguaría, averiguaríamos, averiguaríais, averiguarían**

PRESENT SUBJUNCTIVE **averigüe, averigües, averigüe, averigüemos, averigüéis, averigüen**

IMPERFECT SUBJUNCTIVE **(-ra) averiguara, averiguaras, averiguara, averiguáramos, averiguarais, averiguaran**

IMPERFECT SUBJUNCTIVE **(-se) averiguase, averiguases, averiguase, averiguásemos, averiguaseis, averiguasen**

A regular **-ar** verb, except that a dieresis is used to show that **u** is not silent. The **u** is never stressed (contrast **continuar**, no. 25).

Verbs ending in **-cuar**, e.g. **evacuar** *to evacuate*, are conjugated in the same way (at least in Spain), but without the dieresis. But conjugation like **continuar** (no. 25) is considered correct in much of Latin America and is common in Spain.

14 Balbucir *to stammer*

Gerund **balbuciendo** *Past Participle* **balbucido**

Imperative **balbuce balbucid**
not used

PRESENT NOT USED, **balbuces**, **balbuce**, **balbucimos**, **balbucís**, **balbucen**

PRETERIT **balbucí**, **balbuciste**, **balbució**, **balbucimos**, **balbucisteis**, **balbucieron**

IMPERFECT **balbucía**, **balbucías**, **balbucía**, **balbucíamos**, **balbucíais**, **balbucían**

FUTURE **balbuciré**, **balbucirás**, **balbucirá**, **balbuciremos**, **balbuciréis**, **balbucirán**

CONDITIONAL **balbuciría**, **balbucirías**, **balbuciría**, **balbuciríamos**, **balbuciríais**, **balbucirían**

PRESENT SUBJUNCTIVE *not used*

IMPERFECT SUBJUNCTIVE **(-ra) balbuciera**, **balbucieras**, **balbuciera**, **balbuciéramos**, **balbucierais**, **balbucieran**

IMPERFECT SUBJUNCTIVE **(-se) balbuciese**, **balbucieses**, **balbuciese**, **balbuciésemos**, **balbucieseis**, **balbuciesen**

Balbucir has the unique peculiarity that no form containing a **z** occurs. It is virtually obsolete, although third-person forms are still seen in literary styles. **Balbucear** means the same, is a regular **-ar** verb and is more common.

15 Bullir *to seethe (intransitive)*

Gerund **bullendo** *Past Participle* **bullido**

Imperative **bulle bullid**
bulla bullan

PRESENT **bullo, bulles, bulle, bullimos, bullís, bullen**
PRETERIT **bullí, bulliste, bulló, bullimos, bullisteis, bulleron**
IMPERFECT **bullía, bullías, bullía, bullíamos, bullíais, bullían**
FUTURE **bulliré, bullirás, bullirá, bulliremos, bulliréis, bullirán**
CONDITIONAL **bulliría, bullirías, bulliría, bulliríamos, bulliríais, bullirían**
PRESENT SUBJUNCTIVE **bulla, bullas, bulla, bullamos, bulláis, bullan**
IMPERFECT SUBJUNCTIVE (**-ra**) **bullera, bulleras, bullera, bulléramos, bullerais, bulleran**
IMPERFECT SUBJUNCTIVE (**-se**) **bullese, bulleses, bullese, bullésemos, bulleseis, bullesen**

A regular **-ir** verb affected by the standard spelling rule that **ió** > **ó** and **ie** > **e** after **ll** (because the latter already contains a palatal sound). Similarly affected are:

engulir *to gulp down*
escabullirse *to skive off, to slip away*
mullir *to fluff up (a pillow)*
zambullirse *to dive (into the water)*

16 Caber *to fit (intransitive)*

Gerund **cabiendo** *Past Participle* **cabido**

Imperative **cabe cabed**
quepa quepan

PRESENT **quepo, cabes, cabe, cabemos, cabéis, caben**
PRETERIT **cupe, cupiste, cupo, cupimos, cupisteis, cupieron**
IMPERFECT **cabía, cabías, cabía, cabíamos, cabíais, cabían**
FUTURE **cabré, cabrás, cabrá, cabremos, cabréis, cabrán**
CONDITIONAL **cabría, cabrías, cabría, cabríamos, cabríais, cabrían**
PRESENT SUBJUNCTIVE **quepa, quepas, quepa, quepamos, quepáis, quepan**
IMPERFECT SUBJUNCTIVE **(-ra) cupiera, cupieras, cupiera, cupiéramos, cupierais, cupieran**
IMPERFECT SUBJUNCTIVE **(-se) cupiese, cupieses, cupiese, cupiésemos, cupieseis, cupiesen**

Extremely irregular: Spanish-speaking children constantly make the mistake of saying 'cabo' for **quepo**. Usage:

Esto no cabe aquí *this doesn't fit here*
Tú no cabes *there's no room for you*
¿Quepo yo? *is there any room for me?*

17 Caer *to fall*

Gerund **cayendo** *Past Participle* **caído**

Imperative **cae caed**

caiga caigan

PRESENT **caigo, caes, cae, caemos, caéis, caen**

PRETERIT **caí, caíste, cayó, caímos, caísteis, cayeron**

IMPERFECT **caía, caías, caía, caíamos, caíais, caían**

FUTURE **caeré, caerás, caerá, caeremos, caeréis, caerán**

CONDITIONAL **caería, caerías, caería, caeríamos, caeríais, caerían**

PRESENT SUBJUNCTIVE **caiga, caigas, caiga, caigamos, caigáis, caigan**

IMPERFECT SUBJUNCTIVE **(-ra) cayera, cayeras, cayera, cayéramos, cayerais, cayeran**

IMPERFECT SUBJUNCTIVE **(-se) cayese, cayeses, cayese, cayésemos, cayeseis, cayesen**

The appearance of **g** in some forms constitutes the main irregularity. The preterit is regular. Other verbs similarly conjugated are:

caerse *to fall down/over*
decaer *to decay* (economically, morally; not *to rot*, which is **pudrir**)
raer *to scrape* (rare, usually **raspar**, **fregar**)
recaer *to relapse*

18 Cerrar *to shut/close*

Gerund **cerrando** *Past Participle* **cerrado**

Imperative **cierra cerrad**
cierre cierren

PRESENT **cierro, cierras, cierra, cerramos, cerráis, cierran**
PRETERIT **cerré, cerraste, cerró, cerramos, cerrasteis, cerraron**
IMPERFECT **cerraba, cerrabas, cerraba, cerrábamos, cerrabais, cerraban**
FUTURE **cerraré, cerrarás, cerrará, cerraremos, cerraréis, cerrarán**
CONDITIONAL **cerraría, cerrarías, cerraría, cerraríamos, cerraríais, cerrarían**
PRESENT SUBJUNCTIVE **cierre, cierres, cierre, cerremos, cerréis, cierren**
IMPERFECT SUBJUNCTIVE **(-ra) cerrara, cerraras, cerrara, cerráramos, cerrarais, cerraran**
IMPERFECT SUBJUNCTIVE **(-se) cerrase, cerrases, cerrase, cerrásemos, cerraseis, cerrasen**

A frequently-encountered type of radical changing verb: **e> ie** when stressed. Common verbs of this sort are:

acertar *to get right*
apretar *to squeeze*
atravesar *to cross*
calentar *to heat*
confesar *to confess*
despertar *to wake up*
enterrar *to bury*
helar *to freeze*
nevar *to snow*
pensar *to think*
quebrar *to snap*
recomendar *to recommend*
sentarse *to sit*

Verbs ending in **-egar** are similar, but show spelling changes. See **negar**.(no. 49).

19 Cocer *to cook; to boil*

Gerund **cociendo** *Past Participle* **cocido**

Imperative **cuece coced**
cueza cuezan

PRESENT **cuezo, cueces, cuece, cocemos, cocéis, cuecen**
PRETERIT **cocí, cociste, coció, cocimos, cocisteis, cocieron**
IMPERFECT **cocía, cocías, cocía, cocíamos, cocíais, cocían**
FUTURE **coceré, cocerás, cocerá, coceremos, coceréis, cocerán**
CONDITIONAL **cocería, cocerías, cocería, coceríamos, coceríais, cocerían**
PRESENT SUBJUNCTIVE **cueza, cuezas, cueza, cozamos, cozáis, cuezan**
IMPERFECT SUBJUNCTIVE (**-ra**) **cociera, cocieras, cociera, cociéramos, cocierais, cocieran**
IMPERFECT SUBJUNCTIVE (**-se**) **cociese, cocieses, cociese, cociésemos, cocieseis, cociesen**

Conjugated exactly like **mover** (no. 48), but with the spelling change **c** > **z** before **a** or **o**. Other verbs similarly conjugated are:

escocer *to sting, to smart* (usually **picar**)
retorcerse *to writhe*
torcer *to twist* (transitive)

20 Colgar *to hang up*

Gerund **colgando** *Past Participle* **colgado**

Imperative **cuelga colgad**
cuelgue cuelguen

PRESENT **cuelgo, cuelgas, cuelga, colgamos, colgáis, cuelgan**

PRETERIT **colgué, colgaste, colgó, colgamos, colgasteis, colgaron**

IMPERFECT **colgaba, colgabas, colgaba, colgábamos, colgabais, colgaban**

FUTURE **colgaré, colgarás, colgará, colgaremos, colgaréis, colgarán**

CONDITIONAL **colgaría, colgarías, colgaría, colgaríamos, colgaríais, colgarían**

PRESENT SUBJUNCTIVE **cuelgue, cuelgues, cuelgue, colguemos, colguéis, cuelguen**

IMPERFECT SUBJUNCTIVE (**-ra**) **colgara, colgaras, colgara, colgáramos, colgarais, colgaran**

IMPERFECT SUBJUNCTIVE (**-se**) **colgase, colgases, colgase, colgásemos, colgaseis, colgasen**

Conjugated like **contar** (no. 24: **o** > **ue** when stressed), but with the predictable insertion of a silent **u** before **e** to keep the **g** hard. Similar verbs:

descolgar *to take down*
rogar *to request*

21 Comenzar *to begin*

Gerund **comenzando** *Past Participle* **comenzado**

Imperative **comienza comenzad**
comience comiencen

PRESENT **comienzo, comienzas, comienza, comenzamos, comenzáis, comienzan**

PRETERIT **comencé, comenzaste, comenzó, comenzamos, comenzasteis, comenzaron**

IMPERFECT **comenzaba, comenzabas, comenzaba, comenzábamos, comenzabais, comenzaban**

FUTURE **comenzaré, comenzarás, comenzará, comenzaremos, comenzaréis, comenzarán**

CONDITIONAL **comenzaría, comenzarías, comenzaría, comenzaríamos, comenzaríais, comenzarían**

PRESENT SUBJUNCTIVE **comience, comiences, comience, comencemos, comencéis, comiencen**

IMPERFECT SUBJUNCTIVE **(-ra) comenzara, comenzaras, comenzara, comenzáramos, comenzarais, comenzaran**

IMPERFECT SUBJUNCTIVE **(-se) comenzase, comenzases, comenzase, comenzásemos, comenzaseis, comenzasen**

Conjugated like **cerrar** (no. 18: **e** > **ie** when stressed), but with the predictable spelling change **z** > **c** before **e**. Similar verbs:

empezar *to begin*
tropezar *to stumble*

22 Comer *to eat*

Gerund **comiendo** *Past Participle* **comido**

Imperative **come comed**
coma coman

PRESENT **como, comes, come, comemos, coméis, comen**
PRETERIT **comí, comiste, comió, comimos, comisteis, comieron**
IMPERFECT **comía, comías, comía, comíamos, comíais, comían**
FUTURE **comeré, comerás, comerá, comeremos, comeréis, comerán**
CONDITIONAL **comería, comerías, comería, comeríamos, comeríais, comerían**
PRESENT SUBJUNCTIVE **coma, comas, coma, comamos, comáis, coman**
IMPERFECT SUBJUNCTIVE (**-ra**) **comiera, comieras, comiera, comiéramos, comierais, comieran**
IMPERFECT SUBJUNCTIVE (**-se**) **comiese, comieses, comiese, comiésemos, comieseis, comiesen**

Completely regular, which makes it a convenient model for the **-er** conjugation.

Verbs whose infinitive ends in **-cer** (numerous) should be sought in the list as they may show irregularities. The majority are conjugated like **parecer** (no. 53), but a few are conjugated like **vencer** (no. 86) or **cocer** (no. 19).

For infinitives ending in **-ger** see **proteger** (no. 62), which has predictable spelling changes.

Verbs ending in **-tender** are conjugated like **perder** (no. 55), with the exception of **pretender** *to claim*, which is like **comer**.

23 Construir *to build*

Gerund **construyendo** *Past Participle* **construido**

Imperative **construye construid**
construya construyan

PRESENT **construyo, construyes, construye, construimos, construís, construyen**

PRETERIT **construí, construiste, construyó, construimos, construisteis, construyeron**

IMPERFECT **construía, construías, construía, construíamos, construíais, construían**

FUTURE **construiré, construirás, construirá, construiremos, construiréis, construirán**

CONDITIONAL **construiría, construirías, construiría, construiríamos, construiríais, construirían**

PRESENT SUBJUNCTIVE **construya, construyas, construya, construyamos, construyáis, construyan**

IMPERFECT SUBJUNCTIVE **(-ra) construyera, construyeras, construyera, construyéramos, construyerais, construyeran**

IMPERFECT SUBJUNCTIVE **(-se) construyese, construyeses, construyese, construyésemos, construyeseis, construyesen**

A regular **-ir** verb but for the **y** inserted between **u** and **o** or **a**. The past participle does not have an accent. Similar common verbs are:

atribuir *to attribute*
concluir *to conclude*
contribuir *to contribute*
destruir *to destroy*
distribuir *to distribute*
excluir *to exclude*
huir *to flee*
incluir *to include*
influir *to influence*
intuir *to intuit*
substituir *to substitute*

24 Contar *to count; to tell a story*

Gerund **contando** *Past Participle* **contado**

Imperative **cuenta contad**
cuente cuenten

PRESENT **cuento, cuentas, cuenta, contamos, contáis, cuentan**

PRETERIT **conté, contaste, contó, contamos, contasteis, contaron**

IMPERFECT **contaba, contabas, contaba, contábamos, contabais, contaban**

FUTURE **contaré, contarás, contará, contaremos, contaréis, contarán**

CONDITIONAL **contaría, contarías, contaría, contaríamos, contaríais, contarían**

PRESENT SUBJUNCTIVE **cuente, cuentes, cuente, contemos, contéis, cuenten**

IMPERFECT SUBJUNCTIVE **(-ra) contara, contaras, contara, contáramos, contarais, contaran**

IMPERFECT SUBJUNCTIVE **(-se) contase, contases, contase, contásemos, contaseis, contasen**

A common type of radical changing **-ar** verb in which stressed **o** > **ue**. Similar common verbs:

acordarse de *to remember*
acostarse *to go to bed*
apostar *to bet*
aprobar *to approve; to pass an exam*
colarse *to slip through*
costar *to cost*
demostrar *to demonstrate (a fact)*
desaprobar *to approve*
encontrar *to find*
mostrar *to show*
probar *to prove; to try out*
recordar *to recall*
rodar *to roll*
soltar *to let go*
soñar *to dream*
volar *to fly*

25 Continuar *to continue*

Gerund **continuando** *Past Participle* **continuado**

Imperative **continúa continuad**
continúe continúen

PRESENT **continúo, continúas, continúa, continuamos, continuáis, continúan**

PRETERIT **continué, continuaste, continuó, continuamos, continuasteis, continuaron**

IMPERFECT **continuaba, continuabas, continuaba, continuábamos, continuabais, continuaban**

FUTURE **continuaré, continuarás, continuará, continuaremos, continuaréis, continuarán**

CONDITIONAL **continuaría, continuarías, continuaría, continuaríamos, continuaríais, continuarían**

PRESENT SUBJUNCTIVE **continúe, continúes, continúe, continuemos, continuéis, continúen**

IMPERFECT SUBJUNCTIVE **(-ra) continuara, continuaras, continuara, continuáramos, continuarais, continuaran**

IMPERFECT SUBJUNCTIVE **(-se) continuase, continuases, continuase, continuásemos, continuaseis, continuasen**

This is a regular **-ar** verb, but the **u** is stressed, unlike **averiguar** (no. 13). There are forty similar verbs in the list, the most commonly encountered being:

acentuar *to accentuate*
actuar *to act*
devaluar *to devalue*
efectuar *to effect*
exceptuar *to except*
fluctuar *to fluctuate*
graduar *to graduate; to grade*
insinuar *to insinuate*
perpetuarse *to be perpetuated*
puntuar *to punctuate; to grade*
situar *to situate*

26 Cubrir *to cover*

Gerund **cubriendo** *Past Participle* **cubierto**

Imperative **cubre cubrid**

cubra cubran

PRESENT **cubro, cubres, cubre, cubrimos, cubrís, cubren**

PRETERIT **cubrí, cubriste, cubrió, cubrimos, cubristeis, cubrieron**

IMPERFECT **cubría, cubrías, cubría, cubríamos, cubríais, cubrían**

FUTURE **cubriré, cubrirás, cubrirá, cubriremos, cubriréis, cubrirán**

CONDITIONAL **cubriría, cubrirías, cubriría, cubriríamos, cubriríais, cubrirían**

PRESENT SUBJUNCTIVE **cubra, cubras, cubra, cubramos, cubráis, cubran**

IMPERFECT SUBJUNCTIVE **(-ra) cubriera, cubrieras, cubriera, cubriéramos, cubrierais, cubrieran**

IMPERFECT SUBJUNCTIVE **(-se) cubriese, cubrieses, cubriese, cubriésemos, cubrieseis, cubriesen**

A regular **-ir** verb except for the past participle ending in **-ierto**. Similar verbs are:

descubrir *to discover*
encubrir *to cover up (facts)*
recubrir *to cover; to line (*e.g. *with material)*

27 Dar *to give*

Gerund **dando** *Past Participle* **dado**

Imperative **da dad**
dé den

PRESENT **doy, das, da, damos, dais, dan**
PRETERIT **di, diste, dio** *(no accent!),* **dimos, disteis, dieron**
IMPERFECT **daba, dabas, daba, dábamos, dabais, daban**
FUTURE **daré, darás, dará, daremos, daréis, darán**
CONDITIONAL **daría, darías, daría, daríamos, daríais, darían**
PRESENT SUBJUNCTIVE **dé, des, dé, demos, deis, den**
IMPERFECT SUBJUNCTIVE **(-ra) diera, dieras, diera, diéramos, dierais, dieran**
IMPERFECT SUBJUNCTIVE **(-se) diese, dieses, diese, diésemos, dieseis, diesen**

Irregular verb, the main irregularities being the unexpected form **doy** and the fact that, although it is an **-ar** verb, the preterit and the imperfect subjunctives are conjugated as for **-er** verbs. Note that the preterit forms have no accents: the spelling **dió** for **dio** was abolished in 1959. The accent on the present subjunctive **dé** merely serves to distinguish it from the preposition **de** *of*.

There are no other similar verbs in everyday use.

28 Decir *to say*

Gerund **diciendo** *Past Participle* **dicho**

Imperative **di decid**
diga digan

PRESENT **digo**, **dices**, **dice**, **decimos**, **decís**, **dicen**
PRETERIT **dije**, **dijiste**, **dijo**, **dijimos**, **dijisteis**, **dijeron**
IMPERFECT **decía**, **decías**, **decía**, **decíamos**, **decíais**, **decían**
FUTURE **diré**, **dirás**, **dirá**, **diremos**, **diréis**, **dirán**
CONDITIONAL **diría**, **dirías**, **diría**, **diríamos**, **diríais**, **dirían**
PRESENT SUBJUNCTIVE **diga**, **digas**, **diga**, **digamos**, **digáis**, **digan**
IMPERFECT SUBJUNCTIVE **(-ra) dijera**, **dijeras**, **dijera**, **dijéramos**, **dijerais**, **dijeran**
IMPERFECT SUBJUNCTIVE **(-se) dijese**, **dijeses**, **dijese**, **dijésemos**, **dijeseis**, **dijesen**

Irregular verb. The preterit and imperfect subjunctive endings have a typical feature of irregular verbs: **-ie** becomes **e** when it follows **j**: **dijeron**, **dijera**, **dijese**, not *‘dijieron’, etc. Similar verbs:

contradecir *to contradict*
desdecirse de *to go back on* (a promise)

Predecir *to predict* is usually conjugated like **maldecir** (no. 47).

29 Delinquir *to act delinquently*

Gerund **delinquiendo** *Past Participle* **delinquido**

Imperative **delinque delinquid**
delinca delincan

PRESENT **delinco, delinques, delinque, delinquimos, delinquís, delinquen**

PRETERIT **delinquí, delinquiste, delinquió, delinquimos, delinquisteis, delinquieron**

IMPERFECT **delinquía, delinquías, delinquía, delinquíamos, delinquíais, delinquían**

FUTURE **delinquiré, delinquirás, delinquirá, delinquiremos, delinquiréis, delinquirán**

CONDITIONAL **delinquiría, delinquirías, delinquiría, delinquiríamos, delinquiríais, delinquirían**

PRESENT SUBJUNCTIVE **delinca, delincas, delinca, delincamos, delincáis, delincan**

IMPERFECT SUBJUNCTIVE (**-ra**) **delinquiera, delinquieras, delinquiera, delinquiéramos, delinquierais, delinquieran**

IMPERFECT SUBJUNCTIVE (**-se**) **delinquiese, delinquieses, delinquiese, delinquiésemos, delinquieseis, delinquiesen**

A regular **-ir** verb, except for the predictable spelling change **qu** > **c** before **a** or **o**. This verb is confined to very literary styles and is rarely seen, except occasionally in the infinitive form. No similar verbs are in everyday use in the modern language.

30 **Desosar** *to bone*

Gerund **desosando** *Past Participle* **desosado**

Imperative **deshuesa desosad**
deshuese deshuesen

PRESENT **deshueso, deshuesas, deshuesa, desosamos, desosáis, deshuesan**

PRETERIT **desosé, desosaste, desosó, desosamos, desosasteis, desosaron**

IMPERFECT **desosaba, desosabas, desosaba, desosábamos, desosabais, desosaban**

FUTURE **desosaré, desosarás, desosará, desosaremos, desosaréis, desosarán**

CONDITIONAL **desosaría, desosarías, desosaría, desosaríamos, desosaríais, desosarían**

PRESENT SUBJUNCTIVE **deshuese, deshueses, deshuese, desosemos, desoséis, deshuesen**

IMPERFECT SUBJUNCTIVE (**-ra**) **desosara, desosaras, desosara, desosáramos, desosarais, desosaran**

IMPERFECT SUBJUNCTIVE (**-se**) **desosase, desosases, desosase, desosásemos, desosaseis, desosasen**

An archaic verb, conjugated like **contar** (no. 24), except for the predictable inclusion of **h** before **ue** when this diphthong begins a syllable. **Oler** *to smell* displays the same phenomenon. **Desosar** is nowadays replaced by the regular **deshuesar**.

31 Desvaír *to cause to fade (colors, etc.)*

Gerund **desvayendo** *Past Participle* **desvaído**

Imperative *(the* **tú** *form is not used)* **desvaíd**

(the **ustedes** *forms are not used)*

PRESENT *not used, not used, not used,* **desvaímos, desvaís,** *not used*

PRETERIT **desvaí, desvaíste, desvayó, desvaímos, desvaísteis, desvayeron**

IMPERFECT **desvaía, desvaías, desvaía, desvaíamos, desvaíais, desvaían**

FUTURE **desvairé, desvairás, desvairá, desvairemos, desvairéis, desvairán**

CONDITIONAL **desvairía, desvairías, desvairía, desvairíamos, desvairíais, desvairían**

PRESENT SUBJUNCTIVE *not used*

IMPERFECT SUBJUNCTIVE **(-ra) desvayera, desvayeras, desvayera, desvayéramos, desvayerais, desvayeran**

IMPERFECT SUBJUNCTIVE **(-se) desvayese, desvayeses, desvayese, desvayésemos, desvayeseis, desvayesen**

A rare type of defective verb, similar to **abolir** (no. 1) in that only forms whose endings begin with **i** (or, in this case, **y**) are found. This verb is nowadays seen only in its participle form **desvaído** *faded, washed-out*: **desteñir** is the usual word for *to fade*, applied to colors/(Brit.) colours. **Embaír** *to swindle, to cheat* is conjugated in the same way, but it is virtually extinct, being replaced by the regular verb **estafar**.

32 Discernir *to discern*

Gerund **discerniendo** *Past Participle* **discernido**

Imperative **discierne discernid**
discierna disciernan

PRESENT **discierno, disciernes, discierne, discernimos, discernís, disciernen**

PRETERIT **discerní, discerniste, discernió, discernimos, discernisteis, discernieron**

IMPERFECT **discernía, discernías, discernía, discerníamos, discerníais, discernían**

FUTURE **discerniré, discernirá, discernirá, discerniremos, discerniréis, discernirán**

CONDITIONAL **discerniría, discernirías, discerniría, discerniríamos, discerniríais, discernirían**

PRESENT SUBJUNCTIVE **discierna, disciernas, discierna, discernamos, discernáis, disciernan**

IMPERFECT SUBJUNCTIVE (**-ra**) **discerniera, discernieras, discerniera, discerniéramos, discernierais, discernieran**

IMPERFECT SUBJUNCTIVE (**-se**) **discerniese, discernieses, discerniese, discerniésemos, discernieseis, discerniesen**

This is a radical changing **-ir** verb which shows the common replacement of stressed **e** by **ie**. Such verbs are in fact very uncommon in the **-ir** conjugation (but common in the other two conjugations). Most radical-changing **-ir** verbs are like **sentir** (no. 78), which has the added complication **e** > **i** in the third-person preterit. Similar to **discernir** are

cernir *to sieve,* usually replaced by **cerner**.
cernirse *to loom*, usually replaced by **cernerse**
concernir *to concern* (third-person only)

33 Distinguir *to distinguish*

Gerund **distinguiendo** *Past Participle* **distinguido**

Imperative **distingue distinguid**
distinga distingan

PRESENT **distingo**, **distingues**, **distingue**, **distinguimos**, **distinguís**, **distinguen**

PRETERIT **distinguí**, **distinguiste**, **distinguió**, **distinguimos**, **distinguisteis**, **distinguieron**

IMPERFECT **distinguía**, **distinguías**, **distinguía**, **distinguíamos**, **distinguíais**, **distinguían**

FUTURE **distinguiré**, **distinguirás**, **distinguirá**, **distinguiremos**, **distinguiréis**, **distinguirán**

CONDITIONAL **distinguiría**, **distinguirías**, **distinguiría**, **distinguiríamos**, **distinguiríais**, **distinguirían**

PRESENT SUBJUNCTIVE **distinga**, **distingas**, **distinga**, **distingamos**, **distingáis**, **distingan**

IMPERFECT SUBJUNCTIVE (**-ra**) **distinguiera**, **distinguieras**, **distinguiera**, **distinguiéramos**, **distinguierais**, **distinguieran**

IMPERFECT SUBJUNCTIVE (**-se**) **distinguiese**, **distinguieses**, **distinguiese**, **distinguiésemos**, **distinguieseis**, **distinguiesen**

A regular **-ir** verb which shows the spelling change **gu** > **g** before **a** or **o**, the **g** being hard throughout. Only **extinguir** *to extinguish* is conjugated like it, this verb being literary and usually replaced in everyday speech by **apagar**.

34 Dormir *to sleep*

Gerund **durmiendo** *Past Participle* **dormido**

Imperative **duerme dormid**
duerma duerman

PRESENT **duermo, duermes, duerme, dormimos, dormís, duermen**

PRETERIT **dormí, dormiste, durmió, dormimos, dormisteis, durmieron**

IMPERFECT **dormía, dormías, dormía, dormíamos, dormíais, dormían**

FUTURE **dormiré, dormirás, dormirá, dormiremos, dormiréis, dormirán**

CONDITIONAL **dormiría, dormirías, dormiría, dormiríamos, dormiríais, dormirían**

PRESENT SUBJUNCTIVE **duerma, duermas, duerma, durmamos, durmáis, duerman**

IMPERFECT SUBJUNCTIVE **(-ra) durmiera, durmieras, durmiera, durmiéramos, durmierais, durmieran**

IMPERFECT SUBJUNCTIVE **(-se) durmiese, durmieses, durmiese, durmiésemos, durmieseis, durmiesen**

A special type of radical changing verb showing the changes stressed **o** > **ue** and unstressed **o** > **u** in certain forms of the preterit and present subjunctive, and throughout the imperfect subjunctive. **Dormirse** *to go to sleep* and **morir** (or **morirse**) *to die* are conjugated the same way; the latter has an irregular past participle, **muerto**. All these verbs are in common use.

35 Erguir *to prick up (ears)* (transitive)

Gerund **irguiendo** *Past Participle* **erguido**

Imperative **yergue (irgue) erguid**
yerga (irga) yergan (irgan)

PRESENT **yergo, yergues, yergue, erguimos, erguís, yerguen (irgo, irgues, irgue, erguimos, erguís, irguen)**

PRETERIT **erguí, erguiste, irguió, erguimos, erguisteis, irguieron**

IMPERFECT **erguía, erguías, erguía, erguíamos, erguíais, erguían**

FUTURE **erguiré, erguirás, erguirá, erguiremos, erguiréis, erguirán**

CONDITIONAL **erguiría, erguirías, erguiría, erguiríamos, erguiríais, erguirían**

PRESENT SUBJUNCTIVE **yerga, yergas, yerga, yergamos, yergáis, yergan (irga, irgas, irga, irgamos, irgáis, irgan)**

IMPERFECT SUBJUNCTIVE **(-ra) irguiera, irguieras, irguiera, irguiéramos, irguierais, irguieran**

IMPERFECT SUBJUNCTIVE **(-se) irguiese, irguieses, irguiese, irguiésemos, irguieseis, irguiesen**

Conjugated like **sentir** (no. 78) with the regular spelling change **ie** > **ye** when this occurs at the beginning of a word, and the loss of silent **u** before **o** or **a**. The bracketed forms are optional variants. There are no other exactly similar verbs apart from **erguirse** *to rear up, to sit up straight*.

36 Errar *to wander, err*

Gerund **errando** *Past Participle* **errado**

Imperative **yerra errad**
yerre yerren

PRESENT **yerro, yerras, yerra, erramos, erráis, yerran**

PRETERIT **erré, erraste, erró, erramos, errasteis, erraron**

IMPERFECT **erraba, errabas, erraba, errábamos, errabais, erraban**

FUTURE **erraré, errarás, errará, erraremos, erraréis, errarán**

CONDITIONAL **erraría, errarías, erraría, erraríamos, erraríais, errarían**

PRESENT SUBJUNCTIVE **yerre, yerres, yerre, erremos, erréis, yerren**

IMPERFECT SUBJUNCTIVE **(-ra) errara, erraras, errara, erráramos, errarais, erraran**

IMPERFECT SUBJUNCTIVE **(-se) errase, errases, errase, errásemos, erraseis, errasen**

Conjugated like **cerrar** (no.18: **e** > **ie** when stressed) but with the predictable, spelling change **ie** > **ye** at the beginning of a word. In some Latin-American countries it is conjugated regularly, **erro**, **erra**, etc.

37 **Escribir** *to write*

Gerund **escribiendo** *Past Participle* **escrito**

Imperative **escribe escribid**
escriba escriban

PRESENT **escribo, escribes, escribe, escribimos, escribís, escriben**

PRETERIT **escribí, escribiste, escribió, escribimos, escribisteis, escribieron**

IMPERFECT **escribía, escribías, escribía, escribíamos, escribíais, escribían**

FUTURE **escribiré, escribirás, escribirá, escribiremos, escribiréis, escribirán**

CONDITIONAL **escribiría, escribirías, escribiría, escribiríamos, escribiríais, escribirían**

PRESENT SUBJUNCTIVE **escriba, escribas, escriba, escribamos, escribáis, escriban**

IMPERFECT SUBJUNCTIVE **(-ra) escribiera, escribieras, escribiera, escribiéramos, escribierais, escribieran**

IMPERFECT SUBJUNCTIVE **(-se) escribiese, escribieses, escribiese, escribiésemos, escribieseis, escribiesen**

Regular **-ir** verb except for the past participle ending in **-ito**. The following have the same peculiarity:

circunscribir *to circumscribe*
describir *to describe*
inscribirse *to enroll/*(Brit.) *enrol*
prescribir *to prescribe*
proscribir *to proscribe*
subscribir *to subscribe*
transcribir *to transcribe*

38 Estar *to be*

Gerund **estando** *Past Participle* **estado**

Imperative **está** or **estate** **estad** or **estaos**
esté or **estese** **estén** or **estense**

PRESENT **estoy**, **estás**, **está**, **estamos**, **estáis**, **están**
PRETERIT **estuve**, **estuviste**, **estuvo**, **estuvimos**, **estuvisteis**, **estuvieron**
IMPERFECT **estaba**, **estabas**, **estaba**, **estábamos**, **estabais**, **estaban**
FUTURE **estaré**, **estarás**, **estará**, **estaremos**, **estaréis**, **estarán**
CONDITIONAL **estaría**, **estarías**, **estaría**, **estaríamos**, **estaríais**, **estarían**
PRESENT SUBJUNCTIVE **esté**, **estés**, **esté**, **estemos**, **estéis**, **estén**
IMPERFECT SUBJUNCTIVE **(-ra)** **estuviera**, **estuvieras**, **estuviera**, **estuviéramos**, **estuvierais**, **estuvieran**
IMPERFECT SUBJUNCTIVE **(-se)** **estuviese**, **estuvieses**, **estuviese**, **estuviésemos**, **estuvieseis**, **estuviesen**

Irregular verb of very common occurrence. Note that the pronominal ('reflexive') forms are often used for the imperative: **¡estate quieto!** *sit still!*. By the rules of Spanish spelling, the forms **estate**, **estese** and **estense** should have no accent, but they are often written and printed **estáte**, **estése** and **esténse**.

Estar is used with the gerund to form the Continuous of verbs, e.g. **estoy hablando** *I'm (in the middle of) talking*, etc.

Any good grammar of Spanish will explain the crucial difference of meaning between this verb and **ser**, which also means *to be*.

39 Gruñir *to growl*

Gerund **gruñendo** *Past Participle* **gruñido**

Imperative **gruñe gruñid**
gruña gruñan

PRESENT **gruño**, **gruñes**, **gruñe**, **gruñimos**, **gruñís**, **gruñen**

PRETERIT **gruñí**, **gruñiste**, **gruñó**, **gruñimos**, **gruñisteis**, **gruñeron**

IMPERFECT **gruñía**, **gruñías**, **gruñía**, **gruñíamos**, **gruñíais**, **gruñían**

FUTURE **gruñiré**, **gruñirás**, **gruñirá**, **gruñiremos**, **gruñiréis**, **gruñirán**

CONDITIONAL **gruñiría**, **gruñirías**, **gruñiría**, **gruñiríamos**, **gruñiríais**, **gruñirían**

PRESENT SUBJUNCTIVE **gruña**, **gruñas**, **gruña**, **gruñamos**, **gruñáis**, **gruñan**

IMPERFECT SUBJUNCTIVE (**-ra**) **gruñera**, **gruñeras**, **gruñera**, **gruñéramos**, **gruñerais**, **gruñeran**

IMPERFECT SUBJUNCTIVE (**-se**) **gruñese**, **gruñeses**, **gruñese**, **gruñésemos**, **gruñeseis**, **gruñesen**

A regular **-ir** verb showing the predictable replacement of **ió** by **ó** and **ie** by **e** after a palatal consonant (**ñ**). **Bruñir** *to polish* and **plañir** *to lament* are similarly conjugated, although neither is in common use. Verbs like **reñir** (no. 69) show tho same spelling change, but are radical changing verbs.

40 Haber (auxiliary verb or *there is/there are*)

Gerund **habiendo** *Past Participle* **habido**

Imperative *not used*

PRESENT **he, has, ha (hay), hemos, habéis, han**
PRETERIT **hube, hubiste, hubo, hubimos, hubisteis, hubieron**
IMPERFECT **había, habías, había, habíamos, habíais, habían**
FUTURE **habré, habrás, habrá, habremos, habréis, habrán**
CONDITIONAL **habría, habrías, habría, habríamos, habríais, habrían**
PRESENT SUBJUNCTIVE **haya, hayas, haya, hayamos, hayáis, hayan**
IMPERFECT SUBJUNCTIVE **(-ra) hubiera, hubieras, hubiera, hubiéramos, hubierais, hubieran**
IMPERFECT SUBJUNCTIVE **(-se) hubiese, hubieses, hubiese, hubiésemos, hubieseis, hubiesen**

Irregular verb, in constant use.

Haber is the auxiliary verb used to make compound tenses (perfect, pluperfect, future perfect, conditional perfect, etc.). This is the only auxiliary used for this purpose: there is no Spanish equivalent of the French or Italian verbs conjugated with the auxiliary *to be*.

Haber is also used in the third person only to mean *there is/there are*. When it has this meaning, the present indicative form is **hay**. When it is used with this meaning it should always be singular: **había muchos** = *there were a lot of them*. However, Latin Americans and Catalans constantly use the plural (i.e. **habían muchos**), although this is banned from the written language.

41 Hablar *to speak, talk*

Gerund **hablando** *Past Participle* **hablado**

Imperative **habla hablad**
hable hablen

PRESENT **hablo, hablas, habla, hablamos, habláis, hablan**
PRETERIT **hablé, hablaste, habló, hablamos, hablasteis, hablaron**
IMPERFECT **hablaba, hablabas, hablaba, hablábamos, hablabais, hablaban**
FUTURE **hablaré, hablarás, hablará, hablaremos, hablaréis, hablarán**
CONDITIONAL **hablaría, hablarías, hablaría, hablaríamos, hablaríais, hablarían**
PRESENT SUBJUNCTIVE **hable, hables, hable, hablemos, habléis, hablen**
IMPERFECT SUBJUNCTIVE (-ra) **hablara, hablaras, hablara, habláramos, hablarais, hablaran**
IMPERFECT SUBJUNCTIVE (-se) **hablase, hablases, hablase, hablásemos, hablaseis, hablasen**

A completely regular **-ar** verb and typical of the most common type of Spanish verb (72% of the verbs in the Directory of Verbs follow this pattern if we include verbs like **pagar**, **realizar** and **sacar**, which are of the same type but show predictable spelling changes).

Verbs whose infinitive ends in **-ear** are conjugated like **hablar**. The **e** of the stem is never written with an accent, e.g. **pasear** *to go for a walk, to take for a walk*:

Present Indicative	Present Subjunctive
paseo paseamos	**pasee paseemos**
paseas paseáis	**pasees paseéis**
pasea pasean	**pasee paseen**

42 Hacer *to do; to make*

Gerund **haciendo** *Past Participle* **hecho**

Imperative **haz haced**
haga hagan

PRESENT **hago, haces, hace, hacemos, hacéis, hacen**
PRETERIT **hice, hiciste, hizo, hicimos, hicisteis, hicieron**
IMPERFECT **hacía, hacías, hacía, hacíamos, hacíais, hacían**
FUTURE **haré, harás, hará, haremos, haréis, harán**
CONDITIONAL **haría, harías, haría, haríamos, haríais, harían**
Present Subjunctive **haga, hagas, haga, hagamos, hagáis, hagan**
IMPERFECT SUBJUNCTIVE (**-ra**) **hiciera, hicieras, hiciera, hiciéramos, hicierais, hicieran**
IMPERFECT SUBJUNCTIVE (**-se**) **hiciese, hicieses, hiciese, hiciésemos, hicieseis, hiciesen**

Irregular verb, in frequent use and having many idiomatic meanings. The following less common verbs are conjugated in the same way:

contrahacer *to counterfeit*
deshacer *to undo*
deshacerse *to become loose, undone*
rehacer *to re-do*

43 Ir *to go*

Gerund **yendo** *Past Participle* **ido**

Imperative **ve id**

vaya vayan

PRESENT **voy, vas, va, vamos, vais, van**

PRETERIT **fui, fuiste, fue, fuimos, fuisteis, fueron**

IMPERFECT **iba, ibas, iba, íbamos, ibais, iban**

FUTURE **iré, irás, irá, iremos, iréis, irán**

CONDITIONAL **iría, irías, iría, iríamos, iríais, irían**

PRESENT SUBJUNCTIVE **vaya, vayas, vaya, vayamos, vayáis, vayan**

IMPERFECT SUBJUNCTIVE **(-ra) fuera, fueras, fuera, fuéramos, fuerais, fueran**

IMPERFECT SUBJUNCTIVE **(-se) fuese, fueses, fuese, fuésemos, fueseis, fuesen**

Irregular verb, in frequent use and having many idiomatic meanings. The preterit and the imperfect subjunctive are the same as **ser** *to be*. Apart from **irse** *to go away*, no other verb follows this pattern.

44 Jugar *to play*

Gerund **jugando** *Past Participle* **jugado**

Imperative **juega jugad**

juegue jueguen

PRESENT **juego, juegas, juega, jugamos, jugáis, juegan**

PRETERIT **jugué, jugaste, jugó, jugamos, jugasteis, jugaron**

IMPERFECT **jugaba, jugabas, jugaba, jugábamos, jugabais, jugaban**

FUTURE **jugaré, jugarás, jugará, jugaremos, jugaréis, jugarán**

CONDITIONAL **jugaría, jugarías, jugaría, jugaríamos, jugaríais, jugarían**

PRESENT SUBJUNCTIVE **juegue, juegues, juegue, juguemos, juguéis, jueguen**

IMPERFECT SUBJUNCTIVE **(-ra) jugara, jugaras, jugara, jugáramos, jugarais, jugaran**

IMPERFECT SUBJUNCTIVE **(-se) jugase, jugases, jugase, jugásemos, jugaseis, jugasen**

This verb is unique in that stressed **u** changes to **ue**.

45 Liar *to tie up, tie in a bundle*

Gerund **liando** *Past Participle* **liado**

Imperative **lía liad**
líe líen

PRESENT **lío, lías, lía, liamos, liáis, lían**
PRETERIT **lié, liaste, lió, liamos, liasteis, liaron**
IMPERFECT **liaba, liabas, liaba, liábamos, liabais, liaban**
FUTURE **liaré, liarás, liará, liaremos, liaréis, liarán**
CONDITIONAL **liaría, liarías, liaría, liaríamos, liaríais, liarían**
PRESENT SUBJUNCTIVE **líe, líes, líe, liemos, liéis, líen**
IMPERFECT SUBJUNCTIVE **(-ra) liara, liaras, liara, liáramos, liarais, liaran**
IMPERFECT SUBJUNCTIVE **(-se) liase, liases, liase, liásemos, liaseis, liasen**

The endings are those of a regular **-ar** verb, but verbs like **liar** are unusual in that the **i** may be stressed and then has an accent. Compare **cambiar** *to change*: **cambio, cambias, cambia, cambiamos, cambiáis, cambian**. Similar common verbs:

ampliar *to extend, enlarge*
ansiar *to long for*
averiarse *to break down*
criar *to breed*
desafiar *to challenge*
enviar *to send*
fiar *to sell on credit*
fiarse de *to trust*
fotografiar *to photograph*
guiar *to guide*
vaciar *to empty*
variar *to vary*

46 Lucir *to show off (transitive)*

Gerund **luciendo** *Past Participle* **lucido**

Imperative **luce lucid**
luzca luzcan

PRESENT **luzco**, **luces**, **luce**, **lucimos**, **lucís**, **lucen**
PRETERIT **lucí**, **luciste**, **lució**, **lucimos**, **lucisteis**, **lucieron**
IMPERFECT **lucía**, **lucías**, **lucía**, **lucíamos**, **lucíais**, **lucían**
FUTURE **luciré**, **lucirás**, **lucirá**, **luciremos**, **luciréis**, **lucirán**
CONDITIONAL **luciría**, **lucirías**, **luciría**, **luciríamos**, **luciríais**, **lucirían**
PRESENT SUBJUNCTIVE **luzca**, **luzcas**, **luzca**, **luzcamos**, **luzcáis**, **luzcan**
IMPERFECT SUBJUNCTIVE (**-ra**) **luciera**, **lucieras**, **luciera**, **luciéramos**, **lucierais**, **lucieran**
IMPERFECT SUBJUNCTIVE (**-se**) **luciese**, **lucieses**, **luciese**, **luciésemos**, **lucieseis**, **luciesen**

Shows the common replacement of **c** by **zc** before **a** or **o**. However, this sound change is much more common in the **-er** conjugation, and only four verbs in current use are like **lucir**:

deslucir *to tarnish (*e.g. *reputations*; transitive*)*
deslucirse *to become tarnished*
relucir *to glow*
traslucirse *to show through* (emotions)

47 Maldecir *to curse*

Gerund **maldiciendo** *Past Participle* **maldecido**

Imperative **maldice maldecid**
maldiga maldigan

PRESENT **maldigo, maldices, maldice, maldecimos, maldecís, maldicen**

PRETERIT **maldije, maldijiste, maldijo, maldijimos, maldijisteis, maldijeron**

IMPERFECT **maldecía, maldecías, maldecía, maldecíamos, maldecíais, maldecían**

FUTURE **maldeciré, maldecirás, maldecirá, maldeciremos, maldeciréis, maldecirán**

CONDITIONAL **maldeciría, maldecirías, maldeciría, maldeciríamos, maldeciríais, maldecirían**

PRESENT SUBJUNCTIVE **maldiga, maldigas, maldiga, maldigamos, maldigáis, maldigan**

IMPERFECT SUBJUNCTIVE **(-ra) maldijera, maldijeras, maldijera, maldijéramos, maldijerais, maldijeran**

IMPERFECT SUBJUNCTIVE **(-se) maldijese, maldijeses, maldijese, maldijésemos, maldijeseis, maldijesen**

Conjugated in part like **decir** (no. 28), but with regular future, conditional and imperative forms. **Bendecir** *to bless* is conjugated the same way.

Predecir *to predict* is also normally conjugated like **maldecir**, but alternative future and conditional forms are occasionally found based on **decir**, e.g. **prediré**, **prediría**, etc.

48 Mover *to move*

Gerund **moviendo** *Past Participle* **movido**

Imperative **mueve moved**
mueva muevan

PRESENT **muevo, mueves, mueve, movemos, movéis, mueven**
PRETERIT **moví, moviste, movió, movimos, movisteis, movieron**
IMPERFECT **movía, movías, movía, movíamos, movíais, movían**
FUTURE **moveré, moverás, moverá, moveremos, moveréis, moverán**
CONDITIONAL **movería, moverías, movería, moveríamos, moveríais, moverían**
PRESENT SUBJUNCTIVE **mueva, muevas, mueva, movamos, mováis, muevan**
IMPERFECT SUBJUNCTIVE **(-ra) moviera, movieras, moviera, moviéramos, movierais, movieran**
IMPERFECT SUBJUNCTIVE **(-ra) moviese, movieses, moviese, moviésemos, movieseis, moviesen**

A type of radical changing **-er** verb showing the change **o** to **ue** when stressed. The most common are:

conmover *to move* (emotionally)
conmoverse *to be moved* (emotionally)
demoler *to demolish*
doler *to hurt*
llover *to rain*
morder *to bite*
promover *to encourage*
remorder *to cause remorse*
remover *to stir up; to remove* (latter meaning in Latin America only)

Verbs like **cocer** (no. 19) are similar but for spelling changes.

49 Negar *to deny*

Gerund **negando** *Past Participle* **negado**

Imperative **niega negad**
niegue nieguen

PRESENT **niego, niegas, niega, negamos, negáis, niegan**
PRETERIT **negué, negaste, negó, negamos, negasteis, negaron**
IMPERFECT **negaba, negabas, negaba, negábamos, negabais, negaban**
FUTURE **negaré, negarás, negará, negaremos, negaréis, negarán**
CONDITIONAL **negaría, negarías, negaría, negaríamos, negaríais, negarían**
PRESENT SUBJUNCTIVE **niegue, niegues, niegue, neguemos, neguéis, nieguen**
IMPERFECT SUBJUNCTIVE **(-ra) negara, negaras, negara, negáramos, negarais, negaran**
IMPERFECT SUBJUNCTIVE **(-se) negase, negases, negase, negásemos, negaseis, negasen**

Identical to **cerrar** (no. 18: **e** > **ie** when stressed), but with the spelling change **g** > **gu** before **e** or **i** because the **g** is always hard. Common verbs of this sort are:

cegar *to blind*
denegar *to turn down (a request)*
desasosegarse *to become restless, troubled*
desplegar *to unfold*
fregar *to scrub; to wash up*
negarse a *to refuse to*
plegar *to fold up*
refregar *to scrub hard*
regar *to water*
renegar de *to renounce (beliefs)*
restregar *to rub*
segar *to harvest*
sosegar *to calm*

50 Oír *to hear*

Gerund **oyendo** *Past Participle* **oído**

Imperative **oye oíd**

oiga oigan

PRESENT **oigo, oyes, oye, oímos, oís, oyen**

PRETERIT **oí, oíste, oyó, oímos, oísteis, oyeron**

IMPERFECT **oía, oías, oía, oíamos, oíais, oían**

FUTURE **oiré, oirás, oirá, oiremos, oiréis, oirán**

CONDITIONAL **oiría, oirías, oiría, oiríamos, oiríais, oirían**

PRESENT SUBJUNCTIVE **oiga, oigas, oiga, oigamos, oigáis, oigan**

IMPERFECT SUBJUNCTIVE (**-ra**) **oyera, oyeras, oyera, oyéramos, oyerais, oyeran**

IMPERFECT SUBJUNCTIVE (**-se**) **oyese, oyeses, oyese, oyésemos, oyeseis, oyesen**

Irregular verb. **Desoír** *to turn a deaf ear to* is conjugated the same way, but is confined to literary usage.

51 **Oler** *to smell*

Gerund **oliendo** *Past Participle* **olido**

Imperative **huele oled**
huela huelan

PRESENT **huelo, hueles, huele, olemos, oléis, huelen**
PRETERIT **olí, oliste, olió, olimos, olisteis, olieron**
IMPERFECT **olía, olías, olía, olíamos, olíais, olían**
FUTURE **oleré, olerás, olerá, oleremos, oleréis, olerán**
CONDITIONAL **olería, olerías, olería, oleríamos, oleríais, olerían**
PRESENT SUBJUNCTIVE **huela, huelas, huela, olamos, oláis, huelan**
IMPERFECT SUBJUNCTIVE **(-ra) oliera, olieras, oliera, oliéramos, olierais, olieran**
IMPERFECT SUBJUNCTIVE **(-se) oliese, olieses, oliese, oliésemos, olieseis, oliesen**

Conjugated the same way as **mover** (no. 48), but with the predictable addition of **h** when the diphthong **ue** occurs at the beginning of a word. There are no other similar verbs.

52 Pagar *to pay*

Gerund **pagando** *Past Participle* **pagado**

Imperative **paga pagad**
pague paguen

PRESENT **pago, pagas, paga, pagamos, pagáis, pagan**
PRETERIT **pagué, pagaste, pagó, pagamos, pagasteis, pagaron**
IMPERFECT **pagaba, pagabas, pagaba, pagábamos, pagabais, pagaban**
FUTURE **pagaré, pagarás, pagará, pagaremos, pagaréis, pagarán**
CONDITIONAL **pagaría, pagarías, pagaría, pagaríamos, pagaríais, pagarían**
PRESENT SUBJUNCTIVE **pague, pagues, pague, paguemos, paguéis, paguen**
IMPERFECT SUBJUNCTIVE **(-ra) pagara, pagaras, pagara, pagáramos, pagarais, pagaran**
IMPERFECT SUBJUNCTIVE **(-se) pagase, pagases, pagase, pagásemos, pagaseis, pagasen**

Regular **-ar** verb showing the predictable spelling change **g** > **gu** before **e**. A common type: over 180 similar verbs appear in the Directory of Verbs.

53 Parecer *to seem*

Gerund **pareciendo** *Past Participle* **parecido**

Imperative **parece pareced**
parezca parezcan

PRESENT **parezco, pareces, parece, parecemos, parecéis, parecen**

PRETERIT **parecí, pareciste, pareció, parecimos, parecisteis, parecieron**

IMPERFECT **parecía, parecías, parecía, parecíamos, parecíais, parecían**

FUTURE **pareceré, parecerás, parecerá, pareceremos, pareceréis, parecerán**

CONDITIONAL **parecería, parecerías, parecería, pareceríamos, pareceríais, parecerían**

PRESENT SUBJUNCTIVE **parezca, parezcas, parezca, parezcamos, parezcáis, parezcan**

IMPERFECT SUBJUNCTIVE **(-ra) pareciera, parecieras, pareciera, pareciéramos, parecierais, parecieran**

IMPERFECT SUBJUNCTIVE **(-se) pareciese, parecieses, pareciese, pareciésemos, parecieseis, pareciesen**

Regular except for the change **c** > **zc** before **a** or **o**. The immense majority of verbs whose infinitive ends in **-cer** conjugate like this. Only a few show the more predictable change **c** > **z**; these are listed under **vencer** (no. 86).

54 Pedir *to ask for*

Gerund **pidiendo** *Past Participle* **pedido**

Imperative **pide pedid**
pida pidan

PRESENT **pido, pides, pide, pedimos, pedís, piden**
PRETERIT **pedí, pediste, pidió, pedimos, pedisteis, pidieron**
IMPERFECT **pedía, pedías, pedía, pedíamos, pedíais, pedían**
FUTURE **pediré, pedirás, pedirá, pediremos, pediréis, pedirán**
CONDITIONAL **pediría, pedirías, pediría, pediríamos, pediríais, pedirían**
PRESENT SUBJUNCTIVE **pida, pidas, pida, pidamos, pidáis, pidan**
IMPERFECT SUBJUNCTIVE **(-ra) pidiera, pidieras, pidiera, pidiéramos, pidierais, pidieran**
IMPERFECT SUBJUNCTIVE **(-se) pidiese, pidieses, pidiese, pidiésemos, pidieseis, pidiesen**

Radical changing verb in which **e** > **i** in various forms. This type is not uncommon and certain verbs, e.g. **regir** (66), **reír** (no. 68) and **reñir** (no. 69), are conjugated the same way but for slight spelling changes. Common verbs conjugated like **pedir** are:

competir *to compete*
concebir *to conceive*
derretir *to melt* (transitive)
derretirse *to melt* (intransitive)
despedir *to fire (from a job)*
despedirse de *to say goodbye to*
expedir *to issue (a document)*
gemir *to groan*
impedir *to prevent*
invertir *to invest*
medir *to measure*
rendir *to yield*
rendirse *to surrender*
repetir *to repeat*
servir *to serve*
vestirse *to get dressed*

55 Perder *to lose*

Gerund **perdiendo** *Past Participle* **perdido**

Imperative **pierde perded**
pierda pierdan

PRESENT **pierdo, pierdes, pierde, perdemos, perdéis, pierden**
PRETERIT **perdí, perdiste, perdió, perdimos, perdisteis, perdieron**
IMPERFECT **perdía, perdías, perdía, perdíamos, perdíais, perdían**
FUTURE **perderé, perderás, perderá, perderemos, perderéis, perderán**
CONDITIONAL **perdería, perderías, perdería, perderíamos, perderíais, perderían**
PRESENT SUBJUNCTIVE **pierda, pierdas, pierda, perdamos, perdáis, pierdan**
IMPERFECT SUBJUNCTIVE **(-ra) perdiera, perdieras, perdiera, perdiéramos, perdierais, perdieran**
IMPERFECT SUBJUNCTIVE **(-se) perdiese, perdieses, perdiese, perdiésemos, perdieseis, perdiesen**

Radical changing verb showing the common change stressed **e** > **ie**. The following are common:

ascender *to promote (*i.e. *to a better position at work*)
atender *to attend (*i.e. to pay attention)
cernerse sobre *to loom over*
defender *to defend*
encender *to light*
entender *to understand (*note: **comprender**, same meaning, is less common and is regular*)*
extenderse *to stretch (*intransitive, i.e. *plains, stretches of land)*
tender a *to tend to*
verter *to pour out*

56 Placer *to please*

Gerund **placiendo** *Past Participle* **placido**

Imperative **place placed**

plazca (plega) plazcan (plegan)

PRESENT **plazco**, **places**, **place**, **placemos**, **placéis**, **placen**
PRETERIT **plací**, **placiste**, **plació (plugo)**, **placimos**, **placisteis**, **placieron (pluguieron)**
IMPERFECT **placía**, **placías**, **placía**, **placíamos**, **placíais**, **placían**
FUTURE **placeré**, **placerás**, **placerá**, **placeremos**, **placeréis**, **placerán**
CONDITIONAL **placería**, **placerías**, **placería**, **placeríamos**, **placeríais**, **placerían**
PRESENT SUBJUNCTIVE **plazca**, **plazcas**, **plazca**, **plazcamos**. **plazcáis**, **plazcan**
(plega, plegas, plega, plegamos, plegáis, plegan)
IMPERFECT SUBJUNCTIVE **(-ra) placiera**, **placieras**, **placiera**, **placiéramos**, **placierais**, **placieran**
(pluguiera, pluguieras, pluguiera, pluguiéramos, pluguierais, pluguieran)
IMPERFECT SUBJUNCTIVE **(-se)** **placiese**, **placieses**, **placiese**, **placiésemos**, **placieseis**, **placiesen**
(pluguiese, pluguieses, pluguiese, pluguiésemos, pluguieseis, pluguiesen)

This is conjugated the same way as **parecer** (no. 53) and would not need separate mention but for the existence of the bracketed alternative forms, which are found only in archaic written styles.

Placer is a rare and literary verb, occasionally still seen in third-person forms in phrases like **haz lo que te plazca** *do what you like*. **Gustar** (regular) means the same thing.

57 Poder *to be able*

Gerund **pudiendo** *Past Participle* **podido**

Imperative *not used*

PRESENT **puedo, puedes, puede, podemos, podéis, pueden**
PRETERIT **pude, pudiste, pudo, pudimos, pudisteis, pudieron**
IMPERFECT **podía, podías, podía, podíamos, podíais, podían**
FUTURE **podré, podrás, podrá, podremos, podréis, podrán**
CONDITIONAL **podría, podrías, podría, podríamos, podríais, podrían**
PRESENT SUBJUNCTIVE **pueda, puedas, pueda, podamos, podáis, puedan**
IMPERFECT SUBJUNCTIVE **(-ra) pudiera, pudieras, pudiera, pudiéramos, pudierais, pudieran**
IMPERFECT SUBJUNCTIVE **(-se) pudiese, pudieses, pudiese, pudiésemos, pudieseis, pudiesen**

Irregular verb, in constant use. No other verbs are conjugated like it.

58 Poner *to put*

Gerund **poniendo** *Past Participle* **puesto**

Imperative **pon poned**
ponga pongan

PRESENT **pongo**, **pones**, **pone**, **ponemos**, **ponéis**, **ponen**
PRETERIT **puse**, **pusiste**, **puso**, **pusimos**, **pusisteis**, **pusieron**
IMPERFECT **ponía**, **ponías**, **ponía**, **poníamos**, **poníais**, **ponían**
FUTURE **pondré**, **pondrás**, **pondrá**, **pondremos**, **pondréis**, **pondrán**
CONDITIONAL **pondría**, **pondrías**, **pondría**, **pondríamos**, **pondríais**, **pondrían**
PRESENT SUBJUNCTIVE **ponga**, **pongas**, **ponga**, **pongamos**, **pongáis**, **pongan**
IMPERFECT SUBJUNCTIVE (**-ra**) **pusiera**, **pusieras**, **pusiera**, **pusiéramos**, **pusierais**, **pusieran**
IMPERFECT SUBJUNCTIVE **pusiese**, **pusieses**, **pusiese**, **pusiésemos**, **pusieseis**, **pusiesen**

Irregular verb, in constant use. **Poner** means *to put*, **meter** (regular) has the more restricted meaning of *to put into.* **Ponerse** *to become, to put on clothes* is also important. There are several compounds of **poner** all conjugated in the same way. The following are not uncommon:

componer *to fix; to compose*
componerse de *to be composed of*
descomponerse *to decay; to fall apart*
disponer de *to dispose of* (i.e. *to possess)*
exponer *to expose*
oponerse a *to oppose*
posponer *to postpone*
predisponer *to predispose*
proponer *to propose*
suponer *to suppose*

The final vowel of the **tú** imperative of these compound forms requires an accent: **pospón**, **propón**, etc.

59 Poseer *to possess*

Gerund **poseyendo** *Past Participle* **poseído**

Imperative **posee poseed**
posea posean

PRESENT **poseo, posees, posee, poseemos, poseéis, poseen**
PRETERIT **poseí, poseíste, poseyó, poseímos, poseísteis, poseyeron**
IMPERFECT **poseía, poseías, poseía, poseíamos, poseíais, poseían**
FUTURE **poseeré, poseerás, poseerá, poseeremos, poseeréis, poseerán**
CONDITIONAL **poseería, poseerías, poseería, poseeríamos, poseeríais, poseerían**
PRESENT SUBJUNCTIVE **posea, poseas, posea, poseamos, poseáis, posean**
IMPERFECT SUBJUNCTIVE **(-ra) poseyera, poseyeras, poseyera, poseyéramos, poseyerais, poseyeran**
IMPERFECT SUBJUNCTIVE **(-se) poseyese, poseyeses, poseyese, poseyésemos, poseyeseis, poseyesen**

A regular **-er** verb, showing the common spelling change **i** > **y** when the former vowel is pronounced *y*. Note the accent in the past participle: contrast the **-uido** of verbs like **construir** (no. 23), which has no accent. The following common verbs are conjugated the same way:

creer *to believe*
leer *to read*
releer *to re-read*

For **proveer** *to supply* and **desproveer** *to deprive* see **proveer** (no. 63).

60 **Producir** *to produce*

Gerund **produciendo** *Past Participle* **producido**

Imperative **produce producid**
produzca produzcan

PRESENT **produzco**, **produces**, **produce**, **producimos**, **producís**, **producen**

PRETERIT **produje**, **produjiste**, **produjo**, **produjimos**, **produjisteis**, **produjeron**

IMPERFECT **producía**, **producías**, **producía**, **producíamos**, **producíais**, **producían**

FUTURE **produciré**, **producirás**, **producirá**, **produciremos**, **produciréis**, **producirán**

CONDITIONAL **produciría**, **producirías**, **produciría**, **produciríamos**, **produciríais**, **producirían**

PRESENT SUBJUNCTIVE **produzca**, **produzcas**, **produzca**, **produzcamos**, **produzcáis**, **produzcan**

IMPERFECT SUBJUNCTIVE **(-ra) produjera**, **produjeras**, **produjera**, **produjéramos**, **produjerais**, **produjeran**

IMPERFECT SUBJUNCTIVE **(-se) produjese**, **produjeses**, **produjese**, **produjésemos**, **produjeseis**, **produjesen**

Irregular verb, showing the common change **c** > **zc** before **a** or **o**, and also having a highly irregular preterit stem ending in **-uj**. Note also **-eron**, **-era, -ese**, etc. in the preterit for the predicted **-ieron**, **-iera**, etc. All verbs ending in **-ducir** are conjugated the same way. The most common are:

conducir *to drive*
deducir *to deduce*
introducir en *to insert into*
reducir *to reduce*
reproducir *to reproduce*
seducir *to seduce; to charm*
traducir *to translate*

61 Prohibir *to prohibit*

Gerund **prohibiendo** *Past Participle* **prohibido**

Imperative **prohíbe prohibid**
prohíba prohíban

PRESENT **prohíbo, prohíbes, prohíbe, prohibimos, prohibís, prohíben**

PRETERIT **prohibí, prohibiste, prohibió, prohibimos, prohibisteis, prohibieron**

IMPERFECT **prohibía, prohibías, prohibía, prohibíamos, prohibíais, prohibían**

FUTURE **prohibiré, prohibirás, prohibirá, prohibiremos, prohibiréis, prohibirán**

CONDITIONAL **prohibiría, prohibirías, prohibiría, prohibiríamos, prohibiríais, prohibirían**

PRESENT SUBJUNCTIVE **prohíba, prohíbas, prohíba, prohibamos, prohibáis, prohíban**

IMPERFECT SUBJUNCTIVE **(-ra) prohibiera, prohibieras, prohibiera, prohibiéramos, prohibierais, prohibieran**

IMPERFECT SUBJUNCTIVE **(-se) prohibiese, prohibieses, prohibiese, prohibiésemos, prohibieseis, prohibiesen**

A regular **-ir** verb, unusual only for the appearance of the accent on **i** when this is stressed. The accent was introduced in the spelling reforms of 1959 and even today it does not always appear in printed texts, especially Latin-American ones. **Cohibir** *to inhibit* is conjugated the same way.

62 Proteger *to protect*

Gerund **protegiendo** *Past Participle* **protegido**

Imperative **protege proteged**
proteja protejan

PRESENT **protejo, proteges, protege, protegemos, protegéis, protegen**

PRETERIT **protegí, protegiste, protegió, protegimos, protegisteis, protegieron**

IMPERFECT **protegía, protegías, protegía, protegíamos, protegíais, protegían**

FUTURE **protegeré, protegerás, protegerá, protegeremos, protegeréis, protegerán**

CONDITIONAL **protegería, protegerías, protegería, protegeríamos, protegeríais, protegerían**

PRESENT SUBJUNCTIVE **proteja, protejas, proteja, protejamos, protejáis, protejan**

IMPERFECT SUBJUNCTIVE (**-ra**) **protegiera, protegieras, protegiera, protegiéramos, protegierais, protegieran**

IMPERFECT SUBJUNCTIVE (**-se**) **protegiese, protegieses, protegiese, protegiésemos, protegieseis, protegiesen**

A regular **-er** verb showing the predictable spelling change **g** > **j** before **o, a**.

63 Proveer *to supply*

Gerund **proveyendo** *Past Participle* **provisto (proveído)**

Imperative **provee proveed**
provea provean

PRESENT **proveo, provees, provee, proveemos, proveéis, proveen**

PRETERIT **proveí, proveíste, proveyó, proveímos, proveísteis, proveyeron**

IMPERFECT **proveía, proveías, proveía, proveíamos, proveíais, proveían**

FUTURE **proveeré, proveerás, proveerá, proveeremos, proveeréis, proveerán**

CONDITIONAL **proveería, proveerías, proveería, proveeríamos, proveeríais, proveerían**

PRESENT SUBJUNCTIVE **provea, proveas, provea, proveamos, proveáis, provean**

IMPERFECT SUBJUNCTIVE **(-ra) proveyera, proveyeras, proveyera, proveyéramos, proveyerais, proveyeran**

IMPERFECT SUBJUNCTIVE **(-se) proveyese, proveyeses, proveyese, proveyésemos, proveyeseis, proveyesen**

Conjugated like **poseer** (no. 59) except for the irregular past participle **provisto**. **Desproveer de** *to deprive of* is conjugated the same way, but it is rarely used in its finite forms (the phrase **desprovisto de** *devoid of*, *lacking in* is, however, common).

The alternative past participle is used only in compound tenses.

64 Querer *to want; to love*

Gerund **queriendo** *Past Participle* **querido**

Imperative **quiere quered**
quiera quieran

PRESENT **quiero, quieres, quiere, queremos, queréis, quieren**
PRETERIT **quise, quisiste, quiso, quisimos, quisisteis, quisieron**
IMPERFECT **quería, querías, quería, queríamos, queríais, querían**
FUTURE **querré, querrás, querrá, querremos, querréis, querrán**
CONDITIONAL **querría, querrías, querría, querríamos, querríais, querrían**
PRESENT SUBJUNCTIVE **quiera, quieras, quiera, queramos, queráis, quieran**
IMPERFECT SUBJUNCTIVE **(-ra) quisiera, quisieras, quisiera, quisiéramos, quisierais, quisieran**
IMPERFECT SUBJUNCTIVE **(-se) quisiese, quisieses, quisiese, quisiésemos, quisieseis, quisiesen**

Irregular verb, in constant use. **Malquerer** *to dislike* and **bienquerer** *to like well* are conjugated the same way, but neither is in common use.

65 Realizar *to carry out; to make real*

Gerund **realizando** *Past Participle* **realizado**

Imperative **realiza realizad**

realice realicen

PRESENT **realizo, realizas, realiza, realizamos, realizáis, realizan**

PRETERIT **realicé, realizaste, realizó, realizamos, realizasteis, realizaron**

IMPERFECT **realizaba, realizabas, realizaba, realizábamos, realizabais, realizaban**

FUTURE **realizaré, realizarás, realizará, realizaremos, realizaréis, realizarán**

CONDITIONAL **realizaría, realizarías, realizaría, realizaríamos, realizaríais, realizarían**

PRESENT SUBJUNCTIVE **realice, realices, realice, realicemos, realicéis, realicen**

IMPERFECT SUBJUNCTIVE **(-ra) realizara, realizaras, realizara, realizáramos, realizarais, realizaran**

IMPERFECT SUBJUNCTIVE **(-se) realizase, realizases, realizase, realizásemos, realizaseis, realizasen**

A regular **-ar** verb displaying the usual spelling change **z** > **c** before **e**. A common type: the Directory of Verbs contains 370 examples.

66 Regir *to govern, direct*

Gerund **rigiendo** *Past Participle* **regido**

Imperative **rige regid**
rija rijan

PRESENT **rijo, riges, rige, regimos, regís, rigen**
PRETERIT **regí, registe, rigió, regimos, registeis, rigieron**
IMPERFECT **regía, regías, regía, regíamos, regíais, regían**
FUTURE **regiré, regirás, regirá, regiremos, regiréis, regirán**
CONDITIONAL **regiría, regirías, regiría, regiríamos, regiríais, regirían**
PRESENT SUBJUNCTIVE **rija, rijas, rija, rijamos, rijáis, rijan**
IMPERFECT SUBJUNCTIVE (**-ra**) **rigiera, rigieras, rigiera, rigiéramos, rigierais, rigieran**
IMPERFECT SUBJUNCTIVE (**-se**) **rigiese, rigieses, rigiese, rigiésemos, rigieseis, rigiesen**

Conjugated like **pedir** (no.54) but with the regular spelling change **g** > **j** before **o** or **a**. The following common verbs are conjugated the same way:

colegir *to infer (= to deduce)*
corregir *to correct*
elegir *to elect; to choose*
reelegir (alternative spelling **relegir**) *to re-elect*

67 **Rehuir** *to shy away from*

Gerund **rehuyendo** *Past Participle* **rehuido**

Imperative **rehúye rehuid**
rehúya rehúyan

PRESENT **rehúyo, rehúyes, rehúye, rehuimos, rehuís, rehúyen**

PRETERIT **rehuí, rehuiste, rehuyó, rehuimos, rehuisteis, rehuyeron**

IMPERFECT **rehuía, rehuías, rehuía, rehuíamos, rehuíais, rehuían**

FUTURE **rehuiré, rehuirás, rehuirá, rehuiremos, rehuiréis, rehuirán**

CONDITIONAL **rehuiría, rehuirías, rehuiría, rehuiríamos, rehuiríais, rehuirían**

PRESENT SUBJUNCTIVE **rehúya, rehúyas, rehúya, rehuyamos, rehuyáis, rehúyan**

IMPERFECT SUBJUNCTIVE **(-ra) rehuyera, rehuyeras, rehuyera, rehuyéramos, rehuyerais, rehuyeran**

IMPERFECT SUBJUNCTIVE **(-se) rehuyese, rehuyeses, rehuyese, rehuyésemos, rehuyeseis, rehuyesen**

Conjugated like **construir** (no. 23) except for the accent on the stressed **u**, which was adopted in the spelling changes of 1959.

68 Reír *to laugh*

Gerund **riendo** *Past Participle* **reído**

Imperative **ríe reíd**
ría rían

PRESENT **río, ríes, ríe, reímos, reís, ríen**
PRETERIT **reí, reíste, rió, reímos, reísteis, rieron**
IMPERFECT **reía, reías, reía, reíamos, reíais, reían**
FUTURE **reiré, reirás, reirá, reiremos, reiréis, reirán**
CONDITIONAL **reiría, reirías, reiría, reiríamos, reiríais, reirían**
PRESENT SUBJUNCTIVE **ría, rías, ría, riamos, riáis, rían**
IMPERFECT SUBJUNCTIVE **(-ra) riera, rieras, riera, riéramos, rierais, rieran**
IMPERFECT SUBJUNCTIVE **(-se) riese, rieses, riese, riésemos, rieseis, riesen**

Conjugated like **pedir** (no. 54), although the absence of the consonant between the **e** and the **i** conceals this fact. Verbs like this one are the only verbs that have an accent in the infinitive. The following common verbs are conjugated in the same way:

desleír *to dissolve* (transitive)
desleírse *to dissolve* (intransitive)
freír *to fry* (past part. **frito**)
reírse *to laugh* (more frequent than *reír*)
sofreír *to sauté* (past part. **sofrito**)
sonreír *to smile*

69 **Reñir** *to scold*

Gerund **riñendo** *Past Participle* **reñido**

Imperative **riñe reñid**
riña riñan

PRESENT **riño, riñes, riñe, reñimos, reñís, riñen**
PRETERIT **reñí, reñiste, riñó, reñimos, reñisteis, riñeron**
IMPERFECT **reñía, reñías, reñía, reñíamos, reñíais, reñían**
FUTURE **reñiré, reñirás, reñirá, reñiremos, reñiréis, reñirán**
CONDITIONAL **reñiría, reñirías, reñiría, reñiríamos, reñiríais, reñirían**
PRESENT SUBJUNCTIVE **riña, riñas, riña, riñamos, riñáis, riñan**
IMPERFECT SUBJUNCTIVE **(-ra) riñera, riñeras, riñera, riñéramos, riñerais, riñeran**
IMPERFECT SUBJUNCTIVE **(-se) riñese, riñeses, riñese, riñésemos, riñeseis, riñesen**

Conjugated like **pedir** (no. 54) except for the predictable replacement of **ió** by **ó** and **ie** by **e** after **ñ**. The following verbs are conjugated the same way:

ceñirse a *to stick close to (a topic)*
desteñir *to fade; to lose colour/*(Brit.) *colour*
teñir *to dye*

70 Reunir *to bring together*

Gerund **reuniendo** *Past Participle* **reunido**

Imperative **reúne reunid**

reúna reúnan

PRESENT **reúno, reúnes, reúne, reunimos, reunís, reúnen**

PRETERIT **reuní, reuniste, reunió, reunimos, reunisteis, reunieron**

IMPERFECT **reunía, reunías, reunía, reuníamos, reuníais, reunían**

FUTURE **reuniré, reunirás, reunirá, reuniremos, reuniréis, reunirán**

CONDITIONAL **reuniría, reunirías, reuniría, reuniríamos, reuniríais, reunirían**

PRESENT SUBJUNCTIVE **reúna, reúnas, reúna, reunamos, reunáis, reúnan**

IMPERFECT SUBJUNCTIVE **(-ra) reuniera, reunieras, reuniera, reuniéramos, reunierais, reunieran**

IMPERFECT SUBJUNCTIVE **(-se) reuniese, reunieses, reuniese, reuniésemos, reunieseis, reuniesen**

Regular **-ir** verb except for the appearance of the accent on the stressed **u**. The accent was introduced with the spelling reforms of 1959. **Reunirse** *to meet together* has the same forms.

71 Roer *to gnaw*

Gerund **royendo** *Past Participle* **roído**

Imperative **roe roed**

roa (roiga, roya) roan (roigan, royan)

PRESENT **roo (roigo, royo), roes, roe, roemos, roéis, roen**
PRETERIT **roí, roíste, royó, roímos, roísteis, royeron**
IMPERFECT **roía, roías, roía, roíamos, roíais, roían**
FUTURE **roeré, roerás, roerá, roeremos, roeréis, roerán**
CONDITIONAL **roería, roerías, roería, roeríamos, roeríais, roerían**
PRESENT SUBJUNCTIVE **roa, roas, roa, roamos, roáis, roan (roiga, roigas, roiga, roigamos, roigáis, roigan) (roya, royas, roya, royamos, royáis, royan)**
IMPERFECT SUBJUNCTIVE **(-ra) royera, royeras, royera, royéramos, royerais, royeran**
IMPERFECT SUBJUNCTIVE **(-se) royese, royeses, royese, royésemos, royeseis, royesen**

The alternative forms in brackets are much less common. **Corroer** *to corrode* is conjugated in the same way.

72 Rugir *to roar*

Gerund **rugiendo** *Past Participle* **rugido**

Imperative **ruge rugid**
ruja rujan

PRESENT **rujo, ruges, ruge, rugimos, rugís, rugen**
PRETERIT **rugí, rugiste, rugió, rugimos, rugisteis, rugieron**
IMPERFECT **rugía, rugías, rugía, rugíamos, rugíais, rugían**
FUTURE **rugiré, rugirás, rugirá, rugiremos, rugiréis, rugirán**
CONDITIONAL **rugiría, rugirías, rugiría, rugiríamos, rugiríais, rugirían**
PRESENT SUBJUNCTIVE **ruja, rujas, ruja, rujamos, rujáis, rujan**
IMPERFECT SUBJUNCTIVE (**-ra**)> **rugiera, rugieras, rugiera, rugiéramos, rugierais, rugieran**
IMPERFECT SUBJUNCTIVE (**-se**) **rugiese, rugieses, rugiese, rugiésemos, rugieseis, rugiesen**

Regular **-ir** verb except for the spelling change **g** > **j** before **o** or **a**. Some of the following verbs are commonly found:

afligir *to afflict*
convergir *to converge*
dirigir *to direct; to steer*
dirigirse a *to address; to make for*
exigir *to demand*
fingir *to pretend*
infligir *to inflict*
restringir *to restrict; to constrain*
resurgir *to arise again*
sumergir *to submerge* (transitive)
sumergirse *to submerge* (intransitive)
surgir *to arise*
transigir *to yield; to compromise*

73 Saber *to know*

Gerund **sabiendo** *Past Participle* **sabido**

Imperative **sabe sabed**
sepa sepan

PRESENT **sé, sabes, sabe, sabemos, sabéis, saben**
PRETERIT **supe, supiste, supo, supimos, supisteis, supieron**
IMPERFECT **sabía, sabías, sabía, sabíamos, sabíais, sabían**
FUTURE **sabré, sabrás, sabrá, sabremos, sabréis, sabrán**
CONDITIONAL **sabría, sabrías, sabría, sabríamos, sabríais, sabrían**
PRESENT SUBJUNCTIVE **sepa, sepas, sepa, sepamos, sepáis, sepan**
IMPERFECT SUBJUNCTIVE (**-ra**) **supiera, supieras, supiera, supiéramos, supierais, supieran**
IMPERFECT SUBJUNCTIVE (**-se**) **supiese, supieses, supiese, supiésemos, supieseis, supiesen**

Irregular verb in constant use.

74 Sacar *to take out, extract*

Gerund **sacando** *Past Participle* **sacado**

Imperative **saca sacad**

saque saquen

PRESENT **saco, sacas, saca, sacamos, sacáis, sacan**
PRETERIT **saqué, sacaste, sacó, sacamos, sacasteis, sacaron**
IMPERFECT **sacaba, sacabas, sacaba, sacábamos, sacabais, sacaban**
FUTURE **sacaré, sacarás, sacará, sacaremos, sacaréis, sacarán**
CONDITIONAL **sacaría, sacarías, sacaría, sacaríamos, sacaríais, sacarían**
PRESENT SUBJUNCTIVE **saque, saques, saque, saquemos, saquéis, saquen**
IMPERFECT SUBJUNCTIVE **(-ra) sacara, sacaras, sacara, sacáramos, sacarais, sacaran**
IMPERFECT SUBJUNCTIVE **(-se) sacase, sacases, sacase, sacásemos, sacaseis, sacasen**

Regular **-ar** verb showing the predictable spelling change **c** > **qu** before **e**. There are 260 examples in the Directory of Verbs

75 Salir *to go out, leave*

Gerund **saliendo** *Past Participle* **salido**

Imperative **sal salid**

salga salgan

PRESENT **salgo, sales, sale, salimos, salís, salen**

PRETERIT **salí, saliste, salió, salimos, salisteis, salieron**

IMPERFECT **salía, salías, salía, salíamos, salíais, salían**

FUTURE **saldré, saldrás, saldrá, saldremos, saldréis, saldrán**

CONDITIONAL **saldría, saldrías, saldría, saldríamos, saldríais, saldrían**

PRESENT SUBJUNCTIVE **salga, salgas, salga, salgamos, salgáis, salgan**

IMPERFECT SUBJUNCTIVE **(-ra) saliera, salieras, saliera, saliéramos, salierais, salieran**

IMPERFECT SUBJUNCTIVE **(-se) saliese, salieses, saliese, saliésemos, salieseis, saliesen**

Irregular verb in constant use. **Sobresalir** *to be outstanding* is conjugated the same way.

76 Satisfacer *to satisfy*

Gerund **satisfaciendo** *Past Participle* **satisfecho**

Imperative **satisfaz** *(or* **satisface***)* **satisfaced**
satisfaga satisfagan

PRESENT **satisfago, satisfaces, satisface, satisfacemos, satisfacéis, satisfacen**

PRETERIT **satisfice, satisficiste, satisfizo, satisficimos, satisficisteis, satisficieron**

IMPERFECT **satisfacía, satisfacías, satisfacía, satisfacíamos, satisfacíais, satisfacían**

FUTURE **satisfaré, satisfarás, satisfará, satisfaremos, satisfaréis, satisfarán**

CONDITIONAL **satisfaría, satisfarías, satisfaría, satisfaríamos, satisfaríais, satisfarían**

PRESENT SUBJUNCTIVE **satisfaga, satisfagas, satisfaga, satisfagamos, satisfagáis, satisfagan**

IMPERFECT SUBJUNCTIVE **(-ra) satisficiera, satisficieras, satisficiera, satisficiéramos, satisficierais, satisficieran**

IMPERFECT SUBJUNCTIVE **(-se) satisficiese, satisficieses, satisficiese, satisficiésemos, satisficieseis, satisficiesen**

Irregular verb, similar in conjugation to **hacer** (no. 42). **Licuefacerse** *to liquefy* (intransitive) is conjugated the same way, but it is not in common use, **licuarse** being more usual.

77 Seguir *to follow*

Gerund **siguiendo** *Past Participle* **seguido**

Imperative **sigue seguid**
siga sigan

PRESENT **sigo, sigues, sigue, seguimos, seguís, siguen**

PRETERIT **seguí, seguiste, siguió, seguimos, seguisteis, siguieron**

IMPERFECT **seguía, seguías, seguía, seguíamos, seguíais, seguían**

FUTURE **seguiré, seguirás, seguirá, seguiremos, seguiréis, seguirán**

CONDITIONAL **seguiría, seguirías, seguiría, seguiríamos, seguiríais, seguirían**

PRESENT SUBJUNCTIVE **siga, sigas, siga, sigamos, sigáis, sigan**

IMPERFECT SUBJUNCTIVE (**-ra**)> **siguiera, siguieras, siguiera, siguiéramos, siguierais, siguieran**

IMPERFECT SUBJUNCTIVE (**-se**) **siguiese, siguieses, siguiese, siguiésemos, siguieseis, siguiesen**

Radical-changing verb conjugated like **pedir** (no. 54) but with the spelling change **gu** > **g** before **a** or **o**. The following common verbs are conjugated the same way:

conseguir *to obtain*
perseguir *to persecute*
proseguir *to proceed with*

78 Sentir *to feel*

Gerund **sintiendo** *Past Participle* **sentido**

Imperative **siente sentid**
sienta sientan

PRESENT **siento, sientes, siente, sentimos, sentís, sienten**

PRETERIT **sentí, sentiste, sintió, sentimos, sentisteis, sintieron**

IMPERFECT **sentía, sentías, sentía, sentíamos, sentíais, sentían**

FUTURE **sentiré, sentirás, sentirá, sentiremos, sentiréis, sentirán**

CONDITIONAL **sentiría, sentirías, sentiría, sentiríamos, sentiríais, sentirían**

PRESENT SUBJUNCTIVE **sienta, sientas, sienta, sintamos, sintáis, sientan**

IMPERFECT SUBJUNCTIVE **(-ra) sintiera, sintieras, sintiera, sintiéramos, sintierais, sintieran**

IMPERFECT SUBJUNCTIVE **(-se) sintiese, sintieses, sintiese, sintiésemos, sintieseis, sintiesen**

Radical changing verb showing the common change stressed **e** > **ie**, and also unstressed **e** to **i** in certain forms. The following common verbs are conjugated in the same way:

advertir *to warn*
arrepentirse de *to repent*
consentir *to consent*
convertirse en *to change into*
diferir *to differ*
divertir *to amuse*
herir *to wound*
hervir *to boil*
interferir *to interfere*
invertir *to reverse (order of things); to invest*
mentir *to lie*
preferir *to prefer*
referirse a *to refer to*
sugerir *to suggest*
transferir *to transfer*

79 Ser *to be*

Gerund **siendo** *Past Participle* **sido**

Imperative **sé sed**

sea sean

PRESENT **soy, eres, es, somos, sois, son**

PRETERIT **fui** *(no accent!)*, **fuiste, fue** *(no accent!)*, **fuimos, fuisteis, fueron**

IMPERFECT **era, eras, era, éramos, erais, eran**

FUTURE **seré, serás, será, seremos, seréis, serán**

CONDITIONAL **sería, serías, sería, seríamos, seríais, serían**

PRESENT SUBJUNCTIVE **sea, seas, sea, seamos, seáis, sean**

IMPERFECT SUBJUNCTIVE **(-ra) fuera, fueras, fuera, fuéramos, fuerais, fueran**

IMPERFECT SUBJUNCTIVE **(-se) fuese, fueses, fuese, fuésemos, fueseis, fuesen**

Irregular verb in constant use. The preterit forms have no accents: the spellings **fuí** and **fué** were abolished in 1959.

80 Soler *to be accustomed to*

Gerund **soliendo** *Past Participle* **solido**

Imperative *not used*

PRESENT **suelo, sueles, suele, solemos, soléis, suelen**
PRETERIT **solí, soliste, solió, solimos, solisteis, solieron**
IMPERFECT **solía, solías, solía, solíamos, solíais, solían**
FUTURE *not used*
CONDITIONAL *not used*
PRESENT SUBJUNCTIVE **suela, suelas, suela, solamos, soláis, suelan**
IMPERFECT SUBJUNCTIVE **(-ra) soliera, solieras, soliera, soliéramos, solierais, solieran**
IMPERFECT SUBJUNCTIVE **(-se) soliese, solieses, soliese, soliésemos, solieseis, soliesen**

Conjugated like **mover** (no. 48) except that certain forms are not used. The pluperfect and pluperfect conditional are also not used, but the perfect indicative does occur.

81 Tañer *to chime; to pluck (an instrument)*

Gerund **tañendo** *Past Participle* **tañido**

Imperative **tañe tañed**
taña tañan

PRESENT **taño, tañes, tañe, tañemos, tañéis, tañen**
PRETERIT **tañí, tañiste, tañó, tañimos, tañisteis, tañeron**
IMPERFECT **tañía, tañías, tañía, tañíamos, tañíais, tañían**
FUTURE **tañeré, tañerás, tañerá, tañeremos, tañeréis, tañerán**
CONDITIONAL **tañería, tañerías, tañería, tañeríamos, tañeríais, tañerían**
PRESENT SUBJUNCTIVE **taña, tañas, taña, tañamos, tañáis, tañan**
IMPERFECT SUBJUNCTIVE (**-ra**) **tañera, tañeras, tañera, tañéramos, tañerais, tañeran**
IMPERFECT SUBJUNCTIVE (**-se**) **tañese, tañeses, tañese, tañésemos, tañeseis, tañesen**

Regular **-er** verb showing the usual change **ie** > **e** and **ió** > **o** after **ñ**. **Atañer** *to concern* is conjugated the same way but it is not much used, **concernir** being more usual.

82 Tener *to have*

Gerund **teniendo** *Past Participle* **tenido**

Imperative **ten tened**
tenga tengan

PRESENT **tengo, tienes, tiene, tenemos, tenéis, tienen**
PRETERIT **tuve, tuviste, tuvo, tuvimos, tuvisteis, tuvieron**
IMPERFECT **tenía, tenías, tenía, teníamos, teníais, tenían**
FUTURE **tendré, tendrás, tendrá, tendremos, tendréis, tendrán**
CONDITIONAL **tendría, tendrías, tendría, tendríamos, tendríais, tendrían**
PRESENT SUBJUNCTIVE **tenga, tengas, tenga, tengamos, tengáis, tengan**
IMPERFECT SUBJUNCTIVE **(-ra) tuviera, tuvieras, tuviera, tuviéramos, tuvierais, tuvieran**
IMPERFECT SUBJUNCTIVE **(-se) tuviese, tuvieses, tuviese, tuviésemos, tuvieseis, tuviesen**

Irregular verb in constant use. The following compounds are similar and all are in current use:

abstenerse de *to abstain from*
atenerse a *to abide by*
contener *to contain*
detener *to detain*
detenerse *to halt*
entretener *to hold up (*i.e. *delay someone)*
mantener *to maintain (*i.e. *to look after, support financially)*
obtener *to obtain*
retener *to retain*
sostener *to maintain (an argument); to prop up*

The **tú** imperative of these compound verbs requires an accent on the final vowel: **detén**, **retén**, etc.

83 Traer *to bring*

Gerund **trayendo** *Past Participle* **traído**

Imperative **trae traed**

traiga traigan

PRESENT **traigo, traes, trae, traemos, traéis, traen**
PRETERIT **traje, trajiste, trajo, trajimos, trajisteis, trajeron**
IMPERFECT **traía, traías, traía, traíamos, traíais, traían**
FUTURE **traeré, traerás, traerá, traeremos, traeréis, traerán**
CONDITIONAL **traería, traerías, traería, traeríamos, traeríais, traerían**
PRESENT SUBJUNCTIVE **traiga, traigas, traiga, traigamos, traigáis, traigan**
IMPERFECT SUBJUNCTIVE **(-ra) trajera, trajeras, trajera, trajéramos, trajerais, trajeran**
IMPERFECT SUBJUNCTIVE **(-se) trajese, trajeses, trajese, trajésemos, trajeseis, trajesen**

Irregular verb in constant use. Note the replacement of **ie** by **e** after **j**, normal in irregular verbs that have **-j-** in the preterit. The following similar verbs are found:

abstraer *to abstract*
abstraerse de *to become oblivious to*
atraer *to attract*
contraer *to contract*
distraer *to distract*
distraerse *to be distracted*
sustraer *to steal* (usually **robar**)

84 Trocar *to swap*

Gerund **trocando** *Past Participle* **trocado**

Imperative **trueca trocad**
trueque truequen

PRESENT **trueco, truecas, trueca, trocamos, trocáis, truecan**

PRETERIT **troqué, trocaste, trocó, trocamos, trocasteis, trocaron**

IMPERFECT **trocaba, trocabas, trocaba, trocábamos, trocabais, trocaban**

FUTURE **trocaré, trocarás, trocará, trocaremos, trocaréis, trocarán**

CONDITIONAL **trocaría, trocarías, trocaría, trocaríamos, trocaríais, trocarían**

PRESENT SUBJUNCTIVE **trueque, trueques, trueque, troquemos, troquéis, truequen**

IMPERFECT SUBJUNCTIVE (**-ra**) **trocara, trocaras, trocara, trocáramos, trocarais, trocaran**

IMPERFECT SUBJUNCTIVE (**-se**) **trocase, trocases, trocase, trocásemos, trocaseis, trocasen**

Conjugated like **contar** (no. 24) but with the predictable spelling change stressed **c** > **qu** before **e**. **Trastrocar** *to alter* is conjugated the same way. **Trastocar** *to disorder, muddle up* is constantly confused with it, but is in fact regular (like **sacar**, no. 74). **Derrocar** *to topple* used to be conjugated like **trocar** but nowadays usually follows the pattern of **sacar**.

85 Valer *to be worth; to be useful, valuable*

Gerund **valiendo** *Past Participle* **valido**

Imperative **vale valed**
valga valgan

PRESENT **valgo, vales, vale, valemos, valéis, valen**
PRETERIT **valí, valiste, valió, valimos, valisteis, valieron**
IMPERFECT **valía, valías, valía, valíamos, valíais, valían**
FUTURE **valdré, valdrás, valdrá, valdremos, valdréis, valdrán**
CONDITIONAL **valdría, valdrías, valdría, valdríamos, valdríais, valdrían**
PRESENT SUBJUNCTIVE **valga, valgas, valga, valgamos, valgáis, valgan**
IMPERFECT SUBJUNCTIVE **(-ra) valiera, valieras, valiera, valiéramos, valierais, valieran**
IMPERFECT SUBJUNCTIVE **(-se) valiese, valieses, valiese, valiésemos, valieseis, valiesen**

Irregular (because of the unexpected **g**). The following verbs are conjugated the same way:

equivaler a *to be equivalent to*
prevalerse de *to take advantage of* (literary: usually **aprovecharse de**)
valerse de *to avail oneself of*

86 Vencer *to defeat*

Gerund **venciendo** *Past Participle* **vencido**

Imperative **vence venced**
venza venzan

PRESENT **venzo, vences, vence, vencemos, vencéis, vencen**
PRETERIT **vencí, venciste, venció, vencimos, vencisteis, vencieron**
IMPERFECT **vencía, vencías, vencía, vencíamos, vencíais, vencían**
FUTURE **venceré, vencerás, vencerá, venceremos, venceréis, vencerán**
CONDITIONAL **vencería, vencerías, vencería, venceríamos, venceríais, vencerían**
PRESENT SUBJUNCTIVE **venza, venzas, venza, venzamos, venzáis, venzan**
IMPERFECT SUBJUNCTIVE **(-ra) venciera, vencieras, venciera, venciéramos, vencierais, vencieran**
IMPERFECT SUBJUNCTIVE **(-se) venciese, vencieses, venciese, venciésemos, vencieseis, venciesen**

Regular **-er** verb with the spelling change **c** > **z** before **o** and **a**. The majority of verbs ending in **-cer** are in fact conjugated like **parecer** (no. 46); only a few are conjugated like **vencer**, e.g.

convencer *to convince*
ejercer *to exercise (a profession)*
mecer *to sway* (transitive)
mecerse *to sway* (intransitive)

Torcer *to twist*, **retorcerse** *to writhe*, **escocer** *to sting* and **cocer** *to cook* are conjugated like **cocer** (no. 19)

87 Venir *to come*

Gerund **viniendo** *Past Participle* **venido**

Imperative **ven venid**
venga vengan

PRESENT **vengo, vienes, viene, venimos, venís, vienen**
PRETERIT **vine, viniste, vino, vinimos, vinisteis, vinieron**
IMPERFECT **venía, venías, venía, veníamos, veníais, venían**
FUTURE **vendré, vendrás, vendrá, vendremos, vendréis, vendrán**
CONDITIONAL **vendría, vendrías, vendría, vendríamos, vendríais, vendrían**
PRESENT SUBJUNCTIVE **venga, vengas, venga, vengamos, vengáis, vengan**
IMPERFECT SUBJUNCTIVE **(-ra) viniera, vinieras, viniera, viniéramos, vinierais, vinieran**
IMPERFECT SUBJUNCTIVE **(-se) viniese, vinieses, viniese, viniésemos, vinieseis, viniesen**

Irregular verb in constant use. The following compounds of **venir** follow the same pattern:

avenirse en *to agree on* (literary)
contravenir *to contravene*
convenir en *to agree on*
desavenirse *to fall out* (e.g. friends)
devenir *to become* (philosophical language only: usually **ponerse**, **hacerse** or **volverse**)
intervenir en *to take part in*
prevenir *to prevent*
reconvenir *to reproach*
sobrevenir *to occur* (usually disasters)

The **tú** imperative of the compounds has an accent, e.g. **prevén**, although the imperative of the compounds is hardly ever used.

88 Ver *to see*

Gerund **viendo** *Past Participle* **visto**

Imperative **ve ved**

vea vean

PRESENT **veo, ves, ve, vemos, veis, ven**

PRETERIT **vi, viste, vio** *(no accent!)*, **vimos, visteis, vieron**

IMPERFECT **veía, veías, veía, veíamos, veíais, veían**

FUTURE **veré, verás, verá, veremos, veréis, verán**

CONDITIONAL **vería, verías, vería, veríamos, veríais, verían**

PRESENT SUBJUNCTIVE **vea, veas, veas, veamos, veáis, vean**

IMPERFECT SUBJUNCTIVE **(-ra) viera, vieras, viera, viéramos, vierais, vieran**

IMPERFECT SUBJUNCTIVE **(-se) viese, vieses, viese, viésemos, vieseis, viesen**

Irregular verb, but only insofar as the **e** survives unexpectedly in certain forms (e.g. **veo**, not 'vo', **veía**, not 'vía', etc.). The following common compounds occur, all conjugated like **ver:**

entrever *to glimpse* **prever** *to foresee*

The third-person present indicative of these compounds requires an accent: **prevé, prevén, entrevé, entrevén**. So does the **tú** imperative (if it is ever used): **prevé, entrevé**.

The third-person singular of the preterit of the compounds also requires an accent: **entrevió, previó**. The accent on the third-person singular preterit of the simple form of **ver** was removed in 1959.

89 **Vivir** *to live*

Gerund **viviendo** *Past Participle* **vivido**

Imperative **vive vivid**

viva vivan

PRESENT **vivo, vives, vive, vivimos, vivís, viven**
PRETERIT **viví, viviste, vivió, vivimos, vivisteis, vivieron**
IMPERFECT **vivía, vivías, vivía, vivíamos, vivíais, vivían**
FUTURE **viviré, vivirás, vivirá, viviremos, viviréis, vivirán**
CONDITIONAL **viviría, vivirías, viviría, viviríamos, viviríais, vivirían**
PRESENT SUBJUNCTIVE **viva, vivas, viva, vivamos, viváis, vivan**
IMPERFECT SUBJUNCTIVE (**-ra**) **viviera, vivieras, viviera, viviéramos, vivierais, vivieran**
IMPERFECT SUBJUNCTIVE (**-se**) **viviese, vivieses, viviese, viviésemos, vivieseis, viviesen**

A completely regular **-ir** verb which serves as a good model for the **-ir** conjugation.

90 Volver *to come back*

Gerund **volviendo** *Past Participle* **vuelto**

Imperative **vuelve volved**
vuelva vuelvan

PRESENT **vuelvo, vuelves, vuelve, volvemos, volvéis, vuelven**
PRETERIT **volví, volviste, volvió, volvimos, volvisteis, volvieron**
IMPERFECT **volvía, volvías, volvía, volvíamos, volvíais, volvían**
FUTURE **volveré, volverás, volverá, volveremos, volveréis, volverán**
CONDITIONAL **volvería, volverías, volvería, volveríamos, volveríais, volverían**
PRESENT SUBJUNCTIVE **vuelva, vuelvas, vuelva, volvamos, volváis, vuelvan**
IMPERFECT SUBJUNCTIVE (**-ra**) **volviera, volvieras, volviera, volviéramos, volvierais, volvieran**
IMPERFECT SUBJUNCTIVE (**-se**) **volviese, volvieses, volviese, volviésemos, volvieseis, volviesen**

Conjugated exactly like **mover** (no. 48) except for the irregular past participle **vuelto**. All verbs ending in **-olver** are conjugated this way, the following being commonly found:

absolver *to absolve*
desenvolverse *to develop* (intransitive)
disolver *to dissolve*
envolver *to wrap up*
resolver *to resolve*
revolver *to stir up*
volverse *to become; to turn back;* **v. a** *to turn to*

91 Yacer (Am.) *to lay;* (Brit.) *to lie (as in 'he lay there', 'here lie the mortal remains of', etc.)*

Gerund **yaciendo** *Past Participle* **yacido**

Imperative **yace (yaz) yaced**
yazca (yazga, yaga) yazcan (yazgan, yagan)

PRESENT **yazco (yazgo, yago)**, **yaces**, **yace**, **yacemos**, **yacéis**, **yacen**
PRETERIT **yací**, **yaciste**, **yació**, **yacimos**, **yacisteis**, **yacieron**
IMPERFECT **yacía**, **yacías**, **yacía**, **yacíamos**, **yacíais**, **yacían**
FUTURE **yaceré**, **yacerás**, **yacerá**, **yaceremos**, **yaceréis**, **yacerán**
CONDITIONAL **yacería**, **yacerías**, **yacería**, **yaceríamos**, **yaceríais**, **yacerían**
PRESENT SUBJUNCTIVE **yazca**, **yazcas**, **yazca**, **yazcamos**, **yazcáis**, **yazcan**
(yazga, yazgas, yazga, yazgamos, yazgáis, yazgan)
(yaga, yagas, yaga, yagamos, yagáis, yagan)
IMPERFECT SUBJUNCTIVE **(-ra) yaciera**, **yacieras**, **yaciera**, **yaciéramos**, **yacierais**, **yacieran**
IMPERFECT SUBJUNCTIVE **(-se) yaciese**, **yacieses**, **yaciese**, **yaciésemos**, **yacieseis**, **yaciesen**

Usually conjugated like **parecer** (no. 46). This verb not used in everyday speech, being confined to very formal literary styles. **Echarse**, **tumbarse**, **acostarse** or **descansar** are various ways of expressing the same idea.

The bracketed alternative forms are even rarer.

92 Zurcir *to darn*

Gerund **zurciendo** *Past Participle* **zurcido**

Imperative **zurce zurcid**
zurza zurzan

PRESENT **zurzo, zurces, zurce, zurcimos, zurcís, zurcen**
PRETERIT **zurcí, zurciste, zurció, zurcimos, zurcisteis, zurcieron**
IMPERFECT **zurcía, zurcías, zurcía, zurcíamos, zurcíais, zurcían**
FUTURE **zurciré, zurcirás, zurcirá, zurciremos, zurciréis, zurcirán**
CONDITIONAL **zurciría, zurcirías, zurciría, zurciríamos, zurciríais, zurcirían**
PRESENT SUBJUNCTIVE **zurza, zurzas, zurza, zurzamos, zurzáis, zurzan**
IMPERFECT SUBJUNCTIVE (**-ra**) **zurciera, zurcieras, zurciera, zurciéramos, zurcierais, zurcieran**
IMPERFECT SUBJUNCTIVE (**-se**) **zurciese, zurcieses, zurciese, zurciésemos, zurcieseis, zurciesen**

Regular **-ir** verb with the spelling change **c** > **z**. This is not a common type, most verbs ending in **-cir** having some other type of irregularity as well. Similar verbs :

esparcir *to scatter, strew*
esparcirse *to be scattered*
fruncir *to pucker* (the eyebrows)
resarcir *to compensate* (effort)